AAT

Q2022

Applied Management Accounting

EXAM KIT

This Exam Kit supports study for the following AAT qualifications:

AAT Level 4 Diploma in Professional Accounting

AAT Diploma in Professional Accounting at SCQF Level 8

British Library Cataloguing-in-Publication Data

A catalogue record for this book is available from the British Library.

Published by:

Kaplan Publishing UK

Unit 2 The Business Centre

Molly Millar's Lane

Wokingham

Berkshire

RG41 2QZ

ISBN: 978-1-83996-893-8

© Kaplan Financial Limited, 2024

Printed and bound in Great Britain

The text in this material and any others made available by any Kaplan Group company does not amount to advice on a particular matter and should not be taken as such. No reliance should be placed on the content as the basis for any investment or other decision or in connection with any advice given to third parties. Please consult your appropriate professional adviser as necessary. Kaplan Publishing Limited and all other Kaplan group companies expressly disclaim all liability to any person in respect of any losses or other claims, whether direct, indirect, incidental, consequential or otherwise arising in relation to the use of such materials.

All rights reserved. No part of this examination may be reproduced or transmitted in any form or by any means, electronic or mechanical, including photocopying, recording, or by any information storage and retrieval system, without prior permission from Kaplan Publishing.

This Product includes content from the International Auditing and Assurance Standards Board (IAASB) and the International Ethics Standards Board for Accountants (IESBA), published by the International Federation of Accountants (IFAC) in 2015 and is used with permission of IFAC.

CONTENTS

	Page
Unit specific information	P.4
Index to questions and answers	P.5
Exam technique	P.7
Kaplan's recommended revision approach	P.8

Practice questions	1
Answers to practice questions	195
Mock assessment questions	343
Answers to mock assessment questions	357

Features in this revision kit

In addition to providing a wide ranging bank of real exam style questions, we have also included in this kit:

- unit specific information and advice on exam technique
- our recommended approach to make your revision for this particular subject as effective as possible.

You will find a wealth of other resources to help you with your studies on the AAT website:

www.aat.org.uk/

Quality and accuracy are of the utmost importance to us so if you spot an error in any of our products, please send an email to mykaplanreporting@kaplan.com with full details, or follow the link to the feedback form in MyKaplan.

Our Quality Co-ordinator will work with our technical team to verify the error and take action to ensure it is corrected in future editions.

KAPLAN PUBLISHING

UNIT SPECIFIC INFORMATION

THE EXAM

FORMAT OF THE ASSESSMENT

The assessment will comprise eight independent tasks. Students will normally be assessed by computer-based assessment.

In any one assessment, students may not be assessed on all content, or on the full depth or breadth of a piece of content. The content assessed may change over time to ensure validity of assessment, but all assessment criteria will be tested over time.

The learning outcomes for this unit are as follows:

	Learning outcome	Weighting
1	Understand and implement the organisational planning process	25%
2	Use internal processes to enhance operational control	27%
3	Use techniques to aid short-term and long-term decision making	25%
4	Analyse and report on business performance	23%
	Total	100%

Time allowed

3 hours

PASS MARK

The pass mark for all AAT CBAs is 70%.

 Always keep your eye on the clock and make sure you attempt all questions!

DETAILED SYLLABUS

The detailed syllabus and study guide written by the AAT can be found at:

www.aat.org.uk/

INDEX TO QUESTIONS AND ANSWERS

		Page number	
		Question	Answer
BUDGETING			
1 – 4	Sources of information	1	195
5 – 12	Budgetary responsibilities	2	196
13 – 15	Accounting treatment	6	199
16 – 19	Indices	7	200
20 – 38	Production budgets	9	201
39 – 44	Machine utilisation	15	206
45 – 46	Capacity constraints	17	208
47 – 51	Working schedules and operating budgets	19	209
52 – 57	Cash flow forecasts	23	212
58 – 60	Periodic budgets	27	215
61 – 62	Alternative scenarios	29	216
63 – 77	Sales revenue and costs forecasts	31	218
78 – 84	Written tasks	35	222
85 – 87	Monthly operating reports and variances calculations	46	229
88 – 100	Budget revision and variance analysis	49	231
STANDARD COSTING AND VARIANCES			
101 – 117	Standard costing	55	245
118 – 125	Sale variances	61	248
126 – 134	Material variances	64	250
135 – 153	Labour variances	66	253
154 – 159	Variable overhead variances	73	259
160 – 165	Fixed overhead variances	75	261
166 – 174	Written tasks	77	263
OPERATIONAL CONTROL			
175 – 182	Impact of technology	91	275
183 – 189	Activity based costing	93	277
190 – 199	Life cycle costing	103	284
200 – 214	Target costing	112	288

SHORT TERM DECISION MAKING			
215 – 224	Relevant costing	121	295
225 – 233	Limiting factors and other types of decision	125	298
234 – 244	Linear programming	137	305
LONG TERM DECISION MAKING			
245 – 258	Payback, ARR, NPV and IRR	143	309
PERFORMANCE INDICATORS			
259 – 272	Calculations	152	315
273 – 281	Written tasks	159	319
282 – 284	Ethics	177	329
CALCULATING FORECASTS			
285 – 314	Trend analysis, indexing, linear regression and expected values	178	330
DIVISIONAL PERFORMANCE			
315 – 323	ROI, RI and transfer pricing	189	338

MOCK EXAM		
Questions and answers	343	357

EXAM TECHNIQUE

- **Do not skip any of the material** in the syllabus.

- **Read each question** *very* carefully.

- **Double-check your answer** before committing yourself to it.

- Answer **every** question – if you do not know an answer to a multiple choice question or true/false question, you don't lose anything by guessing. Think carefully before you **guess**.

- If you are answering a multiple-choice question, **eliminate first those answers that you know are wrong**. Then choose the most appropriate answer from those that are left.

- **Don't panic** if you realise you've answered a question incorrectly. Getting one question wrong will not mean the difference between passing and failing.

Computer-based exams – tips

- Do not attempt a CBA until you have **completed all study material** relating to it.

- On the AAT website there is a CBA demonstration. It is **ESSENTIAL** that you attempt this before your real CBA. You will become familiar with how to move around the CBA screens and the way that questions are formatted, increasing your confidence and speed in the actual exam.

- Be sure you understand how to use the **software** before you start the exam. If in doubt, ask the assessment centre staff to explain it to you.

- Questions are **displayed on the screen** and answers are entered using keyboard and mouse. At the end of the exam, you are given a certificate showing the result you have achieved.

- In addition to the traditional multiple-choice question type, CBAs will also contain **other types of questions**, such as number entry questions, drag and drop, true/false, pick lists or drop down menus or hybrids of these.

- You need to be sure you **know how to answer questions** of this type before you sit the exam, through practice.

KAPLAN'S RECOMMENDED REVISION APPROACH

QUESTION PRACTICE IS THE KEY TO SUCCESS

Success in professional examinations relies upon you acquiring a firm grasp of the required knowledge at the tuition phase. In order to be able to do the questions, knowledge is essential.

However, the difference between success and failure often hinges on your exam technique on the day and making the most of the revision phase of your studies.

The **Kaplan textbook** is the starting point, designed to provide the underpinning knowledge to tackle all questions. However, in the revision phase, poring over text books is not the answer.

Kaplan pocket notes are designed to help you quickly revise a topic area; however you then need to practise questions. There is a need to progress to exam style questions as soon as possible, and to tie your exam technique and technical knowledge together.

The importance of question practice cannot be over-emphasised.

The recommended approach below is designed by expert tutors in the field, in conjunction with their knowledge of the examiner and the specimen assessment.

You need to practise as many questions as possible in the time you have left.

OUR AIM

Our aim is to get you to the stage where you can attempt exam questions confidently, to time, in a closed book environment, with no supplementary help (i.e. to simulate the real examination experience).

Practising your exam technique is also vitally important for you to assess your progress and identify areas of weakness that may need more attention in the final run up to the examination.

In order to achieve this we recognise that initially you may feel the need to practice some questions with open book help.

Good exam technique is vital.

THE KAPLAN REVISION PLAN

Stage 1: Assess areas of strengths and weaknesses

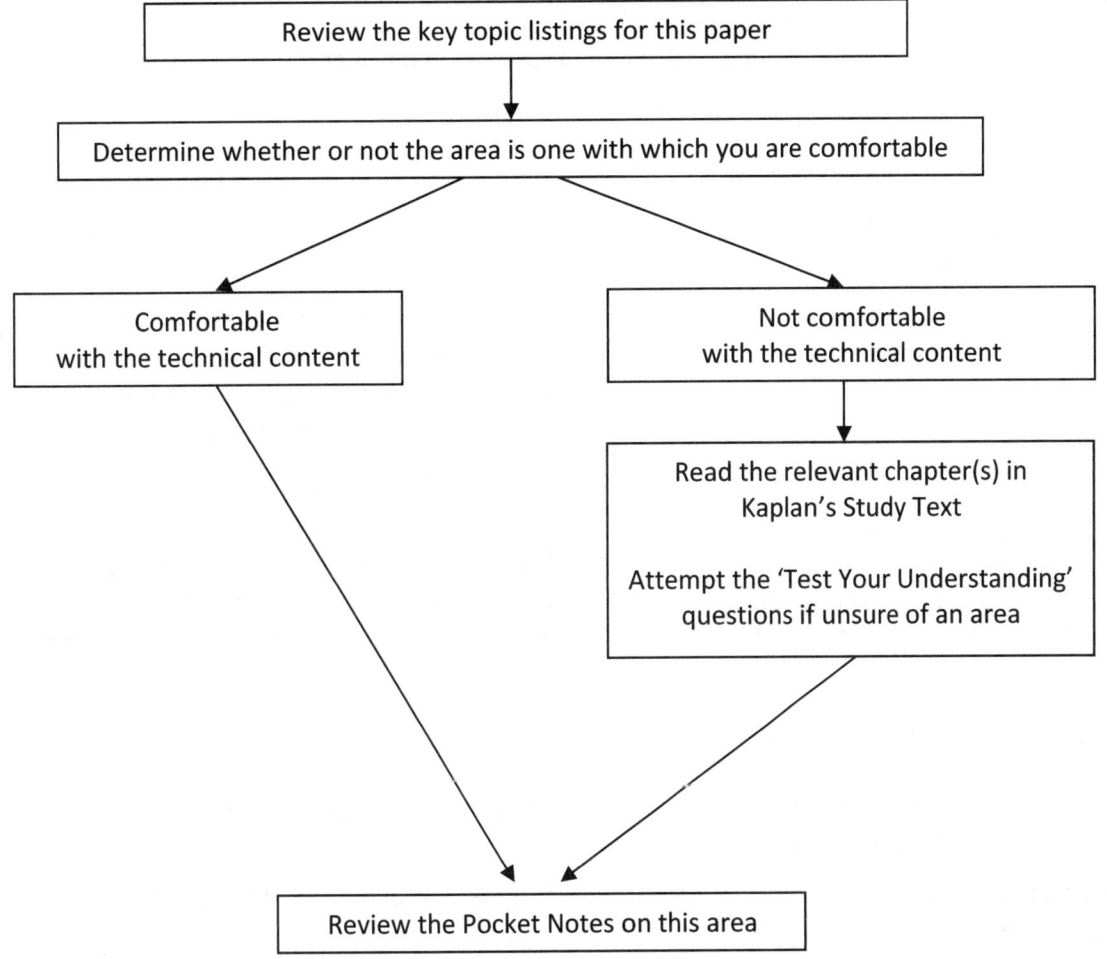

Stage 2: Practise questions

Follow the order of revision of topics as presented in this kit and attempt the questions in the order suggested.

Try to avoid referring to text books and notes and the model answer until you have completed your attempt.

Review your attempt with the model answer and assess how much of the answer you achieved.

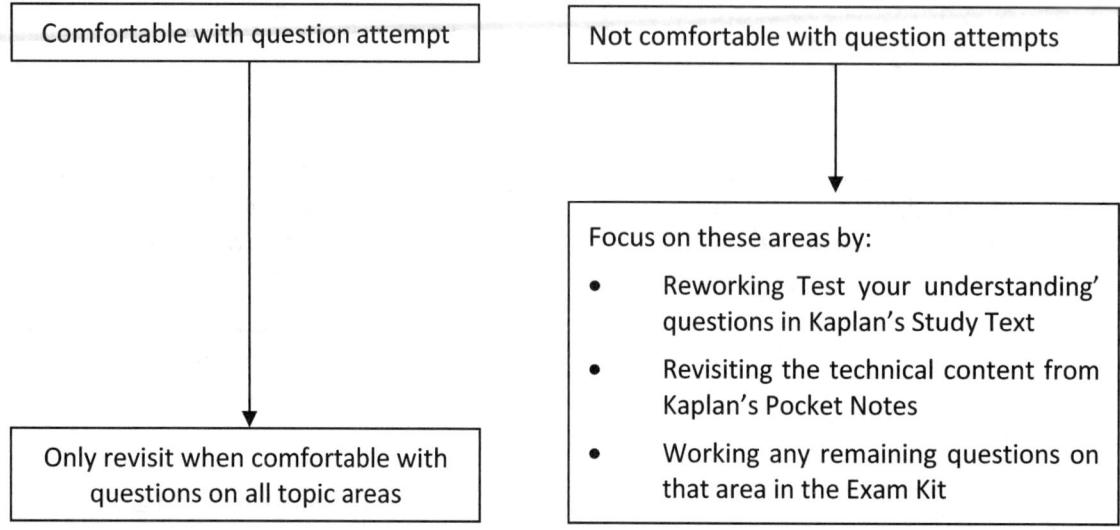

Stage 3: Final pre-exam revision

We recommend that you **attempt at least one three hour mock examination** containing a set of previously unseen exam standard questions.

Attempt the mock CBA online in timed, closed book conditions to simulate the real exam experience.

Section 1

PRACTICE QUESTIONS

BUDGETING

SOURCES OF INFORMATION

1 SOURCES (I)

Match each item of budget data below with its appropriate source.

Data	Source
UK interest rates	SWOT analysis
Competitor prices	European Union
UK economic growth forecasts	Pricing research
	UK Treasury, independent economics consultants
	Bank of England
	Sydney Morning Herald

2 SOURCES (II)

Match each item of budget data below with its appropriate source.

Data	Source
UK tax rates	Internal analysis
UK house prices	European Union
Customer tastes	Market research
	HMRC publications
	Foreign office
	Building society data

3 SOURCES (III)

Match each item of budget data below with its appropriate source.

Data	Source
French tax rates	Building Society data
Political party likely to win power	Market research
Customer preferences	Opinion poll surveys
	HMRC publications
	French government
	New Delhi Times

4 SOURCES (IV)

Match each item of budget data below with its appropriate source.

Data	Source
UK economic growth forecasts	Brazilian government
UK duty rates (tax on alcohol etc.)	New York Times
Brazilian import tax rates	Market research
	HMRC publications
	UK Treasury, independent economics consultants
	Sydney morning herald

BUDGETARY RESPONSIBILITIES

5 CONTACTS (I)

Match each task with the individual or group that you will need to contact for information.

Situation	Contact
You want to identify any production constraints	Trade union representative
You want to forecast the cost of labour	Board of Directors
The budget is ready for final approval	Suppliers
	Budget committee
	Production planning manager

PRACTICE QUESTIONS: SECTION 1

6 CONTACTS (II)

Match each task with the individual or group that you will need to contact for information.

Situation	Contact
You want to know the future strategy of the firm	Pressure group
You want to forecast the cost of machinery	Board of directors
You want to assess the efficiency of labour	Buyer
	Machinery buyers
	Management accountants

7 CONTACTS (III)

Match each task with the individual or group that you will need to contact for information.

Situation	Contact
You want to know day to day regional firm policy	Machine operator
You want to forecast sales	Board of directors
You want to know idle time last period	Regional manager
	Management accountants
	Sales team

8 CONTACTS (IV)

Match each task with the individual or group that you will need to contact for information.

Situation	Contact
You want to forecast the price of raw materials	Managing director
You want to examine competitors' prices	Suppliers
You want to check the availability of skilled labour	Other firms' price lists
	Firms' buying department
	Employment agency

KAPLAN PUBLISHING

9 THE RIGHT BUDGET

Drag each item of revenue or cost in the list below and drop it into its appropriate budget.

Cost
New machinery
Salary of HR Manager
Magazine advertising
New delivery van
Raw material usage
Incentives paid to sales staff
Spare parts for production machines
Salaries of repair engineers
Wages of assembly line workers

Capital expenditure

Marketing

Personnel

Cost of production

Maintenance

10 CUMIN COMPANY

The Cumin Company expects to produce 10,000 units in the month of December. Each unit requires 0.5 kgs of material X. During the production process 2% of material X is wasted. The business will start December with 900 kgs of X and will end the month with 950 kgs. Material X costs £1 per kg.

Complete the following resource budget for materials:

Resource Budget – Material X	Units	December
Needed for production		
Wastage		
Total requirement		
Closing inventory		
Opening Inventory		
Purchases in month		
Cost per kg		
Purchase cost of Material X (2 DP)		

PRACTICE QUESTIONS: **SECTION 1**

11 DRAG AND DROP

Drag each item of revenue or cost in the list below and drop it into its appropriate budget.

Cost
Television advertising
Enhancements to production machines
Wages of IT engineers
Wages of production line workers
New conveyor belt
Salary of IT Manager
Commissions paid to sales staff
Salary of HR Manager

Capital expenditure	Marketing

Personnel	Cost of production

IT

12 ADAM

Drag each item of revenue or cost in the list below and drop it into its appropriate budget.

Cost
New photocopier
Salary of HR Manager
Radio advertising
Raw material usage
Spare parts for production machines
Cost of machinery repairs
Lighting costs for factory
Market research costs
New cars
Cost of HR staff
New building
Cost of heating factory
Bonuses paid to sales team
Internet advertising
Spare parts for old trucks
Wages of assembly line workers

Capital expenditure	Marketing

Personnel	Cost of production

Maintenance

ACCOUNTING TREATMENT

13 ACCOUNTING TREATMENT (I)

Select the most appropriate accounting treatment for each of the following costs.

- Materials used in the production process
- Administrative wages
- Depreciation of production equipment
- Advertising costs
- Rent of the labour intensive production facility
- Office stationery
- Idle time pay for production workers
- Overtime Premium for production workers

Options available in drop down boxes against each item are:

- Allocate to marketing overheads
- Allocate to administrative overheads
- Direct cost
- Charge to production in a machine hour overhead rate
- Charge to production in a labour hour overhead rate

14 ACCOUNTING TREATMENT (II)

Select the most appropriate accounting treatment for each of the following costs.

- Materials used in the production process
- Rent of a machine intensive production facility
- Office paper
- Basic pay for production workers
- Secretarial wages
- Overtime premium for production workers
- Payments to marketing staff

Options available in drop down boxes against each item are:

- Allocate to marketing overheads
- Allocate to administrative overheads
- Direct cost
- Charge to production in a machine hour overhead rate
- Charge to production in a labour hour overhead rate

PRACTICE QUESTIONS: SECTION 1

15 ACCOUNTING TREATMENT (III)

Select the most appropriate accounting treatment for each of the following costs.

- Wood used in the production process
- General postage costs
- Internet advertising costs
- Office stationery
- Chemicals used in the production process
- Idle time pay for production workers
- Power costs for machinery

Options available in drop down boxes against each item are:

- Allocate to marketing overheads
- Allocate to administrative overheads
- Direct cost
- Charge to production in a machine hour overhead rate
- Charge to production in a labour hour overhead rate

INDICES

16 TACO

The budget committee has set the sales volume growth and pricing assumptions for years 2, 3 4 and 5 in the form of indices.

Complete the sales revenue forecast below. Do not show decimals. Round each figure to the nearest whole number.

	Year 1	Year 2	Year 3	Year 4	Year 5
Sales volume index	100	102	107	107	108
Sales price index	110	111	112	113	115

Sales revenue	Actual Year 1 £	Forecast Year 2 £	Forecast Year 3 £	Forecast Year 4 £	Forecast Year 5 £
At Year 1 prices	120,000				
At expected prices					

17 ARCHER

The budget committee has set the sales volume growth and pricing assumptions for years 2, 3 4 and 5 in the form of indices.

Complete the sales revenue forecast below. Do not show decimals. Round each figure to the nearest whole number.

	Year 1	Year 2	Year 3	Year 4	Year 5
Sales volume index	120	121	122	123	124
Sales price index	112	115	120	125	130

Sales revenue	Actual Year 1 £	Forecast Year 2 £	Forecast Year 3 £	Forecast Year 4 £	Forecast Year 5 £
At Year 1 prices	275,000				
At expected prices					

18 FLASH

The budget committee has set the sales volume growth and pricing assumptions for years 2, 3 4 and 5 in the form of indices.

Complete the sales revenue forecast below. Do not show decimals. Round each figure to the nearest whole number.

	Year 1	Year 2	Year 3	Year 4	Year 5
Sales volume index	118	121	122	123	124
Sales price index	112	115	120	125	130

Sales revenue	Actual Year 1 £	Forecast Year 2 £	Forecast Year 3 £	Forecast Year 4 £	Forecast Year 5 £
At Year 1 prices	280,000				
At expected prices					

PRACTICE QUESTIONS: SECTION 1

19 SOPHIE

The budget committee has set the sales volume growth and pricing assumptions for years 2, 3 4 and 5 in the form of indices.

Complete the sales revenue forecast below. Do not show decimals. Round each figure to the nearest whole number.

	Year 1	Year 2	Year 3	Year 4	Year 5
Sales volume index	118	120	125	127	128
Sales price index	112	115	120	125	130

Sales revenue	Actual Year 1 £	Forecast Year 2 £	Forecast Year 3 £	Forecast Year 4 £	Forecast Year 5 £
At Year 1 prices	280,000				
At expected prices					

PRODUCTION BUDGETS

20 TITANIA

Complete the following production forecast for product 'Titania'. Round any decimal figures up to the next whole number of units, if necessary.

Closing inventory should be 30% of the following week's sales volume. 3% of all production fails quality controls checks and is rejected.

Production (units)	Week 1	Week 2	Week 3	Week 4	Week 5
Opening inventory	20,000				
Good production					
Sales Volume	65,000	66,000	67,000	70,000	72,000
Closing inventory					

Rejected Production					
Total manufactured units					

21 PUCK

Complete the following production forecast for product 'Puck'. Round any decimal figures up to the next whole number of units, if necessary.

Closing inventory should be 30% of the following week's sales volume. 4% of all production fails quality controls checks and is rejected.

Production (units)	Week 1	Week 2	Week 3	Week 4	Week 5
Opening inventory	35,000				
Good production					
Sales Volume	80,000	78,000	78,000	70,000	80,000
Closing inventory					

Rejected Production				
Total manufactured units				

22 OBERON

Complete the following production forecast for product 'Oberon'. Round any decimal figures up to the next whole number of units, if necessary.

Closing inventory should be 30% of the following week's sales volume. 10% of all production fails quality controls checks and is rejected.

Production (units)	Week 1	Week 2	Week 3	Week 4	Week 5
Opening inventory	32,000				
Good production					
Sales Volume	78,000	78,000	75,000	70,000	80,000
Closing inventory					

Rejected Production				
Total manufactured units				

23 LYSANDER

Complete the following production forecast for product 'Lysander'. Round any decimal figures up to the next whole number of units, if necessary.

Closing inventory should be 30% of the following week's sales volume. 2% of all production fails quality controls checks and is rejected.

Production (units)	Week 1	Week 2	Week 3	Week 4	Week 5
Opening inventory	20,000				
Good production					
Sales Volume	65,000	65,000	67,000	70,000	72,000
Closing inventory					

Rejected Production				
Total manufactured units				

PRACTICE QUESTIONS: SECTION 1

24 DEMETRIUS

Complete the following production forecast for product 'Demetrius'. Round any decimal figures up to the next whole number of units, if necessary.

Closing inventory should be 30% of the following week's sales volume. 2% of all production fails quality controls checks and is rejected.

Production (units)	Week 1	Week 2	Week 3	Week 4	Week 5
Opening inventory	19,000				
Good production					
Sales Volume	65,000	66,000	67,000	70,000	72,000
Closing inventory					

Rejected Production					
Total manufactured units					

25 HERMIA

Complete the following production forecast for product 'Hermia'. Round any decimal figures up to the next whole number of units, if necessary.

Closing inventory should be 30% of the following week's sales volume. 3% of all production fails quality controls checks and is rejected.

Production (units)	Week 1	Week 2	Week 3	Week 4	Week 5
Opening inventory	19,000				
Good production					
Sales Volume	65,000	66,000	67,000	70,000	80,000
Closing inventory					

Rejected Production					
Total manufactured units					

26 EVIE

Complete the following production forecast for product A.

Units of product A	Week 1	Week 2	Week 3	Week 4	Week 5
Opening inventory	1,000				
Production					
Sub-total					
Sales	7,000	8,000	7,500	7,000	8,000
Closing inventory					

Closing inventory should be 25% of the following week's forecast sales.

(All gaps are numeric.)

KAPLAN PUBLISHING

AAT: APPLIED MANAGEMENT ACCOUNTING

27 EGO

Complete the following production forecast for the 'Ego'.

Units of Ego	Week 1	Week 2	Week 3	Week 4	Week 5
Opening inventory	2,000				
Production					
Sub-total					
Sales	14,000	16,000	15,000	14,000	16,000
Closing inventory					

Closing inventory should be 25% of the following week's forecast sales.

28 PRODUCT C

Complete the following production forecast for product C.

Units of product C	Week 1	Week 2	Week 3	Week 4	Week 5
Opening inventory	500				
Production					
Sub-total					
Sales	3,500	4,000	3,750	3,500	4,000
Closing inventory					

Closing inventory should be 20% of the following week's forecast sales.

(All gaps are numeric.)

29 PRODUCT B

The quarterly production requirements for product B are shown below.

5% of production fails the quality checks and must be scrapped.

How many items of product B must be manufactured to allow for waste?

	Month 1	Month 2	Month 3
Required units	90,250	95,000	99,750
Manufactured units			

30 ROPE

The quarterly production requirements for product 'Rope' are shown below.

5% of production fails the quality checks and must be scrapped.

How many items of 'Rope' must be manufactured to allow for waste?

	Month 1	Month 2	Month 3
Required units	180,670	190,980	185,900
Manufactured units			

PRACTICE QUESTIONS: SECTION 1

31 CAMELIA

Labour hours

104,000 units of product 'Camelia' are to be manufactured in May. Each one takes 3 minutes to produce.

25 staff will each work 176 hours basic time.

How many overtime hours must be worked to complete the production?

Select from   600   5,200   860   800   3,800

32 SAGE

Raw material purchases

20,000 items of product Sage are to be manufactured in April. Each requires 2.5 metres of raw material. You are also told that:

- 20% of raw material is wasted during manufacture.
- The opening inventory will be 10,000 metres.
- The closing inventory will be 14,000 metres.

How much material must be purchased?

Select from   63,000m   66,500m   70,750m   52,000m   68,000m

33 BUMBLEBEE

The quarterly production requirements for product Bumblebee are shown below.

2% of production fails the quality checks and must be scrapped.

How many items of product B must be manufactured to allow for waste?

	Month 1	Month 2	Month 3
Required units	18,900	20,150	22,200
Manufactured units			

34 QUALITY CONTROL

The company has budgeted to make and sell 240,000 units in the coming year.

Each unit takes 1.5 labour hours to make and requires 2.5kg of raw material. The quality control department can test 18,000 units each month. A contract has been placed to purchase 500,000kg of raw material at an agreed price. Further supplies can be obtained on the open market but the price is likely to be much higher. The company employs 198 production workers. Each worker works 1,750 hours in a year in normal time.

Complete the following analysis.

There is labour available to make _____ units in normal time. Therefore, _____ hours of overtime will be needed.

The raw material contract will provide enough material to make _____ units. Therefore, _____ kg will have to be purchased on the open market.

Quality control can test _____ units in the year. It will be necessary to make alternative arrangements for _____ units.

35 COMPANY A

Complete the following analysis.

There is labour available to make **131,250** units in normal time. Therefore, **10,500** hours of overtime will be needed.

The raw material contract will provide enough material to make **100,000** units. Therefore, **72,000** kg will have to be purchased on the open market.

Quality control can test **120,000** units in the year. It will be necessary to make alternative arrangements for **20,000** units.

36 JONES

Complete the following analysis.

There is labour available to make **131,250** units in normal time. Therefore, **15,000** hours of overtime will be needed.

The raw material contract will provide enough material to make **100,000** units. Therefore, **150,000** kg will have to be purchased on the open market.

Quality control can test **144,000** units in the year. It will be necessary to make alternative arrangements for **6,000** units.

37 DONALD

How many overtime hours must be worked to complete the production?

200

38 THEO

Labour hours

48,000 units of product 'Theo' are to be manufactured in May.

Each one takes 6 minutes to produce.

28 staff will each work 170 hours basic time.

How many overtime hours must be worked to complete the production?

Select from   200   4,800   4,760   300   40

MACHINE UTILISATION

39 E, F AND G

Department Y manufactures three products, E, F and G.

Calculate the machine hours required to manufacture these in November.

Product	Units	Hours per unit	Hours required
E	100	1.0	
F	230	2.0	
G	370	3.5	
		Total hours for Department Y	

There are four machines in the department.

Each machine can be used for 300 hours in November. Additional machines can be hired if required.

How many additional machines should be hired? ☐

40 ZEE

Zee manufactures three products, C, D and E.

Calculate the machine hours required to manufacture these in January.

Product	Units	Hours per unit	Hours required
C	200	0.5	
D	460	2.0	
E	740	2.5	
		Total hours for Zee	

There are five machines in the department.

Each machine can be used for 500 hours in January. Additional machines can be hired if required.

How many additional machines should be hired? ☐

41 CLAUDIO

Calculate machine utilisation.

Do not show decimals. Round up to the next whole number of hours or percentage, if necessary. There are 100 machines in the department. Each can be used for 80 hours in the period.

Budgeted machine loading Product	Items	Hours per item	Hours required
A	2,000	1.00	
B	1,750	2.00	
C	610	3.00	
Total machine hours required			
% utilisation			

42 DOGBERRY

Calculate machine utilisation.

Do not show decimals. Round up to the next whole number of hours or percentage, if necessary. There are 50 machines in the department. Each can be used for 50 hours in the period.

Budgeted machine loading Product	Items	Hours per item	Hours required
A	120	3.75	
B	175	1.50	
C	190	1.50	
Total machine hours required			
% utilisation			

43 LEONATO

Calculate machine utilisation.

Do not show decimals. Round up to the next whole number of hours or percentage, if necessary. There are 60 machines in the department. Each can be used for 40 hours in the period.

Budgeted machine loading Product	Items	Hours per item	Hours required
A	250	3.00	
B	1,000	1.00	
C	390	1.50	
Total machine hours required			
% utilisation			

PRACTICE QUESTIONS: SECTION 1

44 BORACHIO

Calculate machine utilisation.

Do not show decimals. Round up to the next whole number of hours or percentage, if necessary.

There are 40 machines in the department. Each can be used for 5 hours in the period.

Budgeted machine loading	Items	Hours per item	Hours required
Product			
A	25	4	
B	10	2	
C	40	1.50	
Total machine hours required			
% utilisation			

CAPACITY CONSTRAINTS

45 GLOUCESTER

Calculate the capacity constraints for product FF by completing the table below.

Round down to the maximum whole number of units, if necessary.

According to the standard cost card, each unit of this product requires:

- 1 kilograms of material
- 40 minutes of direct labour time
- 5 minutes of machine time

Budgets have been drafted by departmental heads which show:

- Maximum sales demand of 1,700 units
- 2,500 kilograms of material available
- 420 hours of direct labour time available without using overtime
- 120 hours of machine time available.

Production capacity	Units
Sufficient materials are budgeted to manufacture	
Without overtime, sufficient direct labour is budgeted to manufacture	
Sufficient machine time is budgeted to manufacture	
Without overtime, the maximum sales volume is	
With unlimited overtime, the maximum sales volume is	

KAPLAN PUBLISHING

46 BEDFORD

Calculate the capacity constraints for product FF by completing the table below.

Round down to the maximum whole number of units, if necessary.

According to the standard cost card, each unit of this product requires:

- 12 kilograms of material
- 120 minutes of direct labour time
- 25 minutes of machine time

Budgets have been drafted by departmental heads which show:

- Maximum sales demand of 350 units
- 1,200 kilograms of material available
- 600 hours of direct labour time available without using overtime
- 180 hours of machine time available.

Production capacity	Units
Sufficient materials are budgeted to manufacture	
Without overtime, sufficient direct labour is budgeted to manufacture	
Sufficient machine time is budgeted to manufacture	
Without overtime, the maximum sales volume is	
With unlimited overtime, the maximum sales volume is	

PRACTICE QUESTIONS: SECTION 1

WORKING SCHEDULES AND OPERATING BUDGETS

47 WASHINGTON

Complete the three working schedules using the information from the production budget and notes below.

Enter all figures as positive values.

Production budget	Units
Opening inventory of finished goods	1,050
Production	20,000
Sub-total	21,050
Sales	18,000
Closing inventory of finished goods	3,050

Materials	Kg	£
Opening inventory	2,200	3,080
Purchases @ £1.50 per kg		
Sub-total		
Used		
Closing inventory	35,000	
Closing inventory to be valued at budgeted purchase price		

Materials

Each unit produced requires 2.5 kilograms of material.

Closing inventory is to be valued at the budgeted price per kilo.

Labour

Each item takes 6 minutes to produce.

8 staff work 200 basic hours each in the period.

Overtime is paid at time and a half (50% above basic rate).

Production overhead

Variable overhead is recovered on total labour hours.

Labour	Hours	£
Basic time @ £16 per hour		
Overtime		
Total		

Production overhead	Hours	£
Variable @ £2.50 per hour		
Fixed		165,020
Total		

48 ADAMS

Use the information provided in the previous question, 'Washington' to complete the operating budget below.

Enter income, costs and inventories as positive figures.

Closing finished goods inventory will be valued at the budgeted production cost per unit.

Operating budget	Units	£ per unit	£
Sales revenue		27.00	
Cost of goods sold			£
Opening inventory of finished goods			40,000
Cost of production		£	
Materials			
Labour			
Production overhead			
Closing inventory of finished goods			
Cost of goods sold			
Gross profit / (loss)			
Overheads		£	
Administration		80,000	
Marketing		25,000	
Operating profit / (loss)			

49 JEFFERSON

Complete the three working schedules using the information from the production budget and notes below.

Enter all figures as positive values.

Production budget	Units
Opening inventory of finished goods	3,000
Production	16,500
Sub-total	19,500
Sales	15,000
Closing inventory of finished goods	4,500

Materials	Kg	£
Opening inventory	20,000	12,000
Purchases @ £2.00 per kg		
Sub-total		
Used		
Closing inventory	35,000	
Closing inventory to be valued at budgeted purchase price		

Materials
Each unit produced requires 5 kilograms of material.
Closing inventory is to be valued at the budgeted price per kilo.

Labour
Each item takes 12 minutes to produce.
35 staff work 60 basic hours each in the period.
Overtime is paid at time and a half (50% above basic rate).

Production overhead
Variable overhead is recovered on total labour hours.

Labour	Hours	£
Basic time @ £8 per hour		
Overtime		
Total		

Production overhead	Hours	£
Variable @ £2.00 per hour		
Fixed		155,200
Total		

AAT: APPLIED MANAGEMENT ACCOUNTING

50 BURR

Use the information provided in the previous question, 'Jefferson' to complete the operating budget below.

Enter income, costs and inventories as positive figures.

Closing finished goods inventory will be valued at the budgeted production cost per unit.

Operating budget	Units	£ per unit	£
Sales revenue		30.00	
Cost of goods sold			£
Opening inventory of finished goods			40,000
Cost of production		£	
Materials			
Labour			
Production overhead			
Closing inventory of finished goods			
Cost of goods sold			
Gross profit / (loss)			
Overheads		£	
Administration		55,000	
Marketing		60,000	

51 SINCLAIR LTD

Sinclair Ltd makes a single product, the Dom. You are Sinclair's management accountant and you are responsible for preparing its operating budgets. The accounting year is divided into 13 four-week periods. There are five days in each week. The sales director of Sinclair has recently completed the following forecast sales volume for the next five periods:

Sales forecast five periods to 18 November 2011

	Period 1	Period 2	Period 3	Period 4	Period 5
4 weeks ending	29 July	26 August	23 Sept	21 Oct	18 Nov
Number of Doms	19,400	21,340	23,280	22,310	22,310

The production director also provides you with the following information:

(i) On completion of production, 3% of the Doms are found to be faulty and have to be scrapped. The faulty Doms are thought to be caused by poor work practices by some of the production workers although this is not known for certain.

The faulty Doms have no scrap value.

(ii) Opening inventories in period 1 were made of finished goods (3,880 Doms) and raw materials (16,500 litres).

(iii) Closing inventories at the end of each period have set rules: finished inventory must equal four days' sales volume of Doms in the next period, and raw materials must equal five days' gross production in the next period.

(iv) Each Dom requires 3 litres of material costing £8 per litre.

(v) Each Dom requires 0.5 hours of labour.

(vi) Sinclair employs 70 production workers who each work a 40-hour week. The 70 production workers work independently of one another in making Doms. Each employee is paid a guaranteed wage of £240 per week, and overtime payments should only be made if absolutely necessary.

(vii) The cost of any overtime is £9 per hour.

Required:

1 Prepare the following budgets for the production director:

(a) **Gross production budget in Doms (including faulty production) for each of the first four periods.**

(b) **Material purchases budget in litres for each of the first three periods.**

(c) **Cost of the material purchases for each of the first three periods.**

(d) **Labour budget in hours for each of the first three periods including any overtime required in each period.**

(e) **Cost of the labour budget for each of the first three periods including the cost of any overtime.**

2 Write a short memo to the production director. In your memo, you should:

(a) explain and quantify the value of any possible overtime savings.

(b) suggest ONE extra cost which might be necessary to achieve the overtime savings.

CASH FLOW FORECASTS

52 WASHINGTON AND ADAMS

Complete the cash flow forecast using the budget data that you have calculated in questions 47 'Washington' and 48 'Adams', as well as the information below. Enter receipts and payments as positive figures.

The sales receivables balance is expected to decrease by 162,000 over the year.

The materials payable balance is expected to increase by 26,800 over the year.

All other payments are made in the year in which they are incurred.

Production overheads include a depreciation charge of 19,000.

AAT: APPLIED MANAGEMENT ACCOUNTING

Cash flow forecast	£	
Opening cash balance / (overdraft)		29,650
Sales receipts		
Payments		
Materials		
Labour		
Production overhead		
Other overheads		
Capital expenditure	50,000	
Closing cash balance / (overdraft)		

53 JEFFERSON AND BURR

Complete the cash flow forecast using the budget data that you have calculated in questions 49 'Jefferson' and 50 'Burr', as well as the information below. Enter receipts and payments as positive figures.

The sales receivables balance is expected to decrease by 15,000 over the year.

The materials payable balance is expected to decrease by 32,600 over the year.

All other payments are made in the year in which they are incurred.

Production overheads include a depreciation charge of 15,000.

Cash flow forecast	£	
Opening cash balance / (overdraft)		90,000
Sales receipts		
Payments		
Materials		
Labour		
Production overhead		
Other overheads		
Capital expenditure	120,000	
Closing cash balance / (overdraft)		

PRACTICE QUESTIONS: SECTION 1

54 CASH FORECAST FOR MAY

Prepare a cash forecast for May from the following budget data.

Budget data	Feb £	Mar £	Apr £	May £	Cash forecast	May £
Invoiced sales	7,000	7,700	7,900	8,300	Opening cash balance	–320
Purchases	6,500	6,300	6,400	6,700	Customer receipts	
Wages	300	340	370	400		
Other overheads	550	540	575	590	**Payments**	
Capital expenditure	0	0	0	3,000	For purchases	
					For wages	
					For overheads	
					For capital exp.	
					Total	
					Closing cash balance	

Average terms

55% of customers take 1 month to pay, the remainder take 2 months

Purchases paid for in the current month

Wages paid in the current month

Other overheads paid after two months

Capital expenditure paid in the following month

Show payments and receipts as plus figures.

Negative balance = overdrawn

55 THE LATEST

Prepare the forecast from the operating budget and statement of financial position assumptions. Enter receipts and payments as positive figures.

Statement of financial position assumptions:

Receivables will increase by £90,000.

Materials payables will reduce by £77,000.

Labour costs are paid in the period in which they are incurred.

Other payables will increase by £2,000.

Operating budget	£	£
Sales revenue		352,000
Expenditure		
Materials	34,200	
Labour	41,250	
Other costs	16,400	91,850
Operating profit		260,150

Cash flow forecast	£	£
Sales receipts		
Payments		
Materials		
Labour		
Other costs		
Cash-flow forecast		

KAPLAN PUBLISHING

56 HARVEST FESTIVAL

Prepare the forecast from the operating budget and balance sheet assumptions.

Enter receipts and payments as positive figures.

Balance sheet assumptions:

Receivables will reduce by £1,500.

Materials payables will increase by £2,500.

Labour costs are paid in the period in which they are incurred.

Other payables will reduce by £650.

Operating budget	£	£
Sales revenue		112,000
Expenditure		
Materials	35,000	
Labour	26,200	
Other costs	16,700	77,900
Operating profit		34,100

Cash flow forecast	£	£
Sales receipts		
Payments		
Materials		
Labour		
Other costs		
Cash-flow forecast		

57 OKTOBERFEST

Prepare the forecast from the operating budget and balance sheet assumptions.

Enter receipts and payments as positive figures.

Balance sheet assumptions:

Receivables will increase by £3,000.

Materials payables will increase by £3,000.

Labour costs are paid in the period in which they are incurred.

Other payables will reduce by £3,150.

Operating budget	£	£
Sales revenue		159,800
Expenditure		
Materials	58,550	
Labour	20,000	
Other costs	19,300	97,850
Operating profit		61,950

Cash flow forecast	£	£
Sales receipts		
Payments		
Materials		
Labour		
Other costs		
Cash Flow forecast		

PERIODIC BUDGETS

58 APRIL BUDGETS

Calculate these sales and cost budgets for April:

	Budget for the year	Budget for April
Units sold	34,000	3,000
Units produced	36,000	3,500
	£	£
Sales	204,000	
Materials used	59,400	
Labour	67,200	
Variable production overhead	54,000	
Fixed overhead	3,600	

Each unit is made from 1.5 kg of material costing £1.10 per kg.

It takes 6 minutes to make each item. 200 hours of basic time is available in the month. Any extra hours must be worked in overtime.

The basic rate is £16 per hour. Overtime is paid at time and a half (50% more than basic rate.) Variable overhead relates to labour hours, including overtime. Fixed overhead costs are incurred evenly through the year.

AAT: APPLIED MANAGEMENT ACCOUNTING

59 ROSE

Rose Ltd manufactures a single product, the Bud.

Calculate these sales and cost budgets for May:

	Budget for the year	Budget for May
Units sold	68,000	6,000
Units produced	72,000	7,000
	£	£
Sales	1,408,000	
Materials used	720,000	
Labour	264,000	
Variable production overhead	96,000	
Fixed overhead	3,600	

Each Bud is made from 2.5 kg of material costing £4 per kg. It takes 10 minutes to make a Bud.

800 hours of basic time is available in the month. Any extra hours must be worked in overtime.

The basic rate is £20 per hour. Overtime is paid at time and a half (50% more than basic rate.)

Variable overhead relates to labour hours, including overtime.

Fixed overhead costs are incurred evenly through the year.

Round to nearest whole number.

60 SALES AND COSTS

Calculate these sales and cost budgets for June:

	Budget for the year	Budget for June
Units sold	120,000	11,000
Units produced	110,000	10,000
	£	£
Sales	1,649,000	
Materials used	1,155,000	
Labour	95,500	
Variable production overhead	55,000	
Fixed overhead	3,600	

Each unit is made from 3.5 kg of material costing £3 per kg.

It takes 5 minutes to make each item.

700 hours of basic time is available in the month.

Any extra hours must be worked in overtime.

The basic rate is £10 per hour.

Overtime is paid at time and a half (50% more than basic rate.)

Variable overhead relates to labour hours, including overtime.

Fixed overhead costs are incurred evenly through the year.

ALTERNATIVE SCENARIOS

61 MADISON

Complete the alternative scenario column in the operating budget table and calculate the increase or decrease in profit.

For the sales price per unit figure, enter any decimal places, if relevant.

For the other figures, round to the nearest whole number, if necessary.

Assumptions in the first scenario

Material and labour costs are variable.

Depreciation is a stepped cost, increasing at every 8,000 units.

There is an allowance for an energy rise of 10.0%.

Alternative scenario

Increase the selling price by 5.0%

Reduce the sales volume by 8.0%.

Revise the energy price rise to 8.0%.

Operating budget	First draft	Alternative scenario
Sales price per unit (£)	15.00	
Sales volume	75,000	
		£
Sales revenue	1,125,000	
Costs		
Material	131,250	
Labour	187,500	
Energy	44,000	
Depreciation	62,400	
Total	425,150	
Gross Profit	699,850	
Increase / (decrease) in gross profit		

62 MONROE

Complete the alternative scenario column in the operating budget table and calculate the increase or decrease in profit.

For the sales price per unit figure, enter any decimal places, if relevant.

For the other figures, round to the nearest whole number, if necessary.

Assumptions in the first scenario

Material and labour costs are variable.

Depreciation is a stepped cost, increasing at every 1,000 units.

There is an allowance for an energy rise of 10.0%.

Alternative scenario

Increase the selling price by 5.0%.

Reduce the sales volume by 2.0%.

Revise the energy price rise to 3.0%.

Operating budget	First draft	Alternative scenario
Sales price per unit (£)	20.00	21.00
Sales volume	6,200	6,076
		£
Sales revenue	124,000	127,596
Costs		
Material	4,650	4,557
Labour	12,400	12,152
Energy	33,000	30,900
Depreciation	14,000	14,000
Total	64,050	61,609
Gross Profit	59,950	65,987
Increase / (decrease) in gross profit		6,037

PRACTICE QUESTIONS: SECTION 1

SALES REVENUE AND COSTS FORECASTS

63 INCOME FORECAST (I)

From the following data revise the income forecast.

Next year, income is forecast at £4,284,000. This assumes a 2% increase in selling price. In the light of increasing competition the marketing manager has decided not to make the increase.

The forecast should be revised to _____.

Select from   £4,198,320   £4,200,000   £4,284,000   £4,369,680

64 INCOME FORECAST (II)

From the following data revise the income forecast.

Next year income is forecast at £7,272,000. This assumes a 1% increase in selling price.

In the light of increasing competition the marketing manager has decided not to make the increase.

The forecast should be revised to _____.

Select from   £7,199,280   £7,200,000   £7,272,000   £7,344,720

65 INCOME FORECAST (III)

From the following data revise the income forecast.

Next year income is forecast at £816,000. This assumes a 2% increase in selling price.

In the light of increasing competition the marketing manager has decided not to make the increase.

The forecast should be revised to _____.

Select from   £799,680   £800,000   £816,000   £832,320

66 ENERGY COSTS

From the following data revise the forecast for energy costs.

Next year energy costs are forecast at £157,590. This assumes a 3% increase in energy consumption and a 2% increase in gas and electricity tariffs.

However energy saving measures are being proposed. Instead of increasing, consumption should be reduced by 6%.

The energy budget should be £_____.

Select from   £143,820   £148,135   £150,000   £153,000

KAPLAN PUBLISHING

67 ELECTRICITY COSTS

From the following data revise the forecast for electricity costs.

Next year energy costs are forecast at £212,160. This assumes a 2% increase in energy consumption and a 4% increase in gas and electricity tariffs.

However energy saving measures are being proposed. Instead of increasing, consumption should be reduced by 5%.

The energy budget should be £_____.

Select from   £197,600   £200,000   £201,552   £208,000

68 FIXED OVERHEADS AND HIGH-LOW

The following data relate to two output levels of a department:

Machine hours	17,000	18,500
Overheads	£246,500	£251,750

The amount of fixed overheads is: £_____.

69 FLUTE

A company incurs the following costs at various activity levels:

Total cost	Activity level
£	Units
250,000	5,000
312,500	7,500
400,000	10,000

Using the high-low method what is the variable cost per unit?

A   £25

B   £30

C   £35

D   £40

70 DISCOUNTS ONE

R Ltd requires 15,000 litres of material S. Material S has a list price of £2.50 per litre. Quantity discounts are available on a tiered basis and are shown in the table below.

Quantity purchased	Discount %
First 1,000 litres	1%
Next 2,000 litres	2%
Next 4,000 litres	4%
All further purchases receive a discount of	5%

If total purchases exceed 12,000 litres a further 2% discount is available on the total amount payable.

Calculate the total amount payable after all available discounts have been claimed. State your answer to two decimal places.

71 DISCOUNTS TWO

QP Ltd requires 8,000 kg of material OM. Material OM has a list price of £3.00 per kg. Quantity discounts are available on a tiered basis and are shown in the table below.

Quantity purchased	Discount %
First 2,000 kg	1%
Next 1,000 kg	2%
Next 1,000 kg	3%
All further purchases receive a discount of	4%

If total purchases exceed 10,000 kg a further 2% discount is available on the total amount payable.

Calculate the total amount payable after all available discounts have been claimed. State your answer to two decimal places.

72 HIGH – LOW

X has recorded their units of production and their total costs for the past six months.

	Production units	Total costs
Jan	11,150	£60,000
Feb	12,345	£66,000
Mar	11,766	£63,080
Apr	13,055	£69,500
May	12,678	£67,500
Jun	13,100	£69,750

The management of X wish to know the total fixed cost and variable cost per unit.

Variable cost per unit is £ ☐

Fixed costs in total are £ ☐

73 HILOW

Y has recorded their units of production and their total costs for the past six months.

	Production units	Total costs £
Jan	420	4,600
Feb	450	4,965
Mar	430	4,750
Apr	460	5,000
May	440	4,900
Jun	410	4,500

The management of Y wish to know the total fixed cost and variable cost per unit.

Variable cost per unit is £ ☐

Fixed costs in total are £ ☐

74 STEPPED

A company has achieved the following output levels and total costs:

Volume of production (units)	25,000	29,000
Total cost	£418,750	£458,750

Total cost includes a fixed element which steps up by £25,000 at an activity level of 27,000 units.

The variable cost per unit is constant.

The variable cost per unit is £ [ ]

75 STEEPLE

A company has achieved the following output levels and total costs:

Volume of production (units)	2,000	2,400
Total cost	£15,000	£21,000

Total cost includes a fixed element which steps up by £5,000 at an activity level of 2,100 units.

The variable cost per unit is constant.

The variable cost per unit is £ [ ]

76 PEN

A company has achieved the following output levels and total costs:

Volume of production (units)	15,000	24,000
Total cost	£125,000	£158,000

There is a bulk buy discount of £0.50 per unit applicable to all units once the purchase quantity exceeds 23,000 units.

The fixed cost is constant.

The variable cost per unit (before the discount) is £ [ ]

The fixed cost is £ [ ]

Forecast the total cost for 25,000 units £ [ ]

77 POPPY

A company has achieved the following output levels and total costs:

Volume of production (units)	28,000	34,000
Total cost	£38,750	£48,750

A bulk buy discount of 16% of the variable cost is applicable to all units once the purchase quantity exceeds 35,000 units.

Total cost includes a fixed element which steps up by £2,500 at an activity level of 30,000 units.

The variable cost per unit (before the discount) is £ ☐

The fixed cost before the step up is £ ☐

Forecast the total cost at an activity level of 40,000 units £ ☐

WRITTEN TASKS

78 NOSEY

You are asked to review the Operating Statement for Nosey Ltd, shown below, and the background information provided, and to make recommendations.

Operating Statement for May 2009
Revenue (units)   3,264,000

	Budget	Actual	Variance Fav/(Adverse)
	£	£	£
Revenue	6,528,000	7,180,800	652,800
Variable costs			
Material	1,958,400	1,960,200	(1,800)
Labour	1,468,800	1,542,200	(73,400)
Distribution	260,400	266,600	(6,200)
Power	326,400	324,700	1,700
Equipment hire	163,200	162,000	1,200
	4,177,200	4,255,700	(78,500)
Contribution	2,350,800	2,925,100	574,300
Fixed costs			
Power	33,600	36,000	(2,400)
Equipment hire	24,000	21,600	2,400
Depreciation	259,200	264,000	(4,800)
Marketing	290,400	307,200	(16,800)
Administration	352,800	362,400	(9,600)
	960,000	991,200	(31,200)
Operating profit	1,390,800	1,933,900	543,100

The budget has been flexed to the actual number of units produced and sold. The original budget had been drawn up by the Chief Executive of Nosey and communicated to senior managers by email.

Despite an unbudgeted price increase, the volume of units sold was higher than expected in the original budget. This seems to have been due to a very successful advertising campaign. Unfortunately, the extra demand could only be met by the work force working overtime, which is paid at time and a half.

One of the raw materials included in the product is a chemical which fell in price by 3% for part of the month.

Although pleased with the overall results, the Chief Executive is concerned that costs were above budget and has asked you to advise how control can be improved.

Write an email to the Chief Executive in which you:

(a) **Suggest possible reasons for the variances on materials, labour, marketing and administration**

(b) **Explain THREE steps that the company can take to motivate managers to achieve budgets.**

To	Chief executive	Date	(Today)
From	Budget accountant	Subject	Review of operating statement

(a) **Reasons for variances**

(b) Three steps to motivate managers to achieve budgets

79 CM LTD

The directors of CM Ltd are putting forward a budget proposal for 2017. Actual results for 2016 are provided for comparison. The Chief Exec's approval of the 2017 budget is requested. You are CM's budget accountant.

Substantial sales growth was achieved in 2016. CM Ltd introduced more than a dozen innovative new products. The key features of these products are patented and therefore protected from direct competition. CM Ltd has a solid customer base.

In 2017, CM Ltd will retain its own identity in the market place. In addition, CM's directors plan to develop a sales channel through George Products Ltd and to be promoted in that company's catalogue.

CM Ltd has 50 products in its catalogue at all stages of the product lifecycle. More exciting new products are being planned. CM's directors are confident that the budgeted 10% growth will be achieved. They have explained that they do not feel it is realistic to try and calculate sales revenue and costs at product level.

The directors have also allowed a 2.5% increase in costs in line with expected inflation. A yearly management bonus (£21,000 in 2016) is linked to these 2017 results, but it has not yet been authorised for payment by the company's remuneration committee.

No increase in selling prices has been assumed, because this is difficult to achieve with high-tech products.

Operating budget for year ended 31/12/2017	2016 results	Draft 2017 budget
Sales volume	7,950	8,745
	£	£
Sales revenue	1,128,900	1,241,790
Costs:		
Materials	246,450	277,256
Labour	409,425	460,603
Production overheads	144,690	162,776
Depreciation	46,800	52,650
Marketing	18,640	20,970
Administration	92,600	104,175
Total	958,605	1,078,430
Operating profit	170,295	163,360
Operating profit as a % to sales	15.1%	13.2%

Write an email to the Chief Executive in which you:

(a) Examine the planning assumptions and calculations in the proposed budget, and identify any weaknesses.

(b) Explain how costs and profitability should be managed in a multi-product manufacturing organisation

(c) Give your opinion, with reasons, on how well the budget would motivate managers to create sustainable, profitable growth.

80 CONTROLLABILITY

Rough & Tumble (R&T) manufactures children's sports clothes for sale online. In the factory, nylon is mostly used in the manufacturing process.

Jon McRae has just joined R&T as Production Manager and has argued that R&T should only use cotton in production, as cotton is superior to nylon for exercise as it 'breathes' more easily. However, cotton is more expensive than nylon. Jon McRae hopes the increased quality of the clothes would stimulate demand, and justify an immediate price increase for the clothes.

R&T operates a responsibility accounting system, which updates raw materials standards every December and allocates variances to specific individuals. Bonuses are only awarded to managers when favourable variances are allocated to them.

Jon Mc Rae's approach was approved and only pure cotton clothes were manufactured from the start of March 2010, although no changes were made to the standard cost cards.

PRACTICE QUESTIONS: SECTION 1

You are the Assistant Management Accountant in R&T and you have been presented with the following extract from a variance report:

Manager responsible:	**Allocated variances**	**February**	**March**
Production manager	Material price (total for all materials)	£ 300 F	£ (3,000) A
	Material usage	£ 100 F	£ (200) A
Sales manager	Sales variance	£ (700) A	£ 10,000 F

Required:

Write an email to the Chief Executive in which you:

(a) Assess the performance of the Production Manager and that of the Sales Manager.

(b) Comment on the controllability of variances in R&T and the fairness of the bonus scheme.

To	Chief executive	**Date**	(Today)
From	Assistant Management Accountant	**Subject**	Review of variances

(a) Performance of production manager and sales manager

(b) Controllability of variances in R&T and the fairness of the bonus scheme

AAT: APPLIED MANAGEMENT ACCOUNTING

81 FRANKA

You are asked to review the operating statement shown below, and the background information provided, and to make recommendations.

Operating statement for May 2009

Revenue (units): 380,000

	Budget £	Actual £	Variance Fav/(Adverse) £
Revenue	8,740,000	8,626,000	(114,000)
Variable costs			
Material	2,040,000	2,116,000	(76,000)
Labour	1,900,000	1,938,000	(38,000)
Distribution	126,000	127,000	(1,000)
Power	1,720,000	1,624,000	96,000
Equipment hire	87,400	86,100	1,300
	5,873,400	5,891,100	(17,700)
Contribution	2,866,600	2,734,900	(131,700)
Fixed costs			
Power	160,000	150,700	9,300
Equipment hire	20,000	21,500	(1,500)
Depreciation	400,000	200,000	200,000
Marketing	480,000	358,000	122,000
Administration	438,600	432,200	6,400
	1,498,600	1,162,400	336,200
Operating profit	1,368,000	1,572,500	204,500

The budget has been flexed to the actual number of units produced and sold. The original budget had been drawn up by the Chief Executive and communicated to senior managers by email. This was part of a new performance-related pay scheme recently introduced for senior managers.

For technical reasons, the same amount of electricity is required for each unit produced and no economies are possible. There is only one possible electricity supplier who has recently reduced both its fixed charge and its variable charge per unit.

The Chief Executive is pleased with the overall results and believes that it was the introduction of the performance-related pay that was the key reason for the actual profit being greater than forecast.

PRACTICE QUESTIONS: **SECTION 1**

Write an email to the Chief Executive in which you:

(a) Explain the key variances and give reasons, other than performance-related pay, to explain why the actual profit for the year was greater than planned.

(b) Give FOUR general conditions necessary for performance-related pay to successfully lead to improved performance in organisations.

To	Chief executive	**Date**	(Today)
From	Budget accountant	**Subject**	Review of operating statement

(a) Key variances and reasons for increase in the actual profit

(b) FOUR general conditions necessary for performance-related pay to successfully lead to improved performance in organisations

KAPLAN PUBLISHING

AAT: **APPLIED MANAGEMENT ACCOUNTING**

82 LABOUR COSTS

You have prepared a draft budget for direct labour costs.

- It is based on this year's costs plus an expected pay rise and increased staffing.
- The manager of human resources has forecast the pay rise.
- You have calculated the required staffing from the agreed production budget.
- You have been asked to suggest appropriate performance measures that would assist managers to monitor direct labour performance against budget.

Direct labour budget

	This year	Next year budget
Production units	1,170,000	1,650,000
Minutes per unit	5.00	5.00
Labour hours	97,500	137,500
Annual hrs per staff member	1,700	1,700
Number of staff	58	81
Average salary p.a.	£30,000	£31,500
Direct labour cost	£1,740,000	£2,551,500

Write an email to the Production director:

(a) Explaining the calculations and assumptions and request approval

(b) Suggesting appropriate direct labour performance indicators for this department

To	Production director	**Date**	(Today)
From	Budget accountant	**Subject**	Direct labour budget

(a) Budget submission

(b) Performance indicators

83 DIEGO

You have prepared a draft budget for direct labour costs.

- Tough economic conditions are likely to hit the firms' sales and profit forecasts.
- It is based on this year's costs minus an expected pay cut and reduced staffing.
- The manager of human resources has forecast the pay cut.
- An increase in productivity is required to help cope with the adverse conditions.
- You have calculated the required staffing from the agreed production budget.
- You have been asked to suggest appropriate performance measures that would assist managers to monitor direct labour performance against budget.

Direct labour budget	Current year	Next year
Prod'n units	1,200,000	950,000
Minutes per unit	6	5.4
Labour hours	120,000	85,500
Annual hrs per staff member	1,800	1,860
Number of staff	67	46
Average salary pa	£35,000	£34,000
Direct labour cost	£2,345,000	£1,564,000

(a) Write an email to the production director explaining the calculations and assumptions and request approval.

(b) Suggest some overall financial performance indicators for the firm.

To	Production director	Date	(Today)
From	Budget accountant	Subject	Direct labour budget

(a) **Budget submission**

(b) Performance indicators (no reference to above numbers required)

84 DRAFT BUDGET

You have prepared a draft budget for direct labour costs.

- It is based on this year's costs plus an expected pay rise and increased staffing.
- There is a favourable economic climate and the sales are forecast to rise.
- The manager of human resources has forecast the pay rise due to labour market shortages.
- Senior management have requested productivity to increase.
- You have calculated the required staffing from the agreed production budget.
- You have been asked to suggest appropriate performance measures that would assist managers to monitor direct labour performance against budget.

Direct labour budget	Current year	Next year
Prod'n units	1,200,000	1,500,000
Minutes per unit	10	9.5
Labour hours	200,000	237,500
Annual hrs per staff member	4,650	4,650
Number of staff	44	52
Average salary pa	£34,000	£36,000
Direct labour cost	£1,496,000	£1,872,000

Write an email to the production director:

(a) Explaining the calculations and assumptions and request approval

(b) Suggesting appropriate direct labour performance indicators for this department

To	Production director	Date	(Today)
From	Budget accountant	Subject	Direct labour budget

(a) Budget submission

(b) Performance indicators

AAT: APPLIED MANAGEMENT ACCOUNTING

MONTHLY OPERATING REPORTS AND VARIANCE CALCULATIONS

85 OS

A monthly operating statement is shown below with some explanatory notes.

You are required to flex the budget, calculate variances and show whether each variance is favourable or adverse.

Monthly operating statement

	Budget	Actual
Volume	76,000	72,000
	£	£
Revenue	3,420,000	3,312,000
Costs		
Material	912,000	836,000
Labour	532,000	509,000
Distribution	19,000	19,500
Energy	215,000	201,250
Equipment hire	48,000	42,000
Depreciation	212,000	206,000
Marketing	268,000	255,000
Administration	184,000	190,000
Total	2,390,000	2,258,750
Operating profit	1,030,000	1,053,250

Monthly operating statement

		Flexed Budget	Actual	Variance Fav/(Adv)
Volume	72,000			
		£	£	£
Revenue		3,240,000	3,312,000	72,000
Costs				
Material		864,000	836,000	28,000
Labour		504,000	509,000	(5,000)
Distribution		18,000	19,500	(1,500)
Energy		205,000	201,250	3,750
Equipment hire		40,000	42,000	(2,000)
Depreciation		212,000	206,000	6,000
Marketing		268,000	255,000	13,000
Administration		184,000	190,000	(6,000)
Total		2,295,000	2,258,750	36,250
Operating profit		945,000	1,053,250	108,250

Enter adverse variances as minus

Notes:

Material, labour and distribution costs are variable.

The budget for energy is semi-variable. The variable element is £2.50 per unit.

The budget for equipment hire is stepped, increasing at every 15,000 units of monthly production.

Depreciation, marketing and administration costs are fixed.

86 OS2

A monthly operating statement is shown below with some explanatory notes.

You are required to flex the budget, calculate variances and show whether each variance is favourable or adverse.

Monthly operating statement

	Budget	Actual
Volume	76,000	80,000
	£	£
Revenue	3,420,000	3,520,000
Costs		
Material	912,000	945,000
Labour	532,000	570,000
Distribution	19,000	19,500
Energy	215,000	219,250
Equipment hire	48,000	50,000
Depreciation	212,000	215,000
Marketing	268,000	253,000
Administration	184,000	166,000
Total	2,390,000	2,437,750
Operating profit	1,030,000	1,082,250

Monthly operating statement

Volume: 80,000

	Flexed Budget £	Actual £	Variance Fav/(Adv) £
Revenue	3,600,000	3,520,000	(80,000)
Costs			
Material	960,000	945,000	15,000
Labour	560,000	570,000	(10,000)
Distribution	20,000	19,500	500
Energy	225,000	219,250	5,750
Equipment hire	48,000	50,000	(2,000)
Depreciation	212,000	215,000	(3,000)
Marketing	268,000	253,000	15,000
Administration	184,000	166,000	18,000
Total	2,477,000	2,437,750	39,250
Operating profit	1,123,000	1,082,250	(40,750)

Enter adverse variances as minus

Notes:

Material, labour and distribution costs are variable.

The budget for energy is semi-variable. The variable element is £2.50 per unit.

The budget for equipment hire is stepped, increasing at every 15,000 units of monthly production.

Depreciation, marketing and administration costs are fixed.

87 OS3

A monthly operating statement is shown below with some explanatory notes.

You are required to flex the budget, calculate variances and show whether each variance is favourable or adverse.

Monthly operating statement

	Budget	Actual
Volume	120,000	110,000
	£	£
Revenue	2,400,000	2,255,000
Costs		
Material	480,000	425,000
Labour	180,000	149,000
Distribution	12,000	12,500
Energy	114,000	110,250
Equipment hire	25,000	32,000
Depreciation	145,000	148,000
Marketing	260,000	255,000
Administration	172,000	181,000
Total	1,388,000	1,312,750
Operating profit	1,012,000	942,250

Monthly operating statement

Volume: 110,000

	Flexed Budget £	Actual £	Variance Fav/(Adv) £
Revenue	2,200,000	2,255,000	55,000
Costs			
Material	440,000	425,000	15,000
Labour	165,000	149,000	16,000
Distribution	11,000	12,500	(1,500)
Energy	106,000	110,250	(4,250)
Equipment hire	25,000	32,000	(7,000)
Depreciation	145,000	148,000	(3,000)
Marketing	260,000	255,000	5,000
Administration	172,000	181,000	(9,000)
Total	1,324,000	1,312,750	11,250
Operating profit	876,000	942,250	66,250

Enter adverse variances as minus

Notes:

Material, labour and distribution costs are variable.

The budget for energy is semi-variable. The variable element is £0.80 per unit.

The budget for equipment hire is stepped, increasing at every 25,000 units of monthly production.

Depreciation, marketing and administration costs are fixed.

PRACTICE QUESTIONS: SECTION 1

BUDGET REVISION AND VARIANCE ANALYSIS

88 LAPEL

Lapel Ltd has produced three forecasts of activity levels for the next period for one of its bins. The original budget involved producing 50,000 bins, but sales and production levels of between 60,000 and 70,000 bins are now more likely.

Complete the table below to estimate the production cost per bin (to 3 decimal places) at the three different activity levels.

Bins made	50,000	60,000	70,000
Costs:	£	£	£
Variable costs:			
Direct materials	5,250		
Direct labour	2,250		
Overheads	11,100		
Fixed costs:			
Indirect labour	9,200		
Overheads	15,600		
Total cost	43,400		
Cost per bin	0.868		

The following budgeted annual sales and cost information relates to bin types A and B:

Product	A	B
Units made and sold	300,000	500,000
Machine hours required	60,000	40,000
Sales revenue (£)	450,000	600,000
Direct materials (£)	60,000	125,000
Direct labour (£)	36,000	70,000
Variable overheads (£)	45,000	95,000

Total fixed costs attributable to A and B are budgeted to be £264,020.

AAT: APPLIED MANAGEMENT ACCOUNTING

Complete the table below (to 2 decimal places) to show the budgeted contribution per unit of A and B sold, and the company's budgeted profit or loss for the year from these two products.

	A (£)	B (£)	Total (£)
Selling price per unit			
Less: variable costs per unit			
Direct materials			
Direct labour			
Variable overheads			
Contribution per unit			
Sales volume (units)			
Total contribution			
Less: fixed costs			
Budgeted profit or loss			

89 SLUSH

A company has produced three forecasts of demand levels for the next quarter. The original budget was to produce 10,000 litres per quarter, but demand levels of 14,000 litres and 18,000 litres are also now feasible.

Complete the table below to estimate the production cost per litre at the three different demand levels.

Litres made	10,000	14,000	18,000
Costs:	£	£	£
Variable costs:			
Direct materials	1,200		
Direct labour	1,000		
Overheads	1,600		
Fixed costs:			
Indirect labour	700		
Overheads	1,600		
Total cost	6,100		
Cost per litre (to 2 d.p.)	0.61		

90 THREE MONTHS

The following production and total cost information relates to a single product organisation for the last three months:

Month	Production units	Total cost £
1	1,200	66,600
2	900	58,200
3	1,400	68,200

The variable cost per unit is constant up to a production level of 2,000 units per month but a step up of £6,000 in the monthly total fixed cost occurs when production reaches 1,100 units per month.

What is the total cost for a month when 1,000 units are produced?

91 EASTERN BUS COMPANY

Eastern Bus Company (EBC) has produced three forecasts of miles to be driven during the next three months for a particular contract. The original contract is for journeys totalling 10,000 miles. It now seems likely, however, that the total journeys involved will increase to either 12,000 or 14,000 miles.

Notes:

- The rate charged by EBC per mile will stay the same irrespective of the total mileage.
- Drivers on this contract are paid entirely on a per mile driven basis.

Complete the table below in order to estimate the profit per mile (in pounds, to 3 decimal places) of this contract for the three likely mileages.

Likely miles	10,000	12,000	14,000
	£	£	£
Sales revenue	100,000		
Variable costs:			
Fuel	8,000		
Drivers' wages and associated costs	5,000		
Overheads	6,000		
Fixed costs:			
Indirect labour	10,600		
Overheads	25,850		
Total cost	55,450		
Total profit	44,550		
Profit per mile to 3 d.p.	4.455		

92 ST DAVIDS

Product X has a standard material cost as follows:

10 kilograms of material Y at £10 per kilogram = £100 per unit of X.

During February 2014, 1,000 units of X were manufactured, using 11,700 kilograms of material Y which cost £98,631.

Calculate the following variances:

(a) The material total variance

(b) The material price variance

(c) The material usage variance

93 EASTER FUN

Prepare the raw material cost statement from the activity data provided.

Activity data	Items produced	Kgs used	Cost
Budget	63,000	31,500	126,000
Actual results	65,000	33,500	112,000

Raw material cost statement	£
Standard raw material cost of production	
Variance (adverse shown as negative)	£ FAV/ – ADV
Material price	
Material usage	
Material cost	

94 ANNIVERSARY

Prepare the raw material cost statement from the activity data provided.

Activity data	Items produced	Kgs used	Cost
Budget	1,200	1,200	12,000
Actual results	1,250	1,300	15,000

Raw material cost statement	£
Standard raw material cost of production	
Variance (adverse shown as negative)	£ FAV/ – ADV
Material price	
Material usage	
Material cost	

95 APPLES AND PEARS

Prepare the raw material cost statement from the activity data provided.

Activity data	Items produced	Kgs used	Cost
Budget	78,000	109,200	65,520
Actual Results	81,500	120,000	83,250

Raw material cost statement	£
Standard raw material cost of production	
Variance (adverse shown as negative)	£ FAV/ – ADV
Material price	
Material usage	
Material cost	

96 INDEPENDENCE DAY

Prepare the raw material cost statement from the activity data provided.

Activity data	Items produced	Kgs used	Cost
Budget	126,000	100,800	50,400
Actual results	130,500	120,000	56,000

Raw material cost statement	£
Standard raw material cost of production	
Variance (adverse shown as negative)	£ FAV/ – ADV
Material price	
Material usage	
Material cost	

97 AUGUST

Prepare the raw material cost statement from the activity data provided.

Activity data	Items produced	Kgs used	Cost
Budget	1,500	4,500	9,000
Actual results	1,550	4,500	9,210

Raw material cost statement	£
Standard raw material cost of production	
Variance (adverse shown as negative)	£ FAV/ – ADV
Material price	
Material usage	
Material cost	

98 BIRTHDAY

Prepare the direct labour cost statement from the activity data provided.

Activity data	Items produced	Hours	Cost
Budget	10,000	7,500	150,000
Actual results	11,000	8,000	168,000

Enter favourable variances as positive figures, for example 500.

Enter adverse variances as negative figures, for example –500.

Direct labour cost statement	£
Standard direct labour cost of production	
Variance (adverse shown as negative)	
Labour rate	
Labour efficiency	
Labour cost	

99 VALENTINE

Prepare the direct labour cost statement from the activity data provided

Activity data	Items produced	Hours	Cost
Budget	6,450	64,500	612,750
Actual results	6,200	62,890	596,412

Enter favourable variances as positive figures, for example 500.

Enter adverse variances as negative figures, for example –500.

Direct labour cost statement	£
Standard direct labour cost of production	
Variance (adverse shown as negative)	
Labour rate	
Labour efficiency	
Labour cost	

100 TRINITY

Trinity Ltd has the following original budget and actual performance for product H for the year ending 31 December.

Calculate the variances as percentages to the 2 decimal places and indicate whether this is Favourable or Adverse. Adverse variances must be denoted with a minus sign or brackets.

	Flexed budget	Actual	Variance
Volume sold	28,800	28,800	
	£000	£000	%
Revenue	4,320	3,877	
Direct materials	252	212	
Direct labour	1,260	912	
Variable overheads	641	448	
Fixed overheads	300	325	
Profit from operations	1,867	1,980	

STANDARD COSTING AND VARIANCES

STANDARD COSTING

101 BUDGIE

The budgeted and actual results for the month of January 20X1 are as follows:

		Budget		Actual
Production (units of A)		3,500		3,600
Direct materials	7,000 litres	£17,500	6,950 litres	£18,070
Direct labour	1,750 hours	£15,750	1,800 hours	£16,020
Fixed overheads (absorbed on a unit basis)		£35,000		£34,500
Total		£68,250		£68,590

Complete the following sentences:

(a) The standard quantity of labour per unit is ☐ minutes.

(b) The budgeted quantity of materials needed to produce 3,000 units of A is ☐

(c) The budgeted labour hours to produce 3,600 units of A is ☐ hours.

(d) The budgeted labour cost to produce 3,600 units of A is £ ☐

(e) The budgeted overhead absorption rate is £ ☐

In February the company budgeted to produce 4,000 units with fixed production overheads of £43,500. The actual volume produced was 4,200 units and the actual fixed overheads were £44,000.

(f) The fixed overheads were (Insert: under or over absorbed) ☐ by £ ☐

102 CARROT

The budgeted and actual results for the month of March 20X1 are as follows:

		Budget		Actual
Production (units of B)		10,000		9,950
Direct materials	4,000 kg	£10,000	3,900 kg	£9,900
Direct labour	250 hours	£2,500	245 hours	£2,695
Fixed overheads (absorbed on a unit basis)		£3,000		£3,100
Total		£15,500		£15,695

Complete the following sentences:

(a) The standard quantity of labour per unit is ☐ minutes.

(b) The budgeted quantity of materials needed to produce 9,950 units of B is ☐

(c) The budgeted labour hours to produce 9,950 units of B is ☐ hours.

(d) The budgeted labour cost to produce 9,950 units of B is £ ☐

(e) The budgeted overhead absorption rate is £ ☐

In April the company budgeted to produce 9,000 units with fixed production overheads of £2,900. The actual volume produced was 10,200 units and the actual fixed overheads were £3,000.

(f) The fixed overheads were (insert: under or over absorbed) ☐ by £ ☐

103 RABBIT

The budgeted and actual results for the month of January 20X1 are as follows:

		Budget		Actual
Production (units of A)		12,500		12,600
Direct materials	25,000 litres	£100,000	26,950 litres	£108,070
Direct labour	12,500 hours	£125,000	13,100 hours	£116,020
Fixed overheads (absorbed on a unit basis)		£75,000		£74,500
Total		£300,000		£298,590

Complete the following sentences:

(a) The standard quantity of labour per unit is ☐ minutes.

(b) The budgeted quantity of materials needed to produce 12,000 units of A is ☐ litres.

(c) The budgeted labour hours to produce 12,600 units of A is ☐ hours.

(d) The budgeted labour cost to produce 12,600 units of A is £ ☐

(e) The budgeted overhead absorption rate is £ ☐

In February the company budgeted to produce 13,000 units with fixed production overheads of £78,000. The actual volume produced was 12,800 units and the actual fixed overheads were £74,000.

(f) The fixed overheads were (insert: under or over absorbed) ☐ by £ ☐

104 BELLS

The following information has been calculated for the production of 1 box of Bells.

- Each box will require 16 kilograms of material at a cost of £1.50 per kilogram.
- Each box will require 3 hours of labour at a total cost of £27.
- Fixed overheads total £324,000 and the estimated output will be 5,400 boxes.

Complete the standard cost card below:

1 box of Bells	Quantity	Cost per unit £	Total cost £
Material			
Labour			
Fixed overheads			
Total			

105 TEA BAGS

The bagging division operates a standard costing system in which:

- purchases of materials are recorded at standard cost
- direct material costs and direct labour costs are variable
- production overheads are fixed

The standard cost card for the coming months is being prepared and you have been provided with the following information:

- Loose tea is expected to cost £5 per kilogram
- 1,000 tea bags require 3 kilograms of loose tea
- Tea bags cost 0.6 pence per bag
- One machine can package 5,000 bags per hour and requires one operator who costs £10 per hour
- Budgeted labour hours are 4,000 per month
- Fixed production overheads are £200,000 per month
- Budgeted production is 20,000 batches of 1,000 tea bags per month
- Fixed production overheads are absorbed on the basis of direct labour hours

Complete the standard cost card for the production of 1,000 tea bags.

1,000 tea bags		Quantity (Units)	Unit price £	Total cost £
Loose tea	Kilograms			
Tea bags	Bags			
Direct labour	Hours			
Fixed production overheads	Hours			

106 GEM

The following information has been calculated for the production of 1 unit of Gem.

- Each unit will require 5.25 litres of material at a cost of £7.00 per litre.
- Each unit will require 3.5 hours of labour at a cost of £3 per hour.
- Fixed overheads, absorbed on a labour hour basis, total £525,000. The expected output of Gem is 10,000 units.

Complete the standard cost card below.

1 unit of Gem	Quantity	Cost per unit	Total cost
Material			
Labour			
Fixed overheads			
Total			

It takes a manufacturing department 750,000 hours to produce 250,000 units of Gem. What are the standard hours per unit? [ ]

107 BESPOKE SUIT

The following information has been calculated for the production of 1 bespoke suit:

- Each suit will require 4.5 metres of fabric at a cost of £48 per metre
- Each suit will require 40 hours of labour at a total cost of £600
- Fixed overheads total £240,000 and the estimated output for the year will be 600 suits. Fixed overheads are absorbed using direct labour hours.

Complete the standard cost card below.

1 bespoke suit	Quantity	Cost per unit	Total cost
Material			
Labour			
Fixed overheads			
Total			

108 GARDEN SHEDS

The following information has been calculated for the production of garden sheds:

- Each shed will require 90 kilograms of material at a cost of £6.50 per kilogram
- Each unit will require 5 hours of labour at a total cost of £50
- Fixed overheads total £500,000 and the estimated output is 5,000 sheds. Fixed overheads are absorbed using direct labour hours.

Complete the standard cost card below.

1 Shed	Quantity	Cost per unit	Total cost
Material			
Labour			
Fixed overheads			
Total			

109 PERFORMANCE

Performance Limited makes car bulbs. The following information has been calculated for the production of a batch of 1,000 bulbs.

- Each batch will require 40 kilograms of material at a total cost of £200
- Each batch will require 2 hours of labour at an hourly cost of £7 per hour.
- Fixed overheads total £240,000 and the estimated output will be 8,000 batches. Fixed overheads are absorbed using direct labour hours.

Complete the standard cost card below.

1000 bulbs	Quantity	Cost per unit	Total cost
Material			
Labour			
Fixed overheads			
Total			

Performance uses 1,500 kilograms of material to manufacture a batch of 1,000 bulbs. The standard quantity in each bulb is ☐

110 DISCO

A disc grinder expects to use 25,000 machine hours to manufacture 5,000 discs in a month.

The standard machine time required for a disc is ☐ **hours.**

111 HARRY

A manufacturer expects to use 2,000 labour hours to manufacture 500 units in a month.

The standard labour time required for a unit is ☐ **hours.**

112 OSCAR

A widget manufacturer expects to use 5,000 machine hours to manufacture 2,000,000 widgets in a month.

The standard machine time required for a widget is [   ] hours.

113 PIZZA

A pizza chain expects to use 300,000 kilograms of flour to manufacture 1,500,000 pizzas per month.

The standard quantity of flour for a pizza is [   ] kilograms

114 SETTING BUDGETS

A company uses standard costing to set budgets.

Which of the following would be useful for controlling costs?

- A Actual results versus flexed budget
- B Actual results versus original budget
- C Seasonal variations versus original budget
- D Seasonal variations versus actual results

115 STANDARD

Which of the following is NOT a characteristic of an ideal standard?

- A It assumes that machines and employees will work with optimal efficiency.
- B It assumes that no materials will be wasted in production.
- C It leads to unachievable objectives being set.
- D It leads to increased motivation to achieve challenging objectives.

116 BASIC

A company uses the basic standard to set budgets.

Which of the following statements is correct?

- A The basic standard reflects current conditions, and is therefore challenging for the staff.
- B The basic standard is a tried and tested target, which should help motivate staff.
- C The basic standard no longer reflects current prices and performance levels.
- D The basic standard is set under perfect conditions and it is difficult to meet, which can be demotivating for staff.

117 SAPPHIRE

A company expects to produce 140,000 units of Sapphire using 280,000 kg of material. The standard cost of material is £6/kg.

If the actual output is 145,000 units what is the total standard material usage? _____ kg

PRACTICE QUESTIONS: **SECTION 1**

SALES VARIANCES

118 GREEN

Green uses standard absorption costing. The following data relate to last month:

	Budget	Actual
Sales and production (units)	1,000	900
	Standard	Actual
	£	£
Selling price per unit	50	52
Total production cost per unit	39	40

What was the adverse sales volume profit variance last month?

£ _____ Adv

119 PURPLE

Purple is reviewing actual performance to budget to see where there are differences. The following standard information is relevant:

	£ per unit
Selling price	50
Direct materials	4
Direct labour	16
Fixed production overheads	5
Variable production overheads	10
Fixed selling costs	1
Variable selling cost	1
Total costs	37
Budgeted sales units	3,000
Actual sales units	3,500

What was the favourable sales volume variance using marginal costing?

A £9,500

B £7,500

C £7,000

D £6,500

KAPLAN PUBLISHING

120 ORANGE

Orange uses variance analysis to control costs and revenues.

Information concerning sales is as follows:

Budgeted selling price	£15 per unit
Budgeted sales units	10,000
Budgeted profit per unit	£5
Actual sales revenue	£151,500
Actual units sold	9,800

What was the sales volume profit variance?

A £500 favourable

B £1,000 favourable

C £1,000 adverse

D £3,000 adverse

121 Z LTD 1

Z Ltd sells computers that it purchases through a regional distributor. An extract from its budget for the 4-week period ended 28 March 20X8 shows that it planned to sell 600 computers at a unit price of £500, which would give a contribution to sales ratio of 25%.

Actual sales were 642 computers at an average selling price of £465. The actual contribution to sales ratio averaged 20%.

What was the sales price variance (to the nearest £1)?

A £22,470 (F)

B £1,470 (A)

C £1,470 (F)

D £22,470 (A)

122 Z LTD 2

Z Ltd sells computers that it purchases through a regional distributor. An extract from its budget for the 4-week period ended 28 March 20X8 shows that it planned to sell 600 computers at a unit price of £500, which would give a contribution to sales ratio of 25%.

Actual sales were 642 computers at an average selling price of £465. The actual contribution to sales ratio averaged 20%.

What was the sales volume contribution variance (to the nearest £1)?

A £5,050 (F)

B £5,150 (F)

C £5,250 (F)

D £5,350 (F)

PRACTICE QUESTIONS: SECTION 1

123 PQR LTD

PQR Ltd operates a standard absorption costing system. Details of budgeted and actual figures are as follows:

	Budget	Actual
Sales volume (units)	100,000	110,000
Selling price per unit	£10	£9.50
Variable cost per unit	£5	£5.25
Total cost per unit	£8	£8.30

The favourable sales volume profit variance for the period was £_____

124 AUDIT

An audit firm budgeted to provide 60 audits in the next month at a fee of £6,000 each. It actually made total sales of £365,400 from 58 audits.

To the nearest £, the favourable sales price variance is £_____

125 MAUVE

Mauve has the following standard information for its product:

	£
Standard selling price	50
Standard contribution	20
Standard profit	15
Marginal cost	30

During the year it produced and sold 60,000 units. Budgeted production and sales was 65,000 units. The firm uses a marginal costing system for determining variances.

What will be the value of the adverse sales volume variance for the year?

A £75,000

B £100,000

C £150,000

D £250,000

KAPLAN PUBLISHING 63

AAT: APPLIED MANAGEMENT ACCOUNTING

MATERIAL VARIANCES

126 MAT (1)

A company bought 1,000 kilograms of material paying £5 per kilogram. It managed to make 200 units whilst the budget had been for 220 units. The standard quantity of material allowed for in the budget was 6 kilograms per unit, and the budgeted price per kilogram was £5.50.

Complete the following table.

			£
Standard cost of materials for actual production			
Variances	Favourable	Adverse	
Direct materials price			
Direct materials usage			
Total variance			
Actual cost of materials for actual production			

127 MAT (2)

A company bought 12,000 kilograms of material paying £4 per kilogram. It managed to make 2,000 units whilst the budget had been for 1,900 units. The standard quantity of material allowed for in the budget was 5 kilograms per unit, and the budgeted price per kilogram was £4.50.

Complete the following table.

			£
Standard cost of materials for actual production			
Variances	Favourable	Adverse	
Direct materials price			
Direct materials usage			
Total variance			
Actual cost of materials for actual production			

128 SMITH

Smith budgets to produce 10,000 units. Each unit requires 3kg. Production does not go as planned and only 9,800 units are produced, using 29,000 kg of materials with a total cost of £8,000. The budgeted cost per kg was £0.27.

What is the material usage variance? £_____.

129 MATERIAL

A company purchases 60,000 tonnes of material at a cost of £720,000. The standard cost per tonne is £11 and the standard quantity per unit is 10 tonnes.

What is the total material price variance? £_____.

130 MOUSE

A drinks manufacturer expects to produce 2,000,000 bottles of cola using 60,000 kilograms of sugar. The standard cost of sugar is £0.75 per kilogram.

If the actual output is 2,450,000 bottles, what is the total standard cost of sugar?

- A £1,837,500
- B £45,000
- C £55,125
- D £1,500,000

131 RAW MATERIALS

A product should require 2kg of raw material costing 75p per kg. In February, 2,500kg of raw materials were purchased at a cost of £2,250; 2,300kg of raw materials were issued to production and 1,200 products were produced.

If raw material inventory is valued at standard cost and there was no opening inventory of raw material, what was the materials usage variance for February?

- A £375 A
- B £150 A
- C £75 A
- D £75 F

132 ALPHA

A company purchases 10,000 kilograms of material at a cost of £55,000. The standard cost per kilogram is £5.

The total material price variance is

- A £5,500 F
- B £5,000 A
- C £5,000 F
- D £5,500 A

133 BETA

A company purchases 5,000 kilograms of material at a cost of £27,500. The standard cost per kilogram is £5.00.

The total material price variance is

- A £2,750 A
- B £2,500 F
- C £2,500 A
- D £2,750 F

134 DELTA

A company purchases and uses 10,000 kilograms of material at a cost of £30,000. Budgeted production was 1,000 units, using 8,000 kg of material at a total standard cost of £28,000. Actual production was 1,000 units.

The total material usage variance is

- A £7,000 A
- B £7,000 F
- C £2,000 A
- D £2,000 F

LABOUR VARIANCES

135 LAB (1)

A company used 12,000 hours of labour paying £8 per hour. During this time it managed to make 2,000 units whilst the budget had been for only 1,900 units. The standard number of hours allowed was 5 per unit, and the budgeted rate per hour was £8.50.

Complete the following table.

			£
Standard cost of labour for actual production			
Variances	**Favourable**	**Adverse**	
Direct labour rate			
Direct labour efficiency			
Total variance			
Actual cost of labour for actual production			

136 LAB (2)

A company used 22,000 hours of labour paying £10 per hour. During this time it managed to make 21,000 units whilst the budget had been for 22,000 units. The standard number of hours allowed was one hour per unit, and the budgeted rate per hour was £9.80.

Complete the following table.

			£
Standard cost of labour for actual production			
Variances	Favourable	Adverse	
Direct labour rate			
Direct labour efficiency			
Total variance			
Actual cost of labour for actual production			

137 BEALE

Beale Limited makes cages. Each cage should take three standard hours to produce at £15 per labour hour. Total labour costs for the period were £5,440 and a total of 340 labour hours were used.

What is the labour rate variance? £_____.

138 MY

My company expects to produce 6,000 units of X using 3,000 labour hours. The standard cost of labour is £7 per hour. The actual output is 7,000 units.

What is the total standard labour cost? £_____

139 GOSSIP

G expects to produce 120,000 units of glug using 60,000 labour hours. The standard cost of labour is £14 per hour.

If actual output is 140,000 units, what is the total standard labour cost? £_____.

140 HIT

HIT expects to produce 10,000 units of glug using 8,000 labour hours. The standard cost of labour is £10 per hour.

If actual output is 11,000 units, what is the total standard labour cost? £_____.

141 JOY

J takes three standard hours to produce a unit at £15 per labour hour. Total labour costs for the period were £53,140 and a total of 3,400 labour hours were used. Units produced were 1,000.

The labour rate variance is

A £2,140 F

B £6,000 A

C £2,140 A

D £6,000 F

142 LEMON

A company pays £62,500 for 7,000 actual labour hours. Actual output was 1,000 units and standard labour hours were 6 hours per unit. The standard rate per hour is £9.

The labour efficiency variance is

A £1,800 F

B £1,800 A

C £9,000 F

D £9,000 A

143 MUFFIN

Actual output was 10,000 units in 16,000 hours at an actual rate of £10 per hour. Standard labour hours were estimated at 1.5 hours per unit. The standard rate per hour is £12.

The labour efficiency variance is

A £32,000 A

B £32,000 F

C £12,000 F

D £12,000 A

PRACTICE QUESTIONS: SECTION 1

144 JAYRO

Jayro Ltd manufactures gas canisters for use in the medical industry.

The Gas Division operates a standard cost system in which:

- purchases of materials are recorded at standard cost
- direct material and direct labour costs are variable
- production overheads are fixed and absorbed on a per unit basis.

The budgeted activity and actual results for the month of August are as follows:

	Budget		Actual	
Production units		50,000		55,000
Direct materials	1,000 litres	£20,000	1,100 litres	£23,100
Direct labour	4,000 hours	£32,000	4,950 hours	£40,095
Fixed overheads		£100,0000		£120,000
Total cost		£152,000		£183,195

Calculate the following variances, if any, for August:

Variance		
	£	A/F
Direct material usage variance		
Direct material price variance		
Direct labour efficiency variance		

145 DIVISION

Division operates a standard costing system in which:

- purchases of materials are recorded at standard cost
- direct material and direct labour costs are variable.

The budgeted activity and actual results for the month of January are as follows:

	Budget	
Production units	5,000	
	Cost per unit £	Budgeted cost £
Direct materials	2.00	10,000
Direct labour	4.00	20,000
Total cost		30,000

KAPLAN PUBLISHING

AAT: APPLIED MANAGEMENT ACCOUNTING

Actual production for the period was 6,000 units and the actual costs incurred were as follows:

	Actual Cost £
Direct materials	11,110
Direct labour	25,000

During the period the actual cost of material was £10.10 per litre and the standard quantity per unit was 0.2 litres.

4,500 actual hours were worked.

The standard time per unit was 0.8 hours per unit.

Complete the following table, for January:

Variance	£	A/F
Actual cost of materials		
Direct material price variance		
Direct material usage variance		
Standard material cost of production		
Actual cost of labour		
Direct labour rate variance		
Direct labour efficiency variance		
Standard labour cost of production		

146 NIGHT

N operates a standard cost system in which:

- purchases of materials are recorded at standard cost
- direct material and direct labour costs are variable.

The budgeted activity and actual results for the month of December are as follows:

	Budget	
Production units		1,000
	Cost per unit £	Budgeted cost £
Direct materials	20.00	20,000
Direct labour	40.00	40,000
Total cost		60,000

Actual production for the period was 900 units and the following costs were incurred:

	Actual cost £
Direct materials	19,100
Direct labour	38,095

During the period the actual amount of material used was 950 litres and the standard quantity per unit was 1 litre.

3,950 actual hours were worked.

The standard time per unit was 4 hours per unit.

Complete the following table, for December:

Variance	£	A/F
Actual cost of materials		
Direct material usage variance		
Direct material total variance		
Standard material cost of production		
Actual cost of labour		
Direct labour rate variance		
Direct labour efficiency variance		
Standard labour cost of production		

147 HINDER

Hinder Limited is obliged to buy sub-standard material at lower than standard price as nothing else is available.

As a result, are the following variances likely to be adverse or favourable?

	Materials price	Materials usage
A	Adverse	Favourable
B	Adverse	No change
C	Favourable	Adverse
D	Favourable	No change

148 LABOUR VARIANCE RATIOS

During a period, the actual hours worked by professional staff totalled 3,471. Budgeted hours were 3,630. The standard hours for the work totalled 3,502. The total hours paid were 3710.

Calculate the: (each to one decimal place)

Labour Activity ratio = ☐ %

Labour Efficiency ratio = ☐ %

Idle time ratio = ☐ %

AAT: APPLIED MANAGEMENT ACCOUNTING

149 LAB VAR RATIOS

During a period, the actual hours worked by employees totalled 31,630. Budgeted hours were 29,470 hours. The standard hours for the work totalled 30,502. The total hours paid were 32,000.

Calculate the: (each to one decimal place)

Labour Activity ratio =		%
Labour Efficiency ratio =		%
Idle time ratio =		%

150 LABOUR

One possible reason for a favourable labour efficiency variance is:

Better quality material used	
Lack of motivation in workers	
Supervisor off sick	

151 TIDLE

Tidle expects to produce 40,000 pots of paint using 5,000 labour hours. The standard cost of labour is £7 per hour. Actual production was 41,000 pots and actual hours paid were 5,200 hours, of which 300 hours were idle due to a machine breakdown. The actual wage bill was £39,000.

The labour rate variance is £	
The idle time variance is £	
The labour efficiency variance is £	
The total labour variance is £	

152 BRIDLE

Bridle expects to produce 4,000 units using 5,000 labour hours. The standard cost of labour is £7 per hour. Actual production was 4,100 units and actual hours paid were 5,200 hours, due to a machine breakdown the hours worked were only 5,100 hours. The actual wage bill was £36,000.

The labour rate variance is £	
The idle time variance is £	
The labour efficiency variance is £	

153 SIDLE

Sidle expects to produce 10,000 pots of paint using 5,000 labour hours. The standard cost of labour is £10 per hour. Actual production was 9,000 pots; 200 hours were idle due to a machine breakdown. The actual rate of pay was £9.61, the actual hours paid were 5,100 hours.

Complete the following table

		£
Standard labour cost for actual production		
Variances	Favourable / adverse / no variance	
Labour rate variance		
Idle time variance		
Labour efficiency variance		
Actual labour cost from actual production		

VARIABLE OVERHEAD VARIANCES

154 VAR (1)

Workers worked 12,000 hours and their company variable overhead rate was £5 per hour. During this time they managed to make 2,000 units whilst the budget had been for only 1,900 units. The standard number of hours allowed was 5 per unit, and the budgeted variable overhead rate per hour was £5.50.

Complete the following table.

			£
Standard cost of variable overheads for actual production			
Variances	Favourable	Adverse	
Variable overhead expenditure			
Variable overhead efficiency			
Total variance			
Actual cost of variable overheads for actual production			

155 JIF

Jif takes three standard hours to produce one unit at a variable overhead rate of £15 per hour. Total variable overhead costs for the period were £53,140 and a total of 3,400 labour hours were worked. Units produced were 1,000.

What is the variable overhead expenditure variance? £_____.

156 CALLUM

A company incurred variable overheads of £55,800 and 10,000 labour hours were worked. Actual output was 10,000 units and standard labour hours were 1.2 hours per unit. The standard variable overhead rate per hour was £5.

What is the variable overhead efficiency variance? £_____.

157 VALERIE (1)

Valerie takes two standard hours to produce one unit at a variable overhead rate of £5 per hour. Total variable overhead costs for the period were £103,140 and a total of 23,400 labour hours were worked. Units produced were 11,000.

The variable overhead expenditure variance is:

- A £13,860 F
- B £13,860 A
- C £7,000 A
- D £7,000 F

158 VALERIE (2)

Valerie takes two standard hours to produce one unit at a variable overhead rate of £5 per hour. Total variable overhead costs for the period were £103,140 and a total of 23,400 labour hours were worked. Units produced were 11,000.

The variable overhead efficiency variance is:

- A £13,860 F
- B £13,860 A
- C £7,000 A
- D £7,000 F

159 SHIRLEY

A company incurred an actual variable overhead cost of £55,800 and 10,000 labour hours were worked. Actual output was 11,000 units and standard labour hours were 0.9 hours per unit. The standard variable overhead rate per hour was £5.

The variable overhead expenditure variance is: £ [   ] F/A

The variable overhead efficiency variance is: £ [   ] F/A

FIXED OVERHEAD VARIANCES

160 OVERHEAD

Budgeted overheads are £20,000

Budgeted output is 10,000 units

Actual output is 12,000 units

Actual overheads are £25,000

The fixed overhead volume variance is £ ☐ A/F

The fixed overhead expenditure variance is £ ☐ A/F

161 FRANK

Budgeted overheads are £800,000

Budgeted output is 40,000 units

Actual output is 42,000 units

Actual overheads are £900,000

The fixed overhead volume variance is £ ☐ A/F

The fixed overhead expenditure variance is £ ☐ A/F

162 TRUMPET

Budgeted production is based on 14,000 labour hours.

Actual fixed overheads are £209,000.

Actual output was 6,000 units and each unit took 2 hours to complete. The standard time allowed was 1.75 hours. The overhead is absorbed at £25 per unit

The budgeted production is ☐ units

The fixed overhead expenditure variance is £ ☐ A/F

The fixed overhead volume variance is £ ☐ A/F

163 FLOPPY

Budgeted production is 100,000 units

Standard labour time per unit is 2 hours

Overheads are absorbed at a rate of £15 per unit

Actual production of 110,000 units took 210,000 hours

Actual overheads were £1,750,000

The fixed overhead expenditure variance is £ ☐ A/F

The fixed overhead volume variance is £ ☐ A/F

164 FIX (1)

A company has budgeted fixed overheads of £400,000 and budgeted output is 20,000 units.

Actual output was 21,000 units and actual overheads were £450,000.

Complete the following table.

			£
Budgeted/Standard fixed cost for actual production			
Variances	Favourable	Adverse	
Fixed overhead expenditure			
Fixed overhead volume			
Total variance			
Actual fixed cost for actual production			

165 FIX (2)

A company has budgeted fixed overheads of £250,000 and budgeted output is 2,000 units.

Actual output was 2,100 units and actual overheads were £245,000.

Complete the following table.

			£
Budgeted/Standard fixed cost for actual production			
Variances	Favourable	Adverse	
Fixed overhead expenditure			
Fixed overhead volume			
Total variance			
Actual fixed cost for actual production			

PRACTICE QUESTIONS: SECTION 1

WRITTEN TASKS

166 ARTETA

You have been provided with the following information for an organisation, which manufactures a product called Persie, for the month just ended:

	Budget		Actual	
Production (units)		10,000		11,000
Direct materials	15,000 kg	£30,000	16,000 kg	£33,500

The finance director has asked you to write a note to help in the training of a junior accounting technician. The note is to explain the calculation of the total direct material variance and how this variance can be split into a price variance and a usage variance.

Prepare a note explaining the total material variance and how it can be split into a price variance and a usage variance. Calculations should be used to illustrate your explanation.

To:	Subject:
From:	Date:

KAPLAN PUBLISHING

77

167 MERTESACKER

You have been provided with the following information for an organisation, which manufactures a product called Wilshere, for the month just ended:

	Budget		Actual	
Production (units)		100		95
Direct labour	1,500 hours	£30,000	1,600 hours	£31,500

The finance director has asked you to write a note to help in the training of a junior accounting technician. The note is to explain the calculation of the total direct labour variance and how this variance can be split into a rate variance and an efficiency variance.

Prepare a note explaining the total labour variance and how it can be split into a rate variance and an efficiency variance. Calculations should be used to illustrate your explanation.

To:	Subject:
From:	Date:

168 TOP DOG

The following budgetary control report has been provided:

	Budget		Actual	
Production (barrels)		2,500		2,400
Material	12,500 litres	£106,250	11,520 litres	£99,072
Direct labour	10,000 hours	£60,000	10,080 hours	£61,488
Fixed overheads		£200,000		£185,808
Total cost		£366,250		£346,368

The following variances have been calculated:

Direct materials price	£1,152
Direct materials usage	£4,080
Direct labour rate	£1,008
Direct labour efficiency	£2,880
Fixed overhead expenditure	£14,192
Fixed overhead volume	£8,000

Using this information, prepare a report to the Managing Director of Top dog to cover an analysis of each variance by

- identifying the sign of the variances
- explaining what the variance means
- providing one possible reason for each variance
- explaining any links between the variances
- Providing an action which could have been taken.

To:	Subject:
From:	Date:

Direct materials price variance

Direct materials usage variance

Labour rate variance
Labour efficiency variance
Fixed overhead expenditure variance
Fixed overhead volume variance

169 O'DOUZIE

(a) Describe the following types of standard

- attainable standards
- ideal standards
- basic standards

Attainable standards
Ideal standards

Basic standards

O'Douzie Ltd produces handmade scones for sales to local cafes.

The existing standard for one batch of fruit scones is shown below:

	£
Flour	1.08
Butter	2.09
Milk	0.50
Dried fruit	1.25
Direct labour	5.00
Total prime cost	9.75

O'Douzie Ltd uses ideal standards for flour and butter; an attainable standard for milk; and basic standards for dried fruit and its direct labour. Inflation in the country that O'Douzie operates has increased by around 10% since O'Douzie started their business.

(b) Discuss the type of variance that may arise under EACH type of standard and how it may affect employee behaviour.

Attainable standards

Ideal standards

AAT: APPLIED MANAGEMENT ACCOUNTING

Basic standards

O'Douzie Ltd has provided the following additional information:

- The standard quantity for flour and butter has been calculated on the basis that there is no wastage during production.

- Last year 10% of flour was wasted & 5% of butter was wasted.

- The standards for dried fruit and direct labour to make each batch were set when O'Douzie formed, several years ago.

- Since then they have invested in some new tools that have reduced the preparation time and the most recent estimate is that productivity has increased by 14%, but labour wage rates have increased in line with inflation.

- The dried fruit is now bought from a better quality supplier because of the improved quality of supply, O'Douzie estimate that they use 8% less, but prices are 6% higher.

O'Douzie have noticed that the staff are more efficient with milk and is therefore considering using attainable standards for all the ingredients and labour.

(c) Recommend possible improvements to the existing standards for ingredients and labour. Use calculations to support your recommendations.

Ingredients

Labour

170 DIXON

Dixon plc manufactures a range of products for use in the electrical industry. The company uses a standard absorption costing system with variances calculated monthly.

It is midway through month 7 of the current financial year and a number of events have occurred which may impact on the month-end variances for one particular product – the ELC.

The production director has asked for a report indicating the possible effects of the various events.

Notes for the production of the ELC

- The ELC uses a specialist industry material – TRI3
- Recent advances in the production of material TR13 have increased its availability which has led to a reduction in its price per metre by 10% in the last month. It is expected that the reduction in price will continue to the year end
- The standard price was set before the decrease in price occurred
- The quality control department has tested the latest batch of TR13 and reported that it is of higher quality than expected
- The company implemented a strict material usage policy at the beginning of the year to monitor levels of wastage. This was overseen by the quality control department and no additional payroll costs were incurred
- Employees usually receive an annual pay rise at the beginning of month 7 and this was included in the standard cost. Due to the current economic climate this pay rise has been suspended indefinitely
- The budgeted production for the month is 1,500 units
- An order for 500 units to be produced in month 7 was cancelled. The company has been unable to replace this order and the actual production for month 7 will only be 1,000 units
- The production machinery settings needed to be altered to deal with the higher quality TR13. In addition, one of the machines was found to be defective and required a complete overhaul. These costs are to be included in the month's fixed production overheads

Complete the report for the production director covering the possible impact of the above events on the TR13 price and usage variances, the labour efficiency variance and the fixed overhead expenditure and volume variances. The report should:

- **Identify whether each variance is likely to be favourable or adverse at the end of the month**
- **Explain what each variance means**
- **Provide one possible reason why each variance is likely to be adverse or favourable at the end of the month**
- **Identify possible links between variances**

You are not required to perform any calculations.

| To: | Subject: |
| From: | Date: |

TR13 price variance

TR13 usage variance

Labour efficiency variance

Fixed overhead expenditure variance

Fixed overhead volume variance

171 GRIPPIT (2)

Grippit Ltd processes old tyres into a product called Crumb. Crumb is used in a variety of applications from road surfaces to brake linings. Grippit Ltd processes the tyres in the Crumbing Division and then either sells Crumb to other companies or uses Crumb in the manufacture of rubberised asphalt in the Road Division.

You work as an Accounting Technician reporting to the Finance Director.

The Crumbing Division operates a standard cost system in which

- purchases of material are recorded at nil cost, as they are delivered free of charge from major tyre companies
- direct labour costs are variable
- production overheads are fixed and absorbed on a unit basis.

The budgeted activity and actual results for the month of May 2008 are as follows:

		Budget		Actual
Production (tonnes)		200		210
Direct labour	600 hours	£4,800	600 hours	£5,100
Fixed overheads		£90,000		£95,000
Total cost		£94,800		£100,100

(a) Calculate the following for May:

(i)	Standard labour rate per hour	
(ii)	Standard labour hours for actual production	
(iii)	Budgeted cost per tonne of Crumb	
(iv)	Budgeted overhead absorption rate per tonne	
(v)	Overheads absorbed into actual production	
(vi)	Total standard cost of actual production	

(b) Calculate the following variances for May:

		£	F/A
(i)	Direct labour rate variance		
(ii)	Direct labour efficiency variance		
(iii)	Fixed overhead expenditure variance		
(iv)	Fixed overhead volume variance		

AAT: **APPLIED MANAGEMENT ACCOUNTING**

(c) The Production Director has reviewed the variances and has given you the following information.

- A pay rise of 25p per hour was awarded after the standard had been set.

- A software upgrade was purchased for the production machinery which cost £120,000 for a 2-year licence. The cost is being amortised (depreciated) on a straight line basis.

- The software upgrade should increase labour efficiency by 10%, reducing the standard labour time to 2.7 hours per tonne.

Using the information provided by the Production Director, draft a report for the Finance Director explaining the variances you calculated above.

To:	Subject:
From:	Date:

(i)　Direct labour rate variance

(ii)　Direct labour efficiency variance

(iii)　Fixed overhead expenditure variance

(iv)　Fixed overhead volume variance

86　　　　　　　　　　　　　　　　　　　　　　　　　　　　　KAPLAN PUBLISHING

172 VARIANCE ETHICS

Below are some of the results for one of the divisions of Variance Ltd for the last month.

Variances	£
Materials price	6,000 adverse
Materials usage	10,000 adverse
Labour rate	2,000 favourable
Labour usage	3,000 favourable

The production managers at Variance Ltd receives a bonus based on labour variances. The bonus is paid if the overall labour variance is favourable.

Explain the ethical issues and any issues with goal congruence.

Ethical issues

Goal congruence issues

173 WOODEN SPOON

Wooden Spoon Ltd manufacture and sell handmade kitchen utensils from rolling pins to porridge stirrers, from chopping boards to wooden spoons.

They use standard costing, and below is an extract from their system:

Standard direct cost of one wooden spoon	£
Wood	3.45
Treatment	0.46
Labour	4.80
Variable overhead	2.40
	11.11

The amount of wood required and treatment used in a wooden spoon was set many years ago and the design has changed in line with fashions from big and bulky to a more streamlined design. They have found that a batch of wood can manufacture around 15% more wooden spoons than from the initial designs.

The labour cost is based on no stoppages or idle time in the production process. Month on month non-productive time has ranged from 3% to 8% and over the last year the average was 4%. The labour rate is also based on the wages that the workers were paid when the company first set up. It is estimated that wages are now 10% higher.

(a) **Write a memo to your manager in which you evaluate the consequences of Wooden Spoon Ltd.'s approach to standard setting. You should:**

    (i) Explain the types of standard being used for the different materials and labour,

    (ii) Explain the behavioural implications of those standards and the consequences for variances analysis,

    (iii) Calculate appropriately revised standards based on the information provided and justify your revised standards.

To:	Manager	Subject:	Standard setting at Wooden Spoon
From:	Accounting Technician	Date:	24/3/20X7
(i) Types of standard			

PRACTICE QUESTIONS: SECTION 1

(ii) Behavioural implications

(iii) Revised standards and justification

Wooden Spoon Ltd's Floor manager will receive a bonus if the net cost variance for the period is favourable. Based on current forecasts the variances will be net adverse. The manager has decided to delay the maintenance of the factory to try to overturn the adverse variance in the current period.

(b) Briefly explain the ethical and goal congruence issues that may arise as a result of this behaviour.

174 FOODRINK

Foodrink Ltd manufactures and distributes nutritional supplements. One of its main products is IQ, a special vitamin supplement which claims to increase the concentration levels of individuals and helps them think carefully, especially when taking an exam. The supplement makes students read questions very carefully and show all their workings.

You work as an Accounting Technician reporting to the Finance Director.

The company operates an integrated standard cost system in which:

- purchases of materials are recorded at standard cost
- direct material costs and direct labour costs are variable
- production overheads are fixed and absorbed on a unit basis.

The budgeted activity and actual results for May are as follows:

		Budget		Actual
Production (units)		9,000		9,900
Direct materials	450 kgs	£5,400	594 kgs	£6,534
Direct labour	300 hours	£4,500	325 hours	£4,225
Fixed overheads		£18,000		£19,000
Total cost		£27,900		£29,759

(a) Calculate the following for May:

(i)	Standard price of materials per kilogram	
(ii)	Standard usage of materials for actual production	
(ii)	Standard labour rate per hour	
(iv)	Standard labour hours for actual production	
(v)	Budgeted overhead absorption rate per unit	
(vi)	Overheads absorbed into actual production	

(b) Calculate the following variances for May:

		£	F/A
(i)	Direct material price variance		
(ii)	Direct material usage variance		
(iii)	Direct labour rate variance		
(iv)	Direct labour efficiency variance		
(v)	Fixed overhead expenditure variance		
(vi)	Fixed overhead volume variance.		

OPERATIONAL CONTROL

IMPACT OF TECHNOLOGY

175 CLOUD

Which THREE of the following are advantages of cloud computing?

- A Cost efficiency
- B Scalability
- C Flexibility
- D Contract management
- E Career opportunities
- F Highlights inefficiencies

176 REMOTE SERVERS

The process by which users log on to remote servers to access and process their files is best known as what?

- A Cloud computing
- B Wide Area Network
- C The internet
- D Remote working

177 RISE OF THE MACHINES

Machines working and reacting like human beings describes what?

- A Robotics
- B Voice recognition
- C Artificial intelligence
- D The 4th Industrial Revolution

178 RELIABILITY

Assessing the reliability of big data refers to which of the 4 Vs?

- A Velocity
- B Volume
- C Visibility
- D Veracity

179 UNDERSTANDABLE

The provision of information in a more appealing and understandable manner is often referred to as what?

A   Artificial Intelligence

B   Data simplification

C   Cloud computing

D   Data visualisation

180 VISUALISATION

Which ONE of the following is not necessarily a benefit of data visualisation

A   Improves the accuracy of the data being analysed

B   Problem areas can be identified sooner

C   Understandable by many users

D   Supports prompt decision making

181 BIG DATA

Which ONE of the following statements about big data and the internal audit function are true?

A   The emergence of big data has improved the accuracy of data which means smaller sample sizes now need to be tested.

B   Internal audit will now be testing and analysing larger populations of data.

C   Big data has no relevance to the internal audit function.

D   Big data will contribute to the development of more efficient and insightful management control systems and budgeting processes.

182 STATEMENTS

Which THREE of the following statements relating to big data are true?

A   Big data refers to any financial data over £1 billion

B   The defining characteristics of big data are velocity, volume, variety and veracity

C   Managing big data effectively can lead to increased competitive advantage

D   The term big data means 'data that comes from many sources'

E   Big data contains both financial and non-financial data

ACTIVITY BASED COSTING

183 CAT

Details of four products and relevant information are given below for one period:

Product	A	B	C	D
Output in units	120	100	80	120
Costs per unit	£	£	£	£
Direct material	40	50	30	60
Direct labour	28	21	14	21
Machine hours (per unit)	4	3	2	3

The four products are similar and are usually produced in production runs of 20 units and sold in batches of 10 units.

The production overhead is currently absorbed by using a machine hour rate, and the total of the production overhead for the period has been analysed as follows:

	£
Machine department costs (rent, business rates, depreciation and supervision)	10,430
Set up costs	5,250
Stores receiving	3,600
Inspection/quality control	2,100
Materials handling and dispatch	4,620
Total	26,000

You have ascertained that the 'cost drivers' to be used are as listed below for the overhead costs shown:

Cost	Cost driver
Set up costs	Number of production runs
Stores receiving	Requisitions raised
Inspection/quality control	Number of production runs
Materials handling and dispatch	Orders executed

The number of requisitions raised on the stores was 20 for each product and the number of orders executed was 42, each order being for a batch of 10 of a product.

The machine hour absorption rate and total costs for each product if all overhead costs are absorbed on a machine hour basis are:

(W1) Machine hour absorption rate = £ ☐ per machine hour.

The cost per unit and total cost per product using absorption costing are:

Per unit	A	B	C	D
	£	£	£	£
Direct materials				
Direct labour				
Production overhead				
	—	—	—	—
Per unit				
	—	—	—	—
Total cost				

The total costs for each product, using activity based costing are:

Total costs	A	B	C	D
	£	£	£	£
Direct materials				
Direct labour				
Machine dept costs				
Set up costs				
Stores receiving				
Inspection/quality control				
Materials handling despatch				
	—	—	—	—
Total cost				
	—	—	—	—

Workings

Cost driver rates:

Machine dept costs (m/c hour basis)

Set up costs

Stores receiving

Inspection/quality control

Material handling despatch

184 SMASH-HIT

Smash-Hit manufactures tennis and squash racquets. Until recently it has recovered its production overhead in a conventional way by using a series of recovery rates based on direct labour hours for each producing costs centre.

The following relates to its budget for quarter ended 30 June 20X3:

Cost centre	Machining	Finishing	Packing
Production and other overhead	£160,000	£65,000	£35,000
Direct labour hours	25,000	12,500	6,500

One of its products the 'Heman 3' has the following specifications (per unit):

Direct material	£38	
Direct labour		
Machining	1.5 hours	
Finishing	1.0 hour	Labour rate per hour £7
Packing	0.2 hours	

In determining the selling price of the product it is company policy to add 15% to cover selling distribution and administration costs and a further 10% to cover profit.

The accounting technician and the production manager have been considering the use of activity based costing as an alternative method of dealing with overheads.

After examining the 'value adding activities' across the business they have prepared the following schedule:

Budget quarter ended 30 June 20X3

Activity	Cost pool	Cost driver volume
	£	
Process set up	80,000	200 set-ups
Material procurement	20,000	100 purchase orders
Maintenance	25,000	20 maintenance plans
Material handling	50,000	4,000 movements
Quality control	45,000	500 inspections
Order processing	40,000	600 customers
	260,000	

A production batch of 'Heman 3' equates to 750 units of output, requiring the following:

- 6 set-ups
- 6 purchase orders
- 2 standard maintenance plans
- 150 material movements
- 75 inspections
- 10 sales customers

Using a traditional absorption costing method based on labour hours for the period:

Determine overhead recovery rates for each cost centre.

Cost centre	Machining	Finishing	Packing
Production overhead			
Direct labour hours			
Recovery rate per labour hour			

Calculate the production cost for one unit of output of 'Heman 3'.

	£
Direct labour	
Direct material	
Production overhead	
Machining	
Finishing	
Packing	
	―――
Production cost	
	―――

Calculate the selling price ex VAT for one unit of 'Heman 3'.

	£
Production cost	
Add: 15% for selling, admin and distribution	
	―――
Add: 10% to cover profit	
	―――
Selling price	
	―――

Using an activity-based costing method calculate the cost driver rates for the period.

Activity	Cost pool	Cost driver volume	Cost driver rate
Process set up			
Material procurement			
Maintenance			
Material handing			
Quality control			
Order processing			

Calculate the overhead chargeable to the batch of units of 'Heman 3'.

	£
Set up	
Order	
Plan	
Material movement	
Inspection	
Customer	
	——
	——

Calculate the production cost of one unit of 'Heman 3'.

	£
Direct labour	
Direct material	
Production and other overhead	
	——
Production cost	
	——

185 ABC LTD

ABC Limited manufactures two products, the DEF and the GHI.

It takes 5 hours of labour to make a DEF and 7 hours of labour to make a GHI.

The overhead activities for these, machine set ups and special parts handling, have budgets of £80,000 and £40,000 respectively.

Other information about the DEF and GHI is below.

	DEF	GHI
Direct materials – £ per unit	8	12
Direct labour – £ per unit	25	35
Number of special parts	300	100
Number of machine set ups	150	50
Budgeted production units	1,000	5,000

(a) Calculate the fixed overheads assuming they are absorbed on a budgeted labour hour basis.

	DEF (£)	GHI (£)
Fixed overheads		

(b) Complete the table below using Activity Based Costing (ABC) principles.

	£	DEF (£)	GHI (£)
Cost driver rate – special parts handling			
Cost driver rate – machine set ups			
Total special parts			
Total machine set ups			

(c) Using the information from (a) and (b) calculate the total cost per unit using traditional absorption costing and using ABC. Give your answers to two decimal places.

	DEF	GHI
Total unit cost – Absorption costing		
Total unit cost – ABC		

ABC Ltd are considering investing in some technological advancements to help with operational control.

(d) **Explain how ABC Ltd could benefit from using technology for operational control processes.**

186 FOUR LIONS LTD

Four Lions Limited manufactures two products, the Lion and the Pride.

The overhead activities for these, material movements and quality control, have budgets of £180,000 and £140,000 respectively.

It takes 3 hours of machine time to make a Lion and 4 hours of machine time to make a Pride.

Other information about the Lion and Pride is below.

	Lion	Pride
Direct materials – £ per unit	12	20
Direct labour – £ per unit	16	24
Material movements	2,000	500
Quality inspections	15	85
Budgeted production units	20,000	10,000

(a) **Calculate the fixed overheads assuming they are absorbed on a budgeted machine hour basis.**

	Lion (£)	Pride (£)
Fixed overheads		

(b) Complete the table below using Activity Based Costing (ABC) principles.

	£	Lion (£)	Pride (£)
Cost driver rate – material movements			
Cost driver rate – quality control			
Total material movements			
Total quality control			

(c) Using the information from (a) and (b) calculate the total cost per unit using traditional absorption costing and using ABC. Give you answers to two decimal places.

	Lion	Pride
Total unit cost – Absorption costing		
Total unit cost – ABC		

(d) Discuss how Activity Based Costing could help improve decision making at Four Lions Ltd.

187 RVI

RVI is a private hospital carrying out 2 procedures, A and B.

The overhead costs for these, nursing costs and remedial visits, have budgets of £300,000 and £500,000 respectively.

It takes 2 hours of surgeon time to carry out a procedure A and 1.5 hours of surgeon time to carry out a procedure B.

Other information about the procedures is below.

	A	B
Surgeon cost – £ per unit	275	235
Total nursing hours	2,000	4,000
Total remedial visits	2,000	3,000
Budgeted procedures	1,000	2,000

(a) Calculate the fixed overheads assuming they are absorbed on a budgeted surgeon hour basis.

	A (£)	B (£)
Fixed overheads		

(b) Complete the table below using Activity Based Costing (ABC) principles.

	£	A (£)	B (£)
Cost driver rate – nurse costs			
Cost driver rate – remedial costs			
Total nursing costs			
Total remedial costs			

(c) Using the information from (a) and (b) calculate the total cost per procedure using traditional absorption costing and using ABC. Give you answers to two decimal places.

	A	B
Total procedure cost – Absorption costing		
Total procedure cost – ABC		

(d) Explain the difficulties that RVI could have switching from traditional absorption costing to Activity Based Costing.

188 ABC STATEMENTS (I)

Complete the following statements:

A cost [ ] is any factor that causes a change in the cost of an activity.

driver/pool/rate/unit

VPS manufactures touchscreens, the most likely cost driver for the cost pool called 'quality control' is number of [ ]

machine hrs/batches/special parts/inspections

189 ABC STATEMENTS (II)

Complete the following statements:

A cost [ ] is an activity which consumes resources and for which overhead costs are identified and allocated.

driver/pool/rate/unit

F supplies pharmaceutical drugs, the most likely cost driver for the cost pool 'invoice processing costs' is the number of [ ]

orders/deliveries/inspections/invoices processed

LIFE CYCLE COSTING

190 NPV

A company is considering installing a new kitchen in which to prepare staff meals. At present, all meals are bought in from a local supplier. The kitchen equipment will cost £40,000 to buy and install and will have a useful life of 4 years with no residual value.

The company uses a discount rate of 10% to appraise all capital projects.

The cash savings from having this facility will be:

Year	0	1	2	3	4
£	0	15,200	14,900	13,585	11,255

Calculate the net present value of the cash flows from the project and present a recommendation as to whether the proposal should go ahead.

The relevant present value factors are:

Year	1	2	3	4
10%	0.909	0.826	0.751	0.683

Year	0	1	2	3	4
Cash flow £					
Discount factor					
Present value £				NPV	

The proposal SHOULD/SHOULD NOT go ahead. *(Delete as appropriate.)*

191 DAFFY

Daffy will be replacing its machines in the next year and needs to decide whether to purchase or lease the machines.

The relevant discount factors are shown below.

Year	Discount factor 10%	Year	Discount factor 10%
0	1.000	3	0.751
1	0.909	4	0.683
2	0.826	5	0.621

(a) Calculate the discounted lifecycle cost of purchasing the machines based upon the following:

- purchase price of £120,000
- annual running costs of £8,000 for the next five years, paid annually in arrears
- a residual value of £20,000 at the end of the five years

AAT: APPLIED MANAGEMENT ACCOUNTING

Year	0	1	2	3	4	5
Cash flow						
DF						
PV						
NPC						

(b) Calculate the discounted lifecycle cost of leasing the machines for five years based upon the total annual costs of £25,000 paid annually in advance.

Year	0	1	2	3	4
Lease costs					
DF					
PV					
NPC					

(c) Based on the calculations it is best to [   ] the machines. This saves £ [   ]

192 LIFECYCLE COSTING

A machine may be purchased at a cost of £30,000 and annual running costs of £2,500 per annum for the next four years paid in arrears. It would have a residual value of £5,500 at the end of the fourth year.

The company has a discount rate of 5% and the discount factors at this rate are:

Year	1	2	3	4
DF at 5%	0.952	0.907	0.864	0.823

The discounted lifecycle cost (DLC) of the machine is:

Year	0	1	2	3	4
Cash flow					
DF at 5%					
Present value					
DLC					

The machine could be leased for the four years instead – at an annual cost of £8,500 per annum, paid in advance.

The discounted lifecycle cost (DLC) of the lease would be:

Year	0	1	2	3	4
Cash flow					
DF at 5%					
Present value					
DLC					

Based on the above calculations, it would be best to [   ] the machine, as it saves £ [   ]

193 HOULTER

Houlter Ltd is considering purchasing a new machine to reduce the labour time taken to produce the X. The machine would cost £300,000. The labour time would be reduced from five hours to two hours without compromising quality and the failure rates will remain at zero.

The discount factors you will need are shown below.

Year	Discount factor 5%
0	1.000
1	0.952
2	0.907
3	0.864
4	0.823
5	0.784

Calculate the discounted lifecycle cost of the machine based upon the following:

(i) purchase price of £300,000

(ii) annual running costs of £30,000 for the next 5 years

(iii) a residual value of £50,000 at the end of the 5 years

Year	0	1	2	3	4	5
Cash flow						
DF						
PV						
NPC						

Calculate the discounted labour savings based upon annual production of 5,000 X, a three hour saving per unit and a labour rate of £7 per hour.

Year	1	2	3	4	5
Labour savings					
DF					
PV					
NPC					

Investing in the new machine saves [ ] and is therefore financially beneficial.

194 YANKEE (1)

Yankee Limited has discovered that instead of buying a machine outright it could lease it. You are required to complete the following tasks to establish whether the company should lease or buy the machine.

The discount factors you will need are shown below:

Year	Discount factor 10%	Year	Discount factor 10%
0	1.000	3	0.751
1	0.909	4	0.683
2	0.826	5	0.621

Calculate the discounted lifecycle cost of purchasing the machine based upon the following:

- purchase price of £1,500,000
- annual running costs of £150,000 for the next five years, paid annually in arrears
- a residual value of £250,000 at the end of the five years

Year	0	1	2	3	4	5
Cash flow						
DF						
PV						
NPC						

Calculate the discounted lifecycle cost of leasing the machine for five years based upon the total annual costs of £450,000 paid annually in advance.

Year	0	1	2	3	4
Lease costs					
DF					
PV					
NPC					

Based on the calculations it is best to ⬚ the machine, in order to save £ ⬚

PRACTICE QUESTIONS: SECTION 1

195 BUDGE

Budge Limited will be replacing some machines in the next year and needs to decide whether to purchase or lease the machines.

The discount factors you will need are shown below.

Year	Discount factor 10%	Year	Discount factor 10%
0	1.00	3	0.751
1	0.909	4	0.683
2	0.826	5	0.621

Calculate the discounted lifecycle cost of purchasing the machine based upon the following:

- purchase price of £600,000
- annual running costs of £45,000 for the next five years, paid annually in arrears
- a residual value of £220,000 at the end of the five years

(Work to the nearest £1,000.)

Year	0	1	2	3	4	5
Cash flow						
DF						
PV						
NPC						

Calculate the discounted lifecycle cost of leasing the machine for five years based upon the total annual costs of £135,000 paid annually in advance. *(Work to the nearest £1,000.)*

Year	0	1	2	3	4
Lease costs					
DF					
PV					
NPC					

Based on the calculations it is best to BUY/LEASE the machine because it saves £ ☐

196 LIFE CYCLE STATEMENTS (I)

Complete the following statements:

Lifecycle costing is a concept which traces all costs to a product over its complete lifecycle, from design through to ☐ .

sales/launch/cessation/production

One of the benefits that adopting lifecycle costing could bring is to improve decision-making and ☐ control.

production/staff/manager/cost

197 LIFE CYCLE STATEMENTS (II)

Complete the following statements:

Life cycle costing recognises that for many products there are significant costs committed by decisions in the [ ] stages of its lifecycle.

early/late/final/unit

One of the benefits of life cycle costing is the visibility of all costs is increased, rather than just costs relating to one period. This facilitates better [ ].

decision-making/maturity/variance analysis/decline

198 ABITFIT CO

Abitfit Co manufactures a small range of technologically advanced products for the fitness market. They are considering the developing a new fitness monitor, which would be the first of its kind in the market. Abitfit estimates it would take one year in the development stage, sales would commence at the beginning of the year two. The product is expected to be in the market for two years, before it will be replaced by a newer model. The following cost estimates have been made.

	Year 1	Year 2	Year 3
Units produced and sold		150,000	250,000
	£	£	£
Research and development costs	250,000		
Marketing costs	500,000	1,000,000	250,000
Administration costs	150,000	300,000	600,000
Production costs			
– Variable cost per unit		55	52
– Fixed production costs		600,000	900,000
Sales and distribution costs			
– Variable cost per unit		10	12
– Fixed sales and distribution costs		200,000	200,000

(a) Calculate the lifecycle cost in total (ignore the time value of money):

	£
Research and development costs	
Marketing costs	
Administration costs	
Total variable production cost	
Fixed production cost	
Total variable sales and distribution cost	
Fixed sales and distribution costs	
Total costs	

Based on the above, calculate the life cycle cost per unit £ [ ]

(Give you answer to 2 decimal places.)

PRACTICE QUESTIONS: **SECTION 1**

(b) **Discuss how the costs change throughout the life of a product, using the different stages of the product life cycle and examples from Abitfit.**

(c) **Explain how data visualisation could benefit Abitfit.**

AAT: APPLIED MANAGEMENT ACCOUNTING

199 LCC PLC

LCC Plc manufacture the latest in satellite navigation accessories, they are looking into developing a new product which could increase their market presence significantly. LCC believe the product will take a year to develop and then makes sales for three years then because of technological advancements it will need to be replaced by a newer model.

The following cost estimates have been made:

	Year 1	Year 2	Year 3	Year 4
Units produced and sold		200,000	250,000	100,000
	£	£	£	£
Research and development costs	500,000			
Marketing and Administration costs	450,000	750,000	800,000	350,000
Production costs				
– Variable cost per unit		28	25	20
– Fixed production costs		200,000	300,000	400,000
Sales and distribution costs				
– Variable cost per unit		18	16	18
– Fixed sales and distribution costs		150,000	150,000	150,000

(a) Calculate the lifecycle cost in total (ignore the time value of money):

	£
Research and development costs	
Marketing and administration costs	
Total variable production cost	
Fixed production cost	
Total variable sales and distribution cost	
Fixed sales and distribution costs	
Total costs	

Based on the above, calculate the life cycle cost per unit £ ☐

(Give you answer to 2 decimal places.)

(b) Discuss how costs can switch between variable and fixed through the different stages of the products life cycle.

(c) Discuss how ethical considerations can be aided by the use of life cycle costing.

TARGET COSTING

200 TARGET COSTING

A new product has been developed. After extensive research it has been estimated that the future selling price will be £10 with a demand of 2,000 units.

Other useful information is given below:

Fixed costs	£1.50 per unit
Labour	4.5 hours
Profit margin required	20%
Material	2 litres at £1 per litre

Assuming no other costs arise, the target cost per hour for labour is £ [1.00]

The labour rate is under negotiation with the union who would like an increase to £1.20 per hour. The personnel department has rejected this because the profit margin will fall to [11] %, which is [unacceptable to] the shareholders.

If management can agree to an increase in the labour rate but the profit margin has to stay at 20%, then material costs would need to fall by [£0.90]

201 HOLDER

Holder Limited is considering designing a new product and will use target costing to arrive at the target cost of the product. You have been given the following information and asked to calculate the target cost for materials so that the purchasing manager can use this as a target in his/her negotiations with suppliers.

The price at which the product will be sold is £50

The company has firm orders for 36,000 units at a price of £50

The fixed costs per unit are £15.50 per unit

The labour requirement is 20 minutes at a cost of £12 per hour

The required profit margin is 20%

The material requirement is 200 grams per unit

Calculate the target cost per kilogram for the materials component of the product.

	£
Sales price per unit	
Profit margin	
Total costs	
Fixed cost per unit	
Labour cost per unit	
Maximum material cost per unit	
Target cost per kilogram	

The trade price per kilogram quoted on the supplier's price list is £120 per kilogram. The purchasing manager has negotiated a discount of 15%. The discount should be ACCEPTED/REJECTED because the £120 reduces to £ [   ] which is ABOVE/BELOW the target cost.

The minimum percentage discount needed to achieve the target cost is [   ] % (to one decimal place).

202 AKEA

Akea is a furniture manufacturer and has just received the results of a market study on the current interest in their new leather sofa range. The study indicates that the maximum price the average customer is prepared to pay for a leather sofa from Akea is £1,500. The following information is also available.

- The company estimates that 2,200 sofas can be sold in a year.
- At this level of production, the fixed overheads per sofa would be £140.
- The labour requirement per sofa is 8 hours at a cost of £25 per hour.
- The wooden frame and the stuffing material cost £110 per sofa.
- The required profit margin is 30%.
- One sofa uses 8 square metres of leather.

Calculate the target cost per square metre of leather.

	£
Sales price per sofa	
Profit margin	
Total costs	
Fixed cost per sofa	
Labour cost per sofa	
Wooden frame and stuffing material	
Maximum leather cost per sofa	
Target cost per square metre	

Akea's leather supplier quotes a list price of £100 per square metre for the grade of leather Akea needs. However, Akea has managed to negotiate a discount of 15% on this price. **The discount should be ACCEPTED/REJECTED because the £100 reduces to £ [   ]**

which is ABOVE/BELOW the target cost. (Delete as appropriate.)

The minimum percentage discount needed to achieve the target cost is [   ] %

203 SHORTY

Shorty has just received the results of a market study on the current interest in their new product range. The study indicates that the maximum price the average customer is prepared to pay for one of their products is £150. The following information is also available.

- The company estimates that 200 units can be sold in a year.
- At this level of production, the fixed overheads per unit would be £40.
- The labour requirement per unit is 4 hours at a cost of £10 per hour.
- The required profit margin is 25%.
- The material (rubber) requirement is 5 kilograms per unit.

Calculate the target cost per kg of rubber.

	£
Sales price per unit	
Profit margin	
Total costs	
Fixed cost per unit	
Labour cost per unit	
Maximum rubber cost per unit	
Target cost per kg	

Shorty's rubber supplier quotes a list price of £10 per kilogram. However, Shorty has managed to negotiate a discount of 25% on this price. **The discount should be ACCEPTED/REJECTED because the £10 reduces to £ ☐ which is ABOVE/BELOW the target cost.** (Delete as appropriate.)

The minimum percentage discount needed to achieve the target cost is ☐ %

204 LONG

Long has designed a new product which it would like to sell for £250. It intends to use target costing to arrive at the target cost for labour. The following information is available.

- The company estimates that 20,000 units can be sold in a year.
- At this level of production, the fixed overheads per unit would be £20.
- The labour requirement per unit is 2 hours.
- The material cost is £110 per unit.
- The required profit margin is 35%.

Calculate the target cost per labour hour.

	£
Sales price per unit	
Profit margin	
Total costs	
Fixed cost per unit	
Material cost per unit	
Maximum labour cost per unit	
Target cost per labour hour	

A recruitment company quotes a rate of £20 per hour for the grade of labour Long needs. Long has managed to negotiate a discount of 15% on this price providing it recruits at least 10 workers. **The discount should be ACCEPTED/REJECTED because the £20 reduces to**

£ ☐ **which is ABOVE/BELOW the target cost.** (Delete as appropriate.)

The minimum percentage discount (to 2 d.p.) needed to achieve the target cost is

☐ %.

205 GRIPPIT (1)

Grippit Limited is developing a new product to monitor energy consumption. There are currently several other companies manufacturing similar products which sell for a price of £25 each. Grippit Ltd wishes to make a margin of 30%.

The target cost of the new product is £ ☐

206 SHOCK

Shock is developing a new product. There are currently several other companies manufacturing similar products which sell for a price of £95 each. Shock wishes to make a margin of 20%.

The target cost of the new product is £ ☐

207 TRICKY (II)

Tricky is developing a new product. There are currently several other companies manufacturing similar products which sell for a price of £205 each. Tricky wishes to make a margin of 10%.

The target cost of the new product is £ ☐

AAT: APPLIED MANAGEMENT ACCOUNTING

208 TC ETHICS

TC is a company attempting to close the cost gap that exists in the target costing exercise they are doing for one of their products. They have decided to reduce the grade of labour they are using and they have also identified a cheaper material they could substitute into the product.

Write a memo to a colleague and briefly explain any ethical issues that may arise

To:	Subject:
From:	Date:

Labour

Material

209 TARGET COSTING STATEMENTS (I)

Complete the following statements:

To calculate the target cost, subtract the ☐ from the target price.

value analysis/target profit/value engineering/cost gap

If there is a cost gap, attempts will be made to close the gap. Techniques such as value engineering and value ☐ may be used to help close the gap.

Analysis/adding/ranging/added tax

210 TARGET COSTING STATEMENTS (II)

Complete the following statements:

The cost gap is the difference between the [   ] and the estimated product cost per unit.

original cost/value engineering/target cost/value added

Target costing works the opposite to [   ] techniques in that it starts by setting a competitive selling price first.

traditional pricing/value added/value analysis/life cycle costing

211 FORMAT

Format is developing a new product and intends to use target costing to price the product. You have been given the following information.

- The price at which the product will be sold has not yet been decided;
- It has been estimated that if the price is set at £4 the demand will be 50,000 units, and if the price is set at £5.00 the demand will be 45,000 units;
- The required profit margin is 20%;
- The variable cost per unit is £1.30 for the 45,000 unit level, and £1.20 at the 50,000 unit level.

Complete the following table:

	Sales price £4	Sales price £5
Target total production cost per unit		
Target fixed production cost per unit		
Total target fixed production cost		

The actual costs of production include fixed production costs of £120,000 which allow a production capacity of 50,000 units. In order to produce above this level the fixed production costs step up by £25,000.

Format should set the price at £ [   ] to achieve the target profit margin.

212 MR WYNN

Winston Wynn (Mr Wynn) runs a company that makes wedding dresses and accessories; he has recently designed a revolutionary new range of accessories. He expects the accessories to have a life cycle of two years, before fashions move on and demand will fall to zero. Mr Wynn has carried out research to determine a target selling price and expected sales units across the two years.

Expected sales volume	8,000 units
Selling price per unit	£500
Profit margin %	45%

(a) **Calculate the profit per unit and target cost per unit**

	£
Profit per unit (£)	
Target cost per unit	

The following information relates to the costs Mr Wynn will incur relating to the new product:

1. Direct material cost is currently £100: all of the materials in the original design for the product are luxury materials. Most of these can be replaced with lower grade material costing 60% less. However, some of the more unique features cannot be replaced, these account for 25% of the total material cost, Mr Wynn has managed to negotiate a 10% discount on the luxury material.

2. Direct labour cost: the accessories require 40 minutes of direct labour, which costs £30 per hour. The use of lower grade material, however, will mean that whilst the first unit would still be expected to take 40 minutes, but as the workers become more familiar with the process the time per unit will reduce to 30 minutes. Mr Wynn expect this to happen after 1,000 units (the first 1,000 will take 40 minutes each, every unit after that will take only 30 minutes).

3. Machining costs: the product is expected to take 2 machine hours costing £20 per hour.

4. Quality costs: It costs £40 to check a unit thoroughly to make sure it is to an acceptable standard, Mr Wynn has decided to check every 20th unit thoroughly, and this means 5% of the total output will be checked in this way.

5. Remedial work: the use of lower grade material means the rate of reworks will be 15% of the total number of units and the cost of each rework will be to £40.

6. The initial design costs were in total £400,000

7. Mr Wynn expects sales and marketing costs to total £1 million across the 2 years.

(b) **Complete the below table to calculate the estimated lifetime cost per unit for the new product after taking into account the points above**

Ignore the time value of money. Give your answer to 2 decimal places

	Per unit cost £
Bought in material	
Direct labour	
Machining costs	
Quality costs	
Remedial work	
Initial design costs	
Sales and Marketing costs	
Estimated lifetime cost per unit	

PRACTICE QUESTIONS: **SECTION 1**

(c) What is the cost gap, if one exists? £ ☐

(d) Discuss how value engineering could be used by Mr Wynn to reduce the cost gap, giving examples specific to Mr Wynn.

(e) Explain FOUR benefits that the use of data analytics could bring to Mr Wynn's cost management processes for any future products.

213 TOPCAT

TopCat Ltd (TC) is planning to introduce a new product which is expected to have a short life. It needs to make a net profit margin of 20%.

TC has commissioned a market research company, Likely Causes & Consequences Plc (LCC) and they believe that, in total, TC will be able to sell 30,000 units of the product at £25 per unit.

The total costs which the TC expects to incur over the life of the product are shown in the table below.

Research and development £000	Market research £000	Variable manufacturing costs £000	Fixed manufacturing costs £000	Closure costs £000
150	35	300	100	75

KAPLAN PUBLISHING

119

(a) Complete the following table to determine the target cost per unit for the new product (to the nearest penny).

	£
Total anticipated sales revenue	
Target total net profit	
Target total costs	
Target cost per unit	

(b) Using the information above, calculate the lifecycle costs per unit (to the nearest penny) and provide a recommendation as to whether or not the product should be introduced.

	£
Total lifecycle costs	
Lifecycle cost per unit	

If a margin of 20% is required, the new product should be / should not be **(delete as appropriate) introduced.**

LCC also reported that customers would purchase more of the product if its selling price was reduced by £0.50 per unit. The company will consider making this price reduction if it can sell enough units to maintain a profit margin of 20%.

(c) Complete the table below and calculate the number of units that TC would need to sell to maintain a profit margin of 20%. Assume the lifecycle costs are expected to be as in (a) and (b) above. Enter your answers in the table below to the nearest penny

	£
Reduced selling price per unit	
Target net profit per unit	
Target total cost per unit	
Expected variable manufacturing cost per unit	
Target fixed costs per unit	

To the nearest whole unit, the required sales volume is [ ] units.

(d) Explain the difference between value analysis and value engineering and discuss how ethical considerations could impact the target costing process.

PRACTICE QUESTIONS: SECTION 1

214 CELSIUS

Celsius is developing a new product and intends to use target costing to price the product. You have been given the following information:

- The price at which the product will be sold has not yet been decided;
- It has been estimated that if the price is set at £20 the demand will be 20,000 units, and if the price is set at £22.00 the demand will be 18,000 units;
- The required profit margin is 25%;
- The variable cost per unit is £10.50 for the 18,000 unit level, and £9.20 at the 20,000 unit level.

Complete the following table:

	Sales price £22	Sales price £20
Target total production cost per unit		
Target fixed production cost per unit		
Total target fixed production cost		

The actual costs of production include fixed production costs of £110,000 which allow a production capacity of 20,000 units. In order to produce above this level the fixed production costs step up by £20,000.

Celsius should set the price at £ ☐ **to achieve the target profit margin.**

SHORT TERM DECISION MAKING TECHNIQUES

RELEVANT COSTING

215 MATERIAL D

An organisation is considering the costs to be incurred in respect of a special order opportunity.

The order would require 1,250 kgs of material D. This is a material that is readily available and regularly used by the organisation on its normal products. There are 265 kgs of material D in stock which cost £795 last week. The current market price is £3.24 per kg.

Material D is normally used to make product X. Each unit of X requires 3 kgs of material D, and if material D is costed at £3 per kg, each unit of X yields a contribution of £15.

What is the relevant cost of material D to be included in the costing of the special order?

KAPLAN PUBLISHING

AAT: APPLIED MANAGEMENT ACCOUNTING

216 H LTD

H Ltd has in stock 15,000 kg of M, a raw material which it bought for £3/kg five years ago, for a product line which was discontinued four years ago.

At present, M has no use in its existing state but could be sold as scrap for £1.00 per kg. One of the company's current products (HN) requires 4 kg of a raw material which is available for £5.00 per kg. M can be modified at a cost of £0.75 per kg so that it may be used as a substitute for this material. However, after modification, 5 kg of M is required for every unit of HN to be produced.

H Ltd has now received an invitation to tender for a product which could use M in its present state.

What is the relevant cost per kg of M to be included in the cost estimate for the tender?

217 LABOUR

A company has been asked to quote for a special contract. The following information is available on the labour required for the contract:

The special contract would require 100 hours of labour. However, the labourers, who are each paid £15 per hour, are working at full capacity. There is a shortage of labour in the market and therefore the labour required to undertake this special contract would have to be taken from another contract, Z, which currently utilises 500 hours of labour and generates £5,000 worth of contribution. If the labour was taken from contract Z, then the whole of contract Z would have to be delayed, and such delay would invoke a penalty fee of £1,000.

What is the relevant cost of labour?

218 NEW CONTRACT

Which of the following costs would not be treated as a relevant cost when making a decision on a potential new contract?

A   A net £2,000 saving from avoiding staff redundancies

B   Extra fixed income of £600 per month

C   A reduction of £4,000 in fixed supervisors' salaries

D   A £4,000 expected increase in the bad debt provision

219 K LTD

In order to utilise some spare capacity, K Ltd is preparing a quotation for a special order which requires 2,000 kg of material J.

K Ltd has 800 kg of material J in stock (original cost £7.00 per kg). Material J is used in the company's main product L. Each unit of L uses 5 kg of material J and, based on an input value of £7.00 per kg of J, each unit of L yields a contribution of £10.00.

The resale value of material J is £5.50 per kg. The present replacement price of material J is £8.00 per kg. Material J is readily available in the market.

The relevant cost of the 2,000 kg of material J to be included in the quotation is £_____

220 CONSULTANT

A company is preparing a quotation for a one-month consultancy project. Currently the company employs a consultant on an annual salary of £36,000.

This consultant is fully employed on current projects and, if they were to be transferred to this new project, then an existing junior consultant would be used to cover the current work. The junior consultant would be paid a bonus of £5,000 for undertaking this additional responsibility.

Alternatively the company could hire an external consultant on a one month contract at a cost of £4,500.

The relevant cost to be used in preparing the quotation is: £_____

221 RELEVANT COST

Which ONE of the following is normally considered to be a relevant cost for decision making?

- A Sunk cost
- B Non-incremental cost
- C Committed cost
- D Opportunity cost

222 LIQUID

A one-off project requires 60 litres of a liquid which was purchased for £12 per litre. The liquid isn't regularly used in the business and there are 40 litres in inventory. The inventory can be sold for £4 per litre and the material would cost £15 per litre to replace.

The relevant cost of using the material in the project is £_____.

223 SKILLED LABOUR

20 hours of skilled labour is required for a one-off project. Existing skilled staff are paid a fixed salary that is equivalent to £35 per hour. These staff are fully employed. Alternatively, the work could be outsourced to an agency who can provide equivalent skilled staff at £45 per hour.

The relevant cost for skilled labour in the project is £_____.

224 NORTH EAST CONTRACT

A company in the civil engineering industry with headquarters located 22 miles from London undertakes contracts anywhere in the United Kingdom.

The company is considering tendering for a job in north-east England at £288,000 and work is due to begin in March 20X3.

The following estimates have been submitted by the company's quantity surveyor:

Cost estimates

	North-east contract £
Materials:	
In inventory at original cost, Material X	21,600
In inventory at original cost, Material Y	30,400
Not yet ordered – current cost, Material X	60,000
Labour – hired locally	86,000
Site management	34,000
Staff accommodation and travel for site management	6,800
Plant on site – depreciation	9,600
Interest on capital, 8%	5,120
Total local contract costs	
Headquarters costs allocated at rate of 5% on total contract costs	12,676
	£
Contract price	288,000
Estimated profit	

(1) X and Y are the building materials. Material X is not in common use and would not realise much money if re-sold; however, it could be used on other contracts but only as a substitute for another material currently quoted at 10% less than the original cost of X. The price of Y, a material in common use, has doubled since it was purchased; its net realisable value if re-sold would be its new price less 15% to cover disposal costs. Alternatively it could be kept for use on other contracts in the following financial year.

(2) With the construction industry not yet recovered from the recent economic difficulties, the company is confident that manual labour, both skilled and unskilled, could be hired locally on a sub-contracting basis to meet the needs of the contract.

(3) Site management for a contract is treated as a specific fixed cost.

(4) It is the company's policy to charge all contracts with notional interest at 8% on estimated working capital involved in contracts. Progress payments would be receivable from the contractee.

(5) Salaries and general costs of operating the small headquarters amount to about £108,000 each year. There are usually ten contracts being supervised at the same time.

(6) The contract is expected to last from March 20X3 to February 20X4 which, coincidentally, is the company's financial year.

Required:

Use relevant costing, calculate the true benefit that they will get from undertaking the contract, complete the below table.

	North-east contract
	£
Materials:	
In inventory at original cost, Material X	
In inventory at original cost, Material Y	
Not yet ordered – current cost, Material X	
Labour – hired locally	
Site management	
Staff accommodation and travel for site management	
Plant on site – depreciation	
Interest on capital, 8%	
	─────
Total local contract costs	
Headquarters costs allocated at rate of 5% on total contract costs	
	─────
Contract price	288,000
	─────
Benefit based on relevant cost principles	
	─────

LIMITING FACTORS AND OTHER TYPES OF DECISION

225 LF

LF manufactures 2 products – L and F. The following information is relevant:

	L	F
Selling price	100	200
Material requirement	4 litres	6 litres
Material price £10 per litre		
Labour requirement	2 hours	8 hours
Labour cost £8 per hour		
Maximum demand	100 units	100 units

LF has found that several of their staff have left to work for a competitor and, until they have recruited and trained new staff, they will be limited to 800 hours of labour per month.

AAT: APPLIED MANAGEMENT ACCOUNTING

Complete the following table:

	L	F
	£	£
Selling price per unit		
Material cost per unit		
Labour cost per unit		
Contribution per unit		
Contribution per limiting factor		
Rank		
Optimal production plan in units		

LF has received an important order from a regular customer requiring 78 units of each product.

The revised production plan would be ▢ **units of L and** ▢ **units of F.**

226 BQ

BQ manufactures 2 products – a B and a Q. The following information is relevant:

	B	Q
Selling price	100	150
Material requirement	4 kg	6 kg
Material price £10 per kg		
Labour requirement	2 hours	3 hours
Labour cost per hour	£8	£10
Maximum demand	100 units	100 units

BQ's supplier has informed them that there is a world shortage of the material they require and that that will be limited to 750 kg per month for the foreseeable future.

Complete the following table:

	B	Q
	£	£
Selling price per unit		
Material cost per unit		
Labour cost per unit		
Contribution per unit		
Contribution per limiting factor		
Rank		
Optimal production plan in units		

BQ has received an important order from a regular customer requiring 65 units of each product.

The revised production plan would be ▢ **units of B and** ▢ **units of Q.**

227 LEARN

Learn makes two products – A and B. The following information is available for the next month:

	A	B
	£ per unit	£ per unit
Selling price	50	60
Variable costs:		
Material cost (£5 per kg)	15	20
Labour cost	10	5
Total variable cost	25	25
Fixed costs:		
Production cost	8	8
Administration cost	12	12
Total fixed costs	20	20
Profit per unit	5	15
Monthly demand	2,000	1,800

Materials are in short supply in the coming month – only 12,000 kg are available.

Complete the table below:

	A	B
The contribution per unit		
The contribution per kg		

☐ should be made first and ☐ should be made second.

The optimal production mix is:

	A	B
Production in units		
Workings		
Total contribution		

Learn has been approached by another material supplier who can supply 500 kg of material at a cost of £6 per kg. This is a premium of £1 above the normal cost per kg.

Should Learn purchase the additional material? YES/NO (delete as appropriate)

228 FROME

Frome makes two products – A and B. The following information is available for the next month:

	A	B
	£ per unit	£ per unit
Selling price	95	80
Variable costs:		
Material cost (£5 per kg)	15	20
Labour cost (£10 per hour)	30	25
Total variable cost	45	45
Fixed costs:		
Production cost	18	18
Administration cost	12	12
Total fixed costs	30	30
Profit per unit	20	5
Monthly demand	200	180

Labour is in short supply in the coming month – only 1,000 hours are available.

Complete the table below:

	A	B
The contribution per unit		
The contribution per hour		

☐ should be made first and ☐ should be made second.

The optimal production mix is:

	A	B
Production in units		
Total contribution		

Frome has been approached by an outsourcer who has surplus labour. They can supply Frome with up to 500 hours of labour at a cost of £25 per hour. This is a premium of £15 above the normal cost per hour.

Should Learn purchase the additional hours? YES/NO (delete as appropriate)

PRACTICE QUESTIONS: SECTION 1

229 US

US Limited, a printing firm, is trying to establish how it can reduce costs and increase efficiency. It has identified two machines, A1 and A2, which it could invest in to achieve these objectives. You have been asked to help US decide which of these two machines it should buy.

The following information for the next year has been forecast for the two machines.

	A1	**A2**
Machine cost	£1.1 million	£1.5 million
Sales revenue	£2.8 million	£3 million
Sales volume (units)	1 million	1.2 million
Variable cost per unit	£1.50	10 % less than A1

Fixed production overheads, currently £500,000, are expected to reduce by £50,000 if the A1 is bought and by £100,000 if the A2 is bought.

Fixed selling and distribution overheads, currently £200,000, are expected to remain the same.

Depreciation is charged at 10% per annum on a straight line basis.

The reduction in fixed production overheads is mainly due to proposed redundancies at an average cost of £20,000 per employee. US will have to make 1 person redundant if it chooses A1 and 2 if it chooses A2.

Calculate the total expected annual profit for each machine by completing the table below.

(Negative figures should be entered using brackets.)

£	**A1**	**A2**
Sales revenue		
Variable costs		
Fixed production overheads		
Fixed selling & distribution overheads		
Depreciation		
Redundancy costs		
Expected annual profit		

The expected return on investment for each machine, to the nearest whole %, is:

A1 [   ]

A2 [   ]

Which of the two machines should US buy? [   ]

AAT: APPLIED MANAGEMENT ACCOUNTING

230 CHATTY

Chatty Ltd (Chatty) manufactures three products I, A and IN which use the same resources (but in different amounts). Chatty also purchase a special component from an external supplier for Product A, this costs £65 per unit. The monthly demand and other financial details of the products are in the table below:

	I	A	IN
Demand (units)	4,000	2,000	6,000
	£	£	£
Selling price	100	200	50
Direct materials (£5 per kg)	10	7.50	15
Specialist labour (£10 per hour)	20	30	5
Unskilled labour (£8 per hour)	16	12	4
Variable overhead (£2 per machine hour)	10	12	2
Special component cost to buy in		65	

In addition to the above, Chatty also have fixed costs of £200,000 per month.

Machine hours limited to 30,000 hours per month, Chatty currently have an abundance of specialist labour and the other resources required. The company bases all short term decisions on profit maximisation.

Complete the table below

	I	A	IN
Contribution per unit (£ to 2DP)			
Contribution per machine hour (£ to 2DP)			
Optimum production plan (units)			

A recent addition to the production management team has suggested that Chatty could potentially make the special component in house, and has estimated the costs to do so as follows:

	£
Direct materials (£5 per kg)	17.50
Specialist labour (£10 per hour)	20
Unskilled labour (£8 per hour)	8
Variable overhead (£2 per machine hour)	4

There would be no incremental fixed costs incurred as a result of making the special component in-house.

Complete the below table to calculate the optimum production plan if Chatty were to make all the special components in house?

	I	A	IN
Contribution per unit (£ to 2DP)			
Contribution per machine hour (£ to 2DP)			
Optimum production plan (units)			

PRACTICE QUESTIONS: SECTION 1

Complete the following sentences

If Chatty base their decision solely on profit maximisation they would **buy in / make** (delete as appropriate) the special component.

The difference in profit between the two options is £ ☐

There are other factors to consider when making an outsourcing decision.

Discuss some of the other considerations that Chatty should take into account before making a final decision.

231 GRAFTERS

Grafters Ltd is a famous furniture maker known for their high quality, unique, hand crafted oak furniture.

Machinery Co, a company producing machinery, has approached Grafters Ltd about automating some of the processes currently undertaken by the craftsmen at Grafters ltd.

Below is a table with information about the current costs:

Average craftsmen salary (£)	55,000 per year
Annual tool replacement costs (£)	200,000
Number of craftsmen	20
Other variable overhead costs (£)	50,000
Oak cost (£)	600/m3
Average oak usage per year	100,000m3

KAPLAN PUBLISHING

Machinery Co has also supplied estimates about the impact their machines can have. These are detailed in the table below:

Rental cost per year (£)	£100,000
Reduction in tool replacement costs	50%
Reduction in workforce	70%
Reduced variable overhead cost	20%
Increase in oak usage	1%

Complete the table below estimating the current annual cost and the cost of using the machinery.

	Current cost per year £	Cost per year with machinery £
Oak costs		
Craftsmen cost		
Tool replacement cost		
Other variable overheads		
Rental cost		
Total cost		

Complete the below sentence

On financial grounds, grafters **should/should not** (delete as appropriate) agree to rent the machinery.

Using the information above. Discuss the other factors that grafters should consider regarding the production process.

Grafters have 100 years of experience producing oak furniture; the craftsmen's activities are considered a tourist attraction and people travel from miles around to see the craftsmen at work. The reputation and the distinctive handcrafting is the main reason customers pay the premium price grafters charge. If they were to go ahead with the change, Grafters do not plan to advertise it and they have also worked out a very low cost way to redesign the viewing area to make sure that the machinery was not on display.

Discuss the ethical issues of introducing the machinery to production at grafters

Machinery Co approached Grafter because they have previously worked with the new finance director at Grafters at her last employers. The finance director has a bonus incentive based on reducing costs within the organisation.

Discuss the operational and ethical issues surrounding the approach and bonus offered to the finance director.

AAT: APPLIED MANAGEMENT ACCOUNTING

232 CCV

CCV manufactures four products: M, D, C, and L in a single factory. Each of the products is manufactured in batches of 50 units, CCV have recently started using a just-in-time manufacturing processes and so have little or no inventory.

This batch size of 50 units cannot be changed in the short term. Despite being manufactured in batches of 50 units, they are sold as single units to CCVs customers. CCV operates in a very competitive market place and there is little differentiation available so they must accept the market price.

CCV are reviewing the profit made from each product, and for the business as a whole. The information has been set out below:

Product	M	D	C	L	Total
Sales units	50,000	75,000	100,000	25,000	
Direct labour hours	200,000	225,000	150,000	125,000	700,000
Machine hours	75,000	75,000	200,000	100,000	450,000
	£000	£000	£000	£000	£000
Sales revenue	1,600	1,875	2,750	2,080	8,305
Direct material	200	825	1,000	900	2,925
Direct labour	400	900	1,200	600	3,100
Overhead costs	225	225	600	300	1,350
Profit/(loss)	775	(75)	(50)	280	930

The board of CCV are concerned that two of its products are losing money and have asked for an analysis of the overhead costs to be carried out before a decision about which, if any, products are shutdown is made. This analysis shows:

(1) The sales of M, D, C & L are completely independent of each other.

(2) An overhead recovery rate of £3 per machine hour has been used to share out the overhead costs in the current analysis.

(3) The analysis of overhead costs shows that some of the overheads are product specific and would no longer be incurred if CCV stopped producing that product, while the rest of the overheads are mostly caused by one specific activity setting up the machinery. The below table shows a breakdown of the findings:

	Total	M	D	C	L
Product specific overhead	651,500	£200,000	£20,000	£10,000	£421,500
Machine set up costs	598,500				
General factory costs	100,000				
Machine set ups per batch		4	1	1	6

134 KAPLAN PUBLISHING

The general factory costs are not specific to any product and could be only be changed if the factory was closed down completely, in which case they would not be incurred.

(a) Complete the below tables to work out the cost driver rate for machine set ups:

	M	D	C	L	Total
Number of batches					
Number of machine setups					

	£
Cost driver rate- per set up	

(b) Using the answers to a) and the other information available, complete the table below to calculate the relevant profit or loss for each product to help make a decision about shutting down any product lines:

	M	D	C	L	Total
	£000	£000	£000	£000	£000
Sales revenue	1,600	1,875	2,750	2,080	8,305
Direct material	200	825	1,000	900	2,925
Direct labour	400	900	1,200	600	3,100
Product specific overhead					
Machine set up costs					
General factory costs					
Profit/(loss)					

(c) Prepare a short report to CCV advising which, if any, of its four products should be discontinued in order to maximise its company profits and explain how CCV could use Value Analysis to improve its profits.

233 WHITLEY

Whitley Co has two divisions, Sea and Bay. Division Sea produces three types of products L, E and A, using a common process. Each of the products can either be sold by Division Sea to the external market at split-off point (after the common process is complete) or can be transferred to Division Bay for individual further processing into products LS, ES and AS.

The normal monthly output from the common process is:

L 6,000 units E 5,000 units A 4,000 units

The market selling prices per unit for the products, at split-off point and after further processing, are as follows:

	£		£
L	4	LS	6.50
E	5	ES	7.50
A	6	AS	8.50

The specific costs for each of the individual further processes are:

	Variable cost per unit £	Additional fixed costs per period £
L to LS	1.20	2,000
E to ES	1.75	750
A to AS	1.50	2,250

Further processing leads to a normal loss of 10% at the beginning of the process for each of the products being processed. Whitley is considering what the most financially beneficial production plan is.

Complete the following table:

	LS £	ES £	AS £
Incremental revenue			
Incremental costs			
Net benefit/(loss)			

Complete the following sentences:

On financial grounds Whitley **should/should not** (delete as appropriate) process L further.

On financial grounds Whitley **should/should not** (delete as appropriate) process E further.

On financial grounds Whitley **should/should not** (delete as appropriate) process A further.

Currently Whitley process exactly half of the output further and sell it as LS, ES & AS. They sell the other half of the output as L, E & A.

What other considerations should Whitley take into account before making the final decision?

LINEAR PROGRAMMING

234 LINEAR PROGRAMMING

Which ONE of the following statements is NOT true?

A   Linear programming techniques should not be used when there is only one scarce resource

B   Linear programming assumes that products must be made in full units

C   Linear programming aims to maximise contribution to profits

D   Linear programming techniques can cope with more than two scarce resources at the same time

235 LP CONSTRAINT

An organisation is preparing a linear programming model. The company makes two products, X and Y. It needs to produce twice as many Y than X.

In the linear programming model, X will be used to represent the number of units of Product X produced and Y will be used to represent the number of units of Product Y produced.

Which ONE of the following represents the correct constraint for the production of the products?

A $2X \geq Y$

B $X \geq 2Y$

C $X = 2Y$

D $2X = Y$

236 SIMULTANEOUS EQUATIONS

An organisation has the following contribution function:

Contribution = 6A + 4B

where

A = the number of units of product A produced, and

B = the number of units of product B produced.

A graph has identified that the optimal production plan exists at the point where the following two constraints cross:

Material X: A + 2B ≤ 9,000

Material Y: 3A + B ≤ 12,000

There is a maximum demand of 10,000 units of each product.

The organisation would like to know the optimum production plan and the contribution that it will earn.

Complete the table below giving each answer to the nearest whole number.

	Units of A	Units of B
Optimum production plan	3,000	3,000
	£	
Contribution from optimum production plan	30,000	

237 UNSKILLED LABOUR

An organisation is preparing a linear programming model. Its production process needs two types of labour, skilled and unskilled. There are only 4,000 hours of each available.

Usage per unit of the two types of labour for the organisation's two products is as follows:

	Skilled labour	**Unskilled labour**
Product A	5 hours	5 hours
Product B	1 hour	1 hour

In the linear programming model, X will be used to represent the number of units of Product A produced and Y will be used to represent the number of units of Product B produced.

Which of the following represents the correct constraint for unskilled labour?

A   5X + 1Y ≤ 4,000

B   5X + 5Y ≤ 4,000

C   1X + 5Y ≤ 4,000

D   1X + 1Y ≤ 4,000

238 LIMITATIONS

Which of the following are limitations of the linear programming technique?

	Limitation?
Linear relationships must exist	
There can only be two products	
There can only be two scarce resources	
All variables must be completely divisible	
A computer must be used to find the optimal point	

239 JRL

JRL manufactures two products from different combinations of the same resources. Unit selling prices and unit cost details for each product are as follows:

	J £/unit	L £/unit
Selling price	115	120
Direct material A (£10 per kg)	20	10
Direct material B (£6 per kg)	12	24
Skilled labour (£14 per hour)	28	21
Variable overhead (£4 per machine hour)	14	18
Fixed overhead	28	36

Which of the following equations represents the iso-contribution line?

A   13J + 11L

B   41J + 47L

C   54J + 58L

D   54J + 65L

240 LP GRAPH

An organization has created the following linear programming solution to represent the position it faces currently in the presence of short term scarce resources:

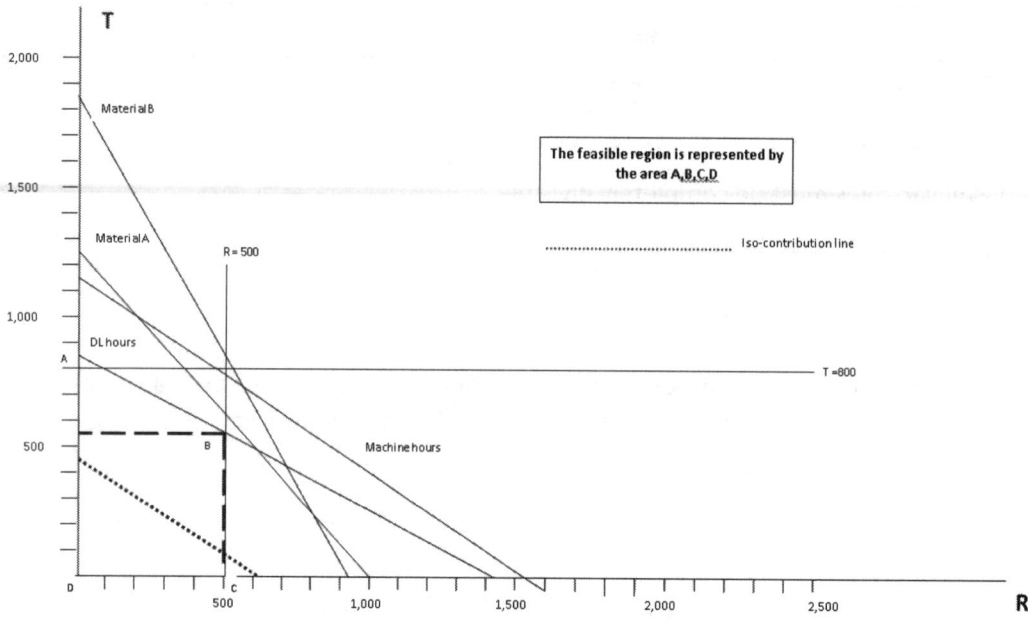

The organisation manufactures two products, T and R. Each T requires 1.4 kgs of material A and each R requires 2 kgs of material A.

The maximum amount of Material A available is _____ kgs

241 LPG CO

LPG Co has the following contribution function:

Contribution = 12A + 8B, where

A = the number of units of product A produced, and

B = the number of units of product B produced.

A graph has identified that the optimal production plan exists at the point where the following two constraints cross:

Material X: A + 2B ≤ 8,000

Material Y: 2A + B ≤ 13,000

There is a maximum demand of 10,000 units of each product.

The organisation would like to know the optimum production plan and the contribution that it will earn.

Complete the table below giving each answer to the nearest whole number.

	Units of A	Units of B
Optimum production plan		
	£	
Contribution from optimum production plan		

242 PRODUCT B

An organisation has graphed the following linear programming model:

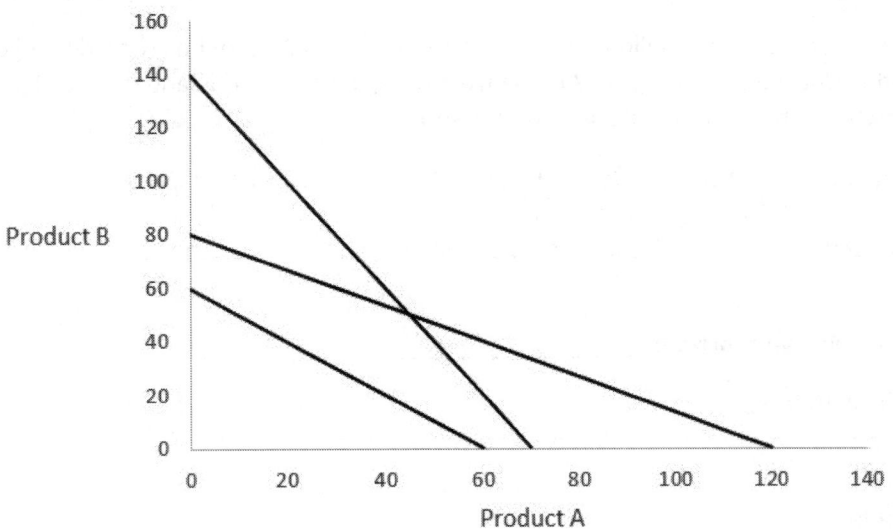

All constraints have less than or equal to limits.

The maximum number of units of Product B which can be produced is _____ units.

243 PRODUCT Y

An organisation has the following contribution function:

Contribution = 5X + 10Y

where

X = the number of units of product X produced, and

Y = the number of units of product Y produced.

A graph has identified that the optimal production plan exists at the point where the following two constraints cross:

Skilled labour: $6X + 4Y \leq 62{,}000$

Unskilled labour: $2X + 5Y \leq 50{,}000$

There is a maximum demand of 12,000 units of each product.

The number of units of Product Y produced in order to maximise contribution (to the nearest whole unit) is _____ units.

244 B CHEMICALS

B Chemicals refines crude oil into petrol. The refining process uses two types of crude oil – heavy and light. A mixture of these oils is blended into either Super or Regular petrol.

In the refining process one gallon (g) of Super is made from 0.7 g of heavy crude and 0.5 g of light crude. One gallon of Regular is made from 0.5 g of heavy crude and 0.7 g of light crude oil. (There is a refining loss of 0.2 g in each case.)

At present, 5,000 g of heavy crude and 6,000 g of light crude oil are available for refining each day. Market conditions suggest that at least two-thirds of the petrol refined should be Super. The company makes contribution of £0.25 per gallon of Super and £0.10 per gallon of Regular.

State the objective function: _____

And the constraints:

heavy crude	
light crude	
market conditions	
Non negativity	

The optimum solution is found to be at the end of the heavy crude constraint.

State the optimum production plan

Super (gallons)	
Regular (gallons)	

Calculate the contribution from this production plan

Contribution	

LONG TERM DECISION MAKING

PAYBACK, ARR, NPV AND IRR

245 JUMP

Jump Ltd is considering a possible capital investment project. It will base its decision upon using three appraisal methods, the results re shown below:

Appraisal method	Notes	Company policy	Project results
Payback period		3 years	3.7 years
Net present value	Discount at 12% cost of capital	Accept if positive	12,000 +ve
Internal Rate of Return	Discount at 12% cost of capital	Must exceed cost of capital	14%

Identify the correct recommendation for each decision below:

Appraisal method	Recommendation
Payback period	
Net present value	
Internal Rate of Return	
Overall	

Options:

- Accept as greater than cost of capital
- Reject as greater than cost of capital
- Reject as per most important investment criterion
- Accept as per most important investment criterion
- Accept as positive
- Reject as positive
- Accept as more than 3 years
- Reject as more than 3 years

246 TRUCK TRANSPORT

Truck Transport Ltd has four possible investment opportunities but is only able to invest in two.

- The first investment needs to be risk limited
- The second investment should provide the best return for the shareholders possible.

The investment opportunities produce the following forecasts.

Method	Option 1	Option 2	Option 3	Option 4
Payback (years)	3.0	4.0	3.3	3.9
Net present value (£000)	16	21	36	52

(a) Complete the sentences below by selecting the most appropriate choices from the options to advise Truck Transport of the options that should be chosen.

For the first investment Truck Transport should invest in option **1 / 2 / 3 / 4** as it has the **highest NPV / lowest NPV / longest payback period / shortest payback period**

For the second investment Truck Transport should invest in option **1 / 2 / 3 / 4** as it has the **highest NPV / lowest NPV / longest payback period / shortest payback period**

(b) Review the statements below and identify whether they are true or false by ticking the correct option.

Statement	True	False
Payback method uses profits from a project to determine the payback period		
If the IRR is less than the cost of capital for a project, then it should be undertaken		
The IRR method uses discounted cash flows		
Projects with a negative NPV should be rejected		

247 CARTCYCLE

One of the finishing machines in Cartcycle Ltd's Wood finishing department is nearing the end of its useful life and the company is considering purchasing a replacement machine.

Estimates have been made for the initial capital cost, sales income and operating costs of the replacement machine, which is expected to have a useful life of three years:

	Year 0 £000	Year 1 £000	Year 2 £000	Year 3 £000
Capital expenditure	1,620			
Other cash flows:				
Sales income		756	1,008	1,440
Operating costs		216	270	342

The company appraises capital investment projects using a 15% cost of capital.

(a) Complete the table below and calculate the net present value of the proposed replacement machine (to the nearest £000).

	Year 0 £000	Year 1 £000	Year 2 £000	Year 3 £000
Capital expenditure				
Sales income				
Operating costs				
Net cash flows				
PV factors	1.0000	0.8696	0.7561	0.6575
Discounted cash flows				
Net present value				

The net present value is of positive/negative*

*delete as appropriate

(b) Calculate the payback of the proposed replacement machine to the nearest whole month.

The payback period is _____Year(s) and _____Months

248 AQUARIUS

One of the finishing machines in Aquarius Ltd's metal finishing department is nearing the end of its useful life and the company is considering purchasing a replacement machine.

Estimates have been made for the initial capital cost, sales income and operating costs of the replacement machine, which is expected to have a useful life of three years:

	Year 0 £000	Year 1 £000	Year 2 £000	Year 3 £000
Capital expenditure	1,200			
Other cash flows:				
Sales income		530	570	710
Operating costs		140	160	170

The company appraises capital investment projects using a 15% cost of capital.

(a) Complete the table below and calculate the net present value of the proposed replacement machine (to the nearest £000).

	Year 0 £000	Year 1 £000	Year 2 £000	Year 3 £000
Capital expenditure				
Sales income				
Operating costs				
Net cash flows				
PV factors	1.0000	0.8696	0.7561	0.6575
Discounted cash flows				
Net present value				

The net present value is positive/negative*

*delete as appropriate

(b) If the net cash inflow in year 4 was £540,000, calculate the payback of the proposed replacement machine to the nearest whole month.

The payback period is _____ Year(s) and _____ Months

249 GRAPE LTD

One of the moulding machines in Grape Ltd's Moulding department is nearing the end of its useful life and the company is considering purchasing a replacement machine.

Estimates have been made for the initial capital cost, sales income and operating costs of the replacement machine, which is expected to have a useful life of three years:

	Year 0 £000	Year 1 £000	Year 2 £000	Year 3 £000
Capital expenditure	500			
Other cash flows:				
Sales income		280	330	370
Operating costs		100	120	140

The company appraises capital investment projects using a 10% cost of capital.

(a) **Complete the table below and calculate the net present value of the proposed replacement machine (to the nearest £000).**

	Year 0 £000	Year 1 £000	Year 2 £000	Year 3 £000
Capital expenditure				
Sales income				
Operating costs				
Net cash flows				
PV factors	1.0000	0.909	0.826	0.751
Discounted cash flows				
Net present value				

The net present value is positive/negative*

*delete as appropriate

(b) **Estimate the IRR of this project.**

A   0%

B   5%

C   10%

D   15%

(c) **Calculate the payback of the proposed replacement machine to the nearest whole month.**

The payback period is _____ Year(s) and _____ Months

250 BARTRUM LTD

Bartrum Ltd needs to purchase a new mashing machine. There are 2 machines available for purchase. Calculate the net present cost of each machine and recommend which machine should be purchased.

Machine A

	Year 0 £000	Year 1 £000	Year 2 £000	Year 3 £000
Capital expenditure	1,085			
Operating costs		200	200	200

Machine B

	Year 0 £000	Year 1 £000	Year 2 £000	Year 3 £000
Capital expenditure	1,200			
Operating costs		150	160	170

The company appraises capital investment projects using a 15% cost of capital.

AAT: APPLIED MANAGEMENT ACCOUNTING

Complete the tables below and calculate the net present cost of each of the proposed replacement machines (to the nearest £000).

Machine A

	Year 0 £000	Year 1 £000	Year 2 £000	Year 3 £000
Capital expenditure				
Net cash flows				
PV factors	1.0000	0.8696	0.7561	0.6575
Discounted cash flows				
Net present cost				

Machine B

	Year 0 £000	Year 1 £000	Year 2 £000	Year 3 £000
Capital expenditure				
Net cash flows				
PV factors	1.0000	0.8696	0.7561	0.6575
Discounted cash flows				
Net present cost				

Bartrum should invest in Machine A/Machine B*

*delete as appropriate

251 CPL

CPL is considering replacing its fleet of delivery vehicles, and has produced the following estimates of capital expenditure and operating costs for two types of van. Both types of van are expected to have a three-year economic life.

Van type P	Year 0 £000	Year 1 £000	Year 2 £000	Year 3 £000
Capital expenditure	600			
Disposal proceeds				150
Operating costs		275	290	315

Van type R	Year 0 £000	Year 1 £000	Year 2 £000	Year 3 £000
Capital expenditure	750			
Disposal proceeds				170
Operating costs		345	365	390

The company's cost of capital is 16%.

Calculate the net present cost for both types of van. (Round the discounted cash flows to the nearest £000).

The net present cost of van type P

	Year 0 £000	Year 1 £000	Year 2 £000	Year 3 £000
Capital expenditure				
Disposal				
Net cash flows				
PV factors	1.0000	0.8621	0.7432	0.6407
Discounted cash flows				
Net present cost				

The net present cost of van type R

	Year 0 £000	Year 1 £000	Year 2 £000	Year 3 £000
Capital expenditure/disposal				
Net cash flows				
PV factors	1.0000	0.8621	0.7432	0.6407
Discounted cash flows				
Net present cost				

CPL should invest in Van type P/Van type R* (*delete as appropriate)

252 GLOBE LTD

(a) Globe Ltd's Finance Director has calculated an IRR of 12% for an investment opportunity. The company's required cost of capital is 15%. Should Globe Ltd take this investment opportunity?

Yes/No

(b) Globe Ltd's Finance Director has calculated an IRR of 17% for another investment opportunity. The companies required cost of capital is 15%. Should Globe Ltd take this investment opportunity?

Yes/No

(c) Globe Ltd's Finance Director has calculated an IRR of 15% for an investment opportunity. The companies required cost of capital is 15%. What is the value of the NPV?

£ ☐

253 MIXING MACHINE

A company is considering investing in a new mixing machine that will cost £3,000,000 to purchase but will reduce operating costs of the company. The following information is relevant to this decision:

- The payback period would be 2.4 years. The company's policy is for projects to pay back within 3 years.
- The net present value is £400,000 negative.
- The internal rate of return is 14%. The company's cost of capital is 16%.

Complete the report below, deleting words/phases where appropriate (marked with *)

REPORT

To: The Chief Accountant

From: AAT student

Subject: Investment appraisal

Date: 3 December 20X2

The payback period of 2.4 years is within/outside* the company's policy of 3 years, and on this criterion the investment should go/should not go* ahead.

The NPV is positive/negative* and on this criterion the investment should go/should not go* ahead.

The IRR, at 14%, is above/below* the company's 16% cost of capital and on this criterion the investment should go/should not go* ahead.

Overall the investment should/should not* proceed because the Payback/NPV/IRR* is the dominant criterion.

---

254 A COMPANY

A company has determined that the net present value of an investment project is £17,706 when using a 10% discount rate and £(4,317) when using a discount rate of 15%.

Calculate the internal rate of return of the project to the nearest 1%.

[   ] %

255 EDUCATION AUTHORITY

An education authority is considering the implementation of a CCTV (closed circuit television) security system in one of its schools. Details of the proposed project are as follows:

Life of project	5 years
Initial cost	£75,000
Annual savings:	
Labour costs	£20,000
Other costs	£5,000
NPV at 15%	£8,800

The discount rates for 20% are:

Year	1	2	3	4	5
PV factors	0.833	0.694	0.579	0.482	0.402

Calculate the internal rate of return for this project to the nearest 1%.

A 16%

B 18%

C 20%

D 22%

256 DPP

A company has the following pattern of cash flow for a project

Year	Cash flow £
0	(100,000)
1	40,000
2	20,000
3	30,000
4	5,000
5	40,000

The company uses a discount rate of 10% and the discount rates for 10% are:

Year	1	2	3	4	5
PV factors	0.909	0.826	0.751	0.683	0.621

In what year does discounted payback occur?

Year ☐

257 STATEMENTS

Which TWO of the following statements about the accounting rate of return (ARR) method and the payback method are true?

A Both methods are affected by changes in the cost of capital

B The ARR does not take account of returns over the entire life of the project

C The payback method is based on the project's cash flows

D A requirement for an early payback can increase a company's liquidity

258 INK CO

Ink Co is considering the following investment opportunity.

Initial capital investment: £1,800,000

The project life is expected to be four years and the finance director thinks the company should use a discount rate of 10% in the evaluation. The investment project has no scrap value.

Using the average investment method and assuming operating cash flows of £729,000 per year, what is the accounting rate of return of the investment project?

A   16%

B   28%

C   31%

D   64%

PERFORMANCE INDICATORS

CALCULATIONS

259 TEES R US

Tees R Us Ltd operates a tea plantation in Kenya. The plantation produces tea for sale to Tees R Us tea bagging division and other wholesalers. The tea crop has been lower than expected due to bad weather. The actual and budgeted information is produced below.

	Actual	Budgeted
	£	£
Turnover	787,500	1,125,000
Cost of sales:		
Tea pickers	132,000	150,000
Tea processor operators	35,000	50,000
Depreciation of tea machines	60,000	60,000
Seeds and fertilizer	75,000	75,000
Total cost of sales	302,000	335,000
Gross profit	485,500	790,000
Administration costs	150,000	150,000
Distribution costs	300,000	350,000
Operating profit	35,500	290,000
Amount of tea in kilograms harvested and sold	1,750,000	2,500,000
Number of harvest days	100	100
Number of tea pickers	440	500
Daily cost of a tea picker	£3	£3
Net assets	£935,500	£1,190,000

Calculate the following performance indicators for the actual and budgeted information (give answers to two decimal places):

	Actual	Budgeted
Cost of tea pickers as a % of turnover		
Cost of tea processor operators as a % of turnover		
Cost of seeds and fertilizer as a % of turnover		
Gross profit margin		
Operating profit margin		
Return on capital employed		
Net asset turnover		

260 PARTY

Party Ltd has developed a skin treatment for spotty teenagers. The product competes with a dozen other companies. Topical Ltd is a major competitor and market leader with over 60% of the market. You have been given the following information about Party and Topical for the year ended 31 May 2014.

Income statement	Party	Topical
	£000	£000
Turnover	45,000	220,000
Cost of production		
Direct (raw) materials	12,000	33,000
Direct labour	7,500	22,000
Fixed production overheads	6,000	30,000
Total cost of sales	25,500	85,000
Gross profit	19,500	135,000
Selling and distribution costs	5,000	10,000
Administration costs	3,750	7,500
Advertising costs	2,500	100,000
Net profit	8,250	17,500

Other information		Party	Topical
Number of units sold (000)	Units	6,000	22,000
Net assets	(£000)	50,000	85,000

Calculate the following performance indicators for Party and Topical (give answers to two decimal places):

	Party	Topical
Selling price per unit		
Material cost per unit		
Labour cost per unit		
Fixed cost per unit		
Gross profit margin		
Net profit margin		
Advertising cost as % of turnover		
Return on capital employed		

261 FUDGE

Fudge Limited has developed a new low calorie chocolate product that does not contain fat. Fudge competes with a dozen other companies making similar products. Stubbed Limited is a major competitor and has recently launched a similar product. You have been given the following information about Fudge and Stubbed for the year ended 31 July 2010.

Income statement	Fudge	Stubbed
	£m	£m
Turnover	3.2	4.0
Cost of production		
Direct (raw) materials	0.5	0.6
Direct labour	0.7	0.5
Fixed production overheads	0.3	0.1
Total cost of sales	1.5	1.2
Gross profit	1.7	2.8
Selling and distribution costs	0.5	0.5
Administration costs	0.1	0.2
Advertising costs	0.6	1.0
Net profit	0.5	1.1

Other information		Fudge	Stubbed
Number of units sold (m)	Units	6.4	6.6
Net assets	£m	10	12

Calculate the following performance indicators for Fudge and Stubbed (give answers to three decimal places:

	Fudge	Stubbed
Selling price per unit		
Material cost per unit		
Labour cost per unit		
Fixed production cost per unit		
Gross profit margin		
Net profit margin		
Advertising cost as % of turnover		
Return on capital employed		

262 DEJAVU

You have been given the following information for the year ended 30 June 2010 for Dejavu, a CD manufacturer and distributor.

Income statement	Budget	Actual
	£000	£000
Turnover	55,000	60,000
Cost of production		
Direct materials	10,000	11,000
Direct labour	3,000	2,850
Fixed production overheads	15,000	15,000
Total cost of sales	28,000	28,850
Gross profit	27,000	31,150
Selling and distribution costs	5,000	6,500
Administration costs	3,500	4,000
Advertising costs	5,550	5,000
Net profit	12,950	15,650

Other information		Budget	Actual
Number of units sold (000)	Units	20,000	20,000
Direct labour hours worked		40,000	38,000

Calculate the following performance indicators for Budget and Actual (give answers to two decimal places):

	Budget	Actual
Selling price per unit		
Material cost per unit		
Labour cost per hour		
Fixed production cost per labour hour		
Gross profit margin		
Net profit margin		
Direct materials cost as % of turnover		

263 GRANSDEN

Gransden Ltd has two divisions, the North Division and the South Division. These are entirely retail operations. Details of their results for the year to 31 May 2010 are reproduced below

Income Statement	North	South
	£000	£000
Turnover	135,000	191,000
Cost of sales		
Opening inventory	25,000	55,000
Purchases	75,000	105,000
Closing inventory	(20,000)	(40,000)
Total cost of sales	80,000	120,000
Gross profit	55,000	71,000
Wages and salaries	10,000	12,000
Depreciation	10,000	16,000
Other costs	9,688	8,620
Operating profit for the year	25,312	34,380

Net assets	North	South
Non-current assets	100,000	160,000
Depreciation	(40,000)	(48,000)
Net book value	60,000	112,000
Inventory	20,000	40,000
Receivables	16,875	46,750
Payables	(12,500)	(8,750)
Capital employed	84,375	190,000

Calculate the following performance indicators for the two divisions (give answers to two decimal places):

	North	South
Gross profit margin		
Operating profit margin		
Wages & salaries as a percentage of turnover		
Inventory turnover in days		
Receivable days		
Payable days (based on cost of sales)		
Return on capital employed		

264 REVENUE

What would the revenue need to have been for the total asset turnover to be 4 times if the total assets are £950,000?

265 OPERATING PROFIT

What would the operating profit need to have been for the ROCE to be 25% if the net assets are £480,000?

266 GROSS PROFIT

What would the gross profit need to have been if sales revenue was £1,000,000 and the gross profit margin was 30%?

267 INVENTORY

What would the inventory value be if the inventory days were 73 and purchases for period were £600,000?

268 RECEIVABLES

What would sales revenue need to be (to the nearest £) if receivable days were 90 days and receivables were £400,000?

269 VALUE ADDED

What would be the 'value added' if sales revenue was £850,000, materials used were £300,000; labour employed was £250,000 and bought in services were £200,000?

[   ]

270 PAYABLES

What would payables need to be (to the nearest £) if sales were £1,000,000, cost of sales were £700,000 and the payables days were 75 days?

[   ]

271 BACKWARDS

A business has sales for the year of £30,000. Its financial performance indicators at the year-end include the following:

Gross profit margin	30%
Receivables collection period	30 days
Creditors payment period	48 days
Inventory	£2,100

Assume there are 360 days in a year.

Complete the following table:

Year-end receivables balance	
Year-end payables balance	

272 REVERSE

A business has provided the following information:

Receivables collection period	45 days
Creditors payment period	64 days
Cash	£5,000
Receivables	£25,000
Payables	£18,000

All sales and purchases were on credit, cost of sales is made up entirely of credit purchases. Assume there are 360 days in a year.

Expenses were budgeted to be £80,000, split equally between fixed and variable costs. The actual fixed costs were 5% higher than expected, while the variable element was 2% higher than expected.

Complete the following table (giving all answers to the nearest £):

	£
Sales revenue	
Cost of sales	
Gross profit	
Expenses	
Net profit	

WRITTEN TASKS

273 PAS

Polina's Accessory Store (PAS) is a new business, selling high quality accessories, from socks to ties, from earrings to cuff links, all via the internet.

Polina is the owner/manager of the company. She has no experience running a company, having become disillusioned with her old job, she decided to take a risk and set up her own business. She believes that buying high quality accessories and selling them online will grow her business very quickly from a relatively low fixed cost base.

The market for accessories is very competitive with all the major high street clothing brands all offering their own accessories both online and in store.

Polina expects that any business takes time to become profitable so is willing to run PAS at a loss in the short term to make sure PAS has a good foundation for future growth. One area she is particularly focussed on is that the website must be secure and be able to handle high levels of traffic. Another area she is prepared to invest in is the initial marketing effort to make sure PAS establishes a good brand image synonymous with quality products. Polina expects that both these costs will be high initially but will not continue at that level for long.

Actual year 1 and 2 figures for PAS are as follows:

	Year 1	Year 2
	£	£
Sales	2,889,598	3,635,746
Cost of sales	(1,405,331)	(2,133,296)
Gross profit	1,484,267	1,502,450
Website development and maintenance	(420,000)	(85,000)
Marketing costs	(340,500)	(170,000)
Distribution costs	(263,575)	(395,565)
Administrative costs	(300,000)	(390,000)
Other overhead costs	(268,000)	(338,000)
Profit/(loss)	(107,808)	123,885

(a) **Complete the table below**

	Year 1	Year 2
Revenue growth (%)		
Gross profit margin (%)		
Net profit margin (%)		

(b) **Using the above information, write a report to Polina commenting on:**

(i) Revenue

(ii) Gross profit

(iii) Net profit

To:	Subject:
From:	Date:

Polina is also very aware of not focussing solely on financial performance indicators. She believes that identifying important non-financial performance indicators and performing well against them will lead to financial success. The tables below show some of the indicators that PAS are tracking and some industry information.

	Year 1	Year 2
Number of units sold	140,956	157,870
Website visits	2,710,692	5,262,333
Sales returns	12,686	33,153
On time delivery	98%	88%
Transactions aborted due to website issues	282	7,453

Industry averages statistics are as follows:

Conversion rate for website visits to number of units sold	4.1%
Sales return rate for internet-based clothing sales	14.2%
On time delivery	95.3%

(c) **Complete the following table. Give % figures to 1 decimal place and £ to 2 decimal places:**

	Year 1	Year 2
Conversion rate for website visits to number of units sold (%)		
% sales returned		
Average price per sale (£ to 2 decimal places)		

(d) **Using the tables above write a report to Polina commenting on the non-financial performance of PAS over the last year, giving reasons for the changes and considering industry averages where possible.**

To:	Subject:
From:	Date:

274 ARCHIMEDES

A division of Archimedes Limited is developing a new product and a colleague has prepared forecast information based upon two scenarios. The forecast income statement and statement of financial position for both scenarios is shown below:

Scenario 1 is to set the price at £7.20 per unit with sales of 120,000 units each year.

Scenario 2 is to set the price at £4.80 per unit with sales of 240,000 units each year.

Forecast Income statement	Scenario 1	Scenario 2
	£	£
Turnover	864,000	1,152,000
Cost of production		
Direct (Raw) Materials	240,000	480,000
Direct Labour	96,000	153,600
Fixed Production overheads	288,000	288,000
Total cost of sales	624,000	921,600
Gross profit	240,000	230,400
Selling and distribution costs	59,200	97,600
Administration costs	40,000	40,000
Operating profit	176,000	116,000
	Scenario 1	Scenario 2
Gross profit margin	27.78%	20.00%
Operating profit margin	16.30%	8.06%
Direct materials as a percentage of turnover	27.78%	41.67%
Direct materials cost per unit	£2.00	£2.00
Direct labour cost per unit	£0.80	£0.64
Fixed production cost per unit	£2.40	£1.20

Draft a report for the finance director covering the following:

(a) An explanation of why the gross profit margins are different, referring to the following.

- Sales price.
- Sales volume.
- Materials.
- Labour.
- fixed costs.

(b) An explanation of why the operating profit margins are different.

(c) A recommendation, with reasons, as to which course of action to take.

To:	Subject:
From:	Date:

(a) Why are the gross profit margins different?

    Sales Price/Sales Volume

    Materials

    Labour

    Fixed costs

(b) Why are the operating profit margins different?

(c) Recommendation, with reasons, as to which course of action to take

275 TEMPEST

Tempest plc is a large public company engaged in the running of cinemas throughout the UK. Some cinemas are very large with multiple screens. Typically these are based on large sites situated out of town, with on-site parking, and often with bar and snack facilities. Other smaller cinemas with only a few screens are typically based in city centres. They have limited parking, but similar facilities for refreshments.

Currently Tempest charges the same fee per film for both types of cinema. However the number of customers per month, and spend per customer on food and drink varies greatly at each type of cinema. The Finance Director wants to know which type of cinema is more profitable per customer.

He/she has prepared forecast information for both types of cinema. A typical forecast income statement and statement of financial position for both type of cinemas is shown below:

Forecast Income statement	Out of Town	City Centre
	£000	£000
Turnover	1,512	501
Cost of production		
Direct costs (90% films, 10% food)	320	108
Fixed costs	450	180
Total cost of sales	770	288
Gross profit	742	213
Administration costs (fixed)	50	50
Operating profit	692	163
Revenue from films	1,209	451
Revenue from food and drink	303	50
Gross profit margin	49%	42%
Operating profit margin	46%	32%
Number of customers per month (thousand)	150	56
Average spend per customer – Films	£8.06	£8.05
Average spend per customer – Food	£2.02	£0.89
Direct cost per customer	£2.13	£2.16
Fixed cost per customer	£3.00	£3.24

Draft a report for the Finance Director covering the following:

Explain why the gross profit margins are not significantly different using sales price, direct costs and fixed costs to illustrate your answer.

Explain why the operating profit margins are different.

Which is the most profitable type of cinema and why?

PRACTICE QUESTIONS: SECTION 1

Apart from reducing fixed costs what could Tempest do to improve the profitability of the City Centre Cinemas? Use numbers to demonstrate your answer if necessary.

Tempest suspect City Centre customers are smuggling in their own sweets and snacks – give ONE way that Tempest could investigate the extent of this smuggling? What could be done to combat it?

To:	Subject:
From:	Date:

Why are the gross profit margins not significantly different?

Sales Price

Direct costs

Fixed costs

Why are the operating profit margins different?

Which is the most profitable type of cinema and why?

Apart from reducing fixed costs what could Tempest do to improve the profitability of the City Centre Cinemas?

Tempest suspect City Centre customers are smuggling in their own sweets and snacks – what could Tempest do to combat this smuggling?

276 ANIMAL

You have been provided with the information for Animal Limited:

Current position

The price is £25 per unit. At this price demand is 15,000 units each year. Advertising costs are £50,000 per year. The factory can produce a maximum of 40,000 units per year. Labour and material costs are the only variable costs.

Proposed position

The price will fall to £22 per unit. Advertising costs will increase to £75,000 per year and it is expected that this will increase demand to 30,000 units per year. The factory will still be limited to 40,000 units per year. The labour and material costs are the only variable costs.

Forecast information for each scenario is shown below.

	Current position (actual)	Proposed position (forecast)
Sales price per unit	£25	£22
Sales volume	15,000	30,000
	£	£
Revenue	375,000	660,000
Materials	75,000	120,000
Labour	90,000	180,000
Fixed production costs	60,000	60,000
Total cost of sales	225,000	360,000
Gross profit	150,000	300,000
Fixed advertising costs	50,000	75,000
Administration costs	30,000	40,000
Profit	70,000	185,000
Material cost per unit	£5.00	£4.00
Labour cost per unit	£6.00	£6.00
Fixed production cost per unit	£4.00	£2.00
Fixed advertising cost per unit	£3.33	£2.50
Gross profit margin	40%	45%
Profit margin	19%	28%
Inventory of finished goods	£35,000	
Trade receivables	£50,000	

Draft a report for the finance director covering the following:

(a) An explanation of why the gross profit margin for the proposed position is higher than the current position, referring to the following:

- sales volume
- material cost
- labour cost
- fixed production cost

(b) An explanation of what is likely to happen to the current asset position of the business by considering the following:

- inventory levels (include a prediction of the proposed inventory level based upon the current holding period)
- trade receivable levels (include a prediction of the proposed level based upon current trade receivables collection period).

To:	Subject:
From:	Date:

Why are the gross profit margin for the proposed position is higher than the current position:

Sales volume

Material costs

Labour costs

Fixed production cost

What is likely to happen to the current asset position:

Inventory levels

Trade receivable levels

277 FRUITY

Fruity manufactures fruit juices for sale in supermarkets. Fruity has several products including Apple fruit juice and Cranberry fruit juice. The finance department has produced the following information for each product.

Quarterly information	Apple	Cranberry
Unit information		
Sales price	£1	£1.25
Quantity of material in grams	500	550
Material cost per unit	£0.40	£0.50
Fixed production overheads	£0.20	£0.12
Full production cost per unit	£0.60	£0.62
Gross profit per unit	£0.40	£0.63
Gross profit margin	40.0%	50.4%
Volume of sales	500,000	1,000,000
Sales revenue	500,000	1,250,000
Variable production costs	200,000	500,000
Fixed production overhead	100,000	120,000
Gross profit	200,000	630,000
Marketing costs	50,000	120,000
Net profit	150,000	510,000
Net profit margin	30.0%	40.8%

A new manager has asked for your help in understanding the figures for Apple and Cranberry. The information has been reviewed and the following questions have arisen:

1. Why is the gross profit margin of Cranberry less than 50% higher than that of Apple when the gross profit per unit is more than 50% higher?

2. I was told that the material cost is £0.80 per kilogram for Apple and £0.91 per kilogram for Cranberry. Therefore I do not understand why the material cost per unit for Apple is £0.40 and for Cranberry is £0.50. Is this correct?

3. If the fixed production overheads are constant does that mean they have no effect on the profit margin? And if the fixed production overheads increase will they affect the profit margin?

4. Can you explain why Cranberry is more profitable than Apple?

Draft an email to the new manager answering the questions.

To:	Subject:
From:	Date:

Gross profit margin

Material cost

Fixed production overheads

Profitability

PRACTICE QUESTIONS: SECTION 1

278 PI ETHICS

Below are some of the results for one of the divisions of PI Ltd for the last two quarters.

Performance indicator	Qtr 1 20X5	Qtr 2 20X5
Revenue growth	9%	11%
Gross profit margin	40%	30%
Average selling price	£50	£40
Number of customers	10	9

One of the managers at PI receives a bonus based on some of the financial measures in the table above. They receive a bonus if revenue growth is over 10%.

Explain the ethical issues and any issues with goal congruence.

Ethical issues

Goal congruence issues

AAT: APPLIED MANAGEMENT ACCOUNTING

279 SSS

Stuart is the owner and manager of Stu's Snipping Station (SSS) which is a premium hairdressing salon in the upmarket town of Gosford; being in such a premium location, there are several similar salons trying to differentiate their service, so SSS are in a very competitive market. When Stuart first set up the salon his main focus was female clients, but he has recently turned his attention to the male market too.

The salon offers the usual range of hair services to female clients, including cuts, colouring and straightening. The male market is, overall, much simpler; usually haircuts only, so the time taken per client is much lower.

The price and mix of services provided to female clients has stayed the same over the last 4 years. Below is a table detailing the financial performance of SSS over the last 2 years:

	2015		2016	
	£	£	£	£
Sales		500,000		550,600
Cost of Sales:				
Stylists salaries	122,500		162,725	
Hair products	75,000		80,000	
		197,500		242,725
Gross profit		302,500		307,875
Property rental	15,000		15,000	
Administrative assistant	14,000		14,140	
Rates	8,000		9,000	
Marketing and advertising	3,000		9,000	
Total Expenses		40,000		47,140
Profit		262,500		260,735

Stuart feels the business is much busier than a year ago and is concerned that the financial results do not back this up. He has identified that the number of client visits to the salon are as follows:

	2015	2016
Female client visits	10,000	8,802
Male client visits	0	4,420

(a) **Using the figures above complete the table below:**

	£
Average price for hair services per female client visit in 2016 (assuming prices remained the same as 2015)	
Average price for hair services per male client visit in 2016	

Additional information:

(1) Stuart hired two stylists at the start of 2016; one was a dedicated stylist for male customers. The other was a trainee stylist on an apprentice contract and salary of £13,000.

(2) The other stylists all received a 1% pay rise at the start of 2016.

(b) Complete the following table stating your answer to 2 decimal places.

	2015	2016
Gross profit margin		
Net profit margin		

Write a report to Stuart about how the financial performance of SSS has changed over the last year.

(c) Comment on revenue, giving reasons for the change between 2015 and 2016.

(d) Comment on gross profit margin, giving reasons for the change between 2015 and 2016.

(e) Comment on net profit margin, giving reasons for the change between 2015 and 2016.

To:	Subject:
From:	Date:

Revenue

Gross profit margin

Net profit margin

AAT: APPLIED MANAGEMENT ACCOUNTING

Stuart is considering introducing some non-financial measures of success, the table below shows some figures that he thinks will help set up some measures.

	2015	2016
Complaints	16	176
Stylists for female clients	5	6
Stylists for male clients	0	1

The complaints related to two main factors and were from the loyal customer base that SSS had developed over the years. One of those factors was the introduction of male customers had changed the atmosphere at the salon.

(f) **Complete the below table analysing the non-financial performance of the business.**

	2015	2016
Customer		
% of visits that had complaints (to 2 decimal places)		
Internal business		
Number of female client visits per stylist		
Number of male client visits per stylist		
Innovation and growth		
% revenue from new male hairdressing service (to 2 decimal places)		

(g) **Comment on the non-financial performance of SSS, giving reasons for the changes in the non-financial performance indicators over the last year.**

280 COST REDUCTION

Distinguish between the terms 'cost reduction' and 'cost control', and outline the process of a cost reduction programme.

Cost reduction

Cost control

Outline process of a cost reduction programme

281 VALUE ANALYSIS

Value analysis is a technique widely used in cost reduction programmes. **Outline the process of value analysis.**

Value analysis

ETHICS

282 ETHICS STATEMENTS (I)

A company that takes a strong ethical stance in the way they behave will usually find their relationship with investors [   ]

improves/stays the same/gets worse/deteriorates

A worker in the accounts department who receives a profit based bonus decides to manipulate some of the expenses, artificially increasing the profits and allowing them to get a bonus has not breached the ethical principle of [   ]

professional behaviour/integrity/objectivity/confidentiality

283 ETHICS STATEMENTS (II)

Consumers may be willing to pay [   ] price for Fairtrade products, knowing that the products are grown in an ethical and sustainable fashion

a lower/a premium/a discounted/a penetration

An advantage of using life cycle costing is it could help an organisation make more *sustainable* [   ] they will consider all costs throughout the projects including any potential closure and clean-up costs.

sustainable/confidential/expensive/irresponsible

284 ETHICS STATEMENTS (III)

Products that have [   ] packaging could be considered unethical because they are using more of the world's resources and could potentially cost the company more money.

excess/no/sustainable/limited

Ethical actions by a business may help them achieve long term [   ].

costs/penalties/success/expense

CALCULATING FORECASTS

TREND ANALYSIS, INDEXING, LINEAR REGRESSION AND EXPECTED VALUES

285 TREND

The actual purchase price per tonne of materials, together with its estimated seasonal variation, is as below:

	Q1	Q2	Q3	Q4
Actual price	£30	£34	£54	£66
Seasonal variation	–£4	–£8	+£4	+£8

The trend in prices is an increase of ☐ per quarter.

286 RPI

A company has provided the following information:

	2008	2009	2010
Cost per kg of materials	£17.00	£18.60	£19.40
Retail price index	184	192	200

The percentage increase in purchase costs, after removing the effect of general inflation, between 2008 and 2010 was:

A 14.12%

B 8.70%

C 4.99%

D 24.04%

287 PRODUCT Z

The cost per unit of a product has decreased from £36 in October 20X7 to £32 in December 20X7. The cost per unit was £30 when the index was rebased to 100 in January 20X7.

A The cost index in December was 107 and the decrease from October to December is 11.11%

B The cost index in December was 89 and the decrease from October to December is 11.11%

C The cost index in December is 107 and the decrease from October to December is 12.5%

D The cost index in December is 89 and the decrease from October to December is 12.5%

288 TANZANITE

The table below contains the last three months cost per metre for product Tanzanite.

Jan	Feb	Mar
Actual price was £6.90	Actual price was £7.00	Actual price was £7.40
Seasonal variation was −10p	Seasonal variation was −15p	Seasonal variation was 10p

The trend in prices is an increase of £ [0.15] per month

289 MARCH

A company has provided the following information:

	Jan	Feb	March
Total cost	£450,000	£500,000	£650,000
Total quantity purchased	20,000 m	25,000 m	27,500 m

The cost index for March, based upon January being the base period with an index of 100, is:

A   105

B   138

C   144

D   167

290 COST PER UNIT

The cost per unit of a product has increased from £52 in February to £56 in April. The cost per unit was £50 in January when the index was rebased to 100.

Which of the following statements is correct?

A   The cost index in April was 112 and the increase from January to April is 12%

B   The cost index in April was 112 and the increase from January to April is 8%

C   The cost index in April was 108 and the increase from January to April is 12%

D   The cost index in April was 108 and the increase from January to April is 8%

291 PRODUCT Y

The table below contains the last three months cost per kilogram for product Y

Apr	May	Jun
Actual price was £6.56	Actual price was £7.14	Actual price was £7.35
Seasonal variation was (£0.30)	Seasonal variation was £0.14	Seasonal variation was £0.21

The trend in prices is an increase of £ [0.14] per month

292 A COMPANY

A company has provided the following information:

	Jan	Feb	March
Total cost	£100,000	£132,000	£127,000
Total quantity purchased	10,000 kgs	12,000 kgs	11,500 kgs

The cost index (to the nearest whole number) for March based upon January being the base period of 100 is:

A 120

B 110

C 127

D 115

293 PRODUCT X

The cost per unit of a product has increased from £46 in January to £52 in April. The cost per unit was £42 when the index was rebased to 100. (Assume an inflationary economy.)

A The cost index in April was 123.8 and the increase from January to April is 13.0%

B The cost index in April was 113 and the increase from January to April is 13.0%

C The cost index in April is 123.8 and the increase from January to April is 11.5%

D The cost index in April is 113 and the increase from January to April is 11.5%

294 INDEX

The cost per unit of a product has increased from £82 in May to £96 in July. The cost per unit was £70 when the index was 100. (Assume an inflationary economy.)

A The cost index in July is 137, and the increase from May to July is 17%

B The cost index in July is 127, and the increase from May to July is 17%

C The cost index in July is 137, and the increase from May to July is 15%

D The cost index in July is 127, and the increase from May to July is 15%

295 DEXTER

The cost per unit of a product has increased from £1,350 in June to £1,710 in September. The cost per unit was £1,080 when the index was rebased to 100.

A The cost index in September is 126 and the increase from June to September is 21.05%

B The cost index in September is 158 and the increase from June to September is 21.05%

C The cost index in September is 126 and the increase from June to September is 26.67%

D The cost index in September is 158 and the increase from June to September is 26.67%

PRACTICE QUESTIONS: SECTION 1

296 WASTE

A company has provided the following information for kilograms of waste sent to landfill by Moody Co.

	Jan	**Feb**	**March**
Kgs	1000	1250	1100
Price per kilo	5	6	7
Total cost	£5000	£7500	£7700

The cost index for March based upon January being the base period of 100 is:

A   120

B   140

C   117

D   83

297 FIZZ

The table below contains the last three months cost per litre for Fizz.

Jan	Feb	Mar
Actual price was £550	Actual price was £675	Actual price was £650
Seasonal variation was –£50	Seasonal variation was +£50	Seasonal variation was Nil

The trend in prices is an increase of £ ☐ **per month**

298 ACRID

The table below contains the last three months cost per tonne for product Acrid.

Jan	Feb	Mar
Actual price was £50	Actual price was £50	Actual price was £65
Seasonal variation was £5	Seasonal variation was –£5	Seasonal variation was Nil

The trend in prices is an increase of £ ☐ **per month.**

299 PRODUCT J

The table below contains the last three months cost per litre for product J.

	April	**May**	**June**
Actual price	£7.20	£7.50	£6.90
Seasonal variation	£0.10	£0.20	(£0.60)

The trend in prices is an increase of £ ☐ **per month.**

300 ABCO

A company has provided the following information:

	October	November	December
Total cost	£1,250	£1,390	£1,610
Quantity purchased	1,000 kg	1,100 kg	1,200 kg

The cost index for December based upon October prices is:

A 101

B 107

C 125

D 134

301 SOAP

The soap industry maintains a price index for soap. The index for May was 105 and the actual price per tonne was £1,200. The forecast index for the three months ending November 2009 is shown below.

Month	September	October	November
Underlying trend in index	120	125	130
Seasonal variation in index	+6	−6	+3
Seasonally adjusted index	126	119	133

Calculate the expected cost of one tonne of soap for each of the three months.

September	£
October	£
November	£

302 ASPHALT

The Production Director has asked for your help and has been given you an equation and information to estimate the cost of asphalt for the coming three months.

The equation is Y = a + bX, where

X is the time period in months

the value for X in April is 24 and May is 25

Y is the cost of asphalt

The constant "a" is 125 and constant "b" is 2.

The cost of asphalt is set on the first day of each month and is not changed during the month. The cost of asphalt in May was £175 per tonne.

The expected price of asphalt per tonne for June is £ [   ] and for July is £ [   ]

Convert into index numbers (to 2 d.p.) the asphalt prices per tonne for June and July, using May as the base.

June	
July	

303 BEST FIT

You have calculated the line of best fit as y = 25.97 + 3.56x, where y is the cost per litre and x is the period. January 20X3 is period 21.

The forecast cost per litre, using the line of best fit, for June 20X3 is £ 118.53

304 LEAST

You have calculated the line of best fit as y = 105.97 + 12.56x, where y is the cost per kilogram and x is the period. March 20X1 is period 45.

The forecast cost per kilogram, using the line of best fit, for July 20X1 is £ 721.41

305 MOST

The Production Director has asked for your help and has been given you an equation and information to estimate the cost of a supply for the coming months.

The equation is Y = a + bX, where

X is the time period in months

the value for X in April 20X9 is 19 and May 20X9 is 20

Y is the cost of the supply

The constant "a" is 15 and constant "b" is 4.

The expected price of the supply for June 20X9 is £ 99 **and for July 20X9 is £** 103

Convert in to index numbers (to 2 d.p.) the supply prices for June and July, using May 20X9 as the base.

June	104.21
July	108.42

306 TEA

Tea is imported from India and the historical cost per kilogram is shown below.

	June X7 £	July X7 £	Aug X7 £	Sept X7 £	Oct X7 £	Nov X7 £
Cost per kg of tea	4.95	4.97	4.99	5.05	5.08	5.10

Convert the costs per kilogram for June and November to index numbers using January 20X7 as the base year. The cost per kilogram in January 20X7 was £4.80.

	June X7 £	Nov X7 £
Cost per kg of tea	4.95	5.10
Base cost	4.80	4.80
Index	103.13	106.25

It is expected that the index number for tea for January 20X8 will be 108.25. The expected cost per kilogram for January 20X8 is £ 5.20

The percentage increase in the price of tea from January 20X7 to January 20X8 is: 8.25 **%.**

AAT: APPLIED MANAGEMENT ACCOUNTING

307 FRUIT

The vitamin which is derived from soft fruit is either imported or purchased from UK farmers. The price of the vitamin fluctuates month by month depending on the time of year. The cost information for the 4 months ending August 20X6 is given below.

	May X6	June X6	July X6	August X6
Cost per 1,000 kg of vitamin	£1,000	£900	£700	£800

The underlying cost does not change during the period May to August. The change in cost over the 4 months is due only to the seasonal variations which are given below.

	May X6	June X6	July X6	August X6
Seasonal variations	£200	£100	(£100)	£0

Calculate the underlying cost per 1,000 kilograms for the period May to August 20X6.

	May X6	Jun X6	Jul X6	Aug X6
Cost per 1,000 kg				
Seasonal variation				
Trend				

Indications are that the underlying cost per 1,000 kilograms for the period May 20X7 to August 20X7 will be £850. The percentage increase in the underlying cost from 20X6 to 20X7 is ☐ %.

Calculate the forecast cost per 1,000 kilograms for the period May 20X7 to August 20X7 using the underlying cost and the seasonal variations given above.

	May X7	June X7	July X7	Aug X7
Trend				
Seasonal variation				
Cost per 1,000 kgs				

308 YANKEE (2)

The Sales Manager for Yankee Limited is reviewing the company's quarterly sales (shown below) for the last financial year. External information for the label printing market indicates average annual growth of 16%. The Sales Manager's analysis suggests Yankee's sales have increased by 18% over the last year. As this is better than the market average the Manager will be awarded a performance related bonus.

	Q1	Q2	Q3	Q4
Actual sales volume	224,000	196,000	215,000	265,000

Before the Sales Manager's bonus is calculated and paid you have been asked to verify the findings. Having carried out some research you have established the following seasonal variations.

PRACTICE QUESTIONS: SECTION 1

	Q1	Q2	Q3	Q4
Seasonal variations	14,000	−24,000	−15,000	25,000

Calculate the seasonally adjusted sales volume for EACH of the FOUR quarters for Yankee Ltd.

[   ]   [   ]   [   ]   [   ]

Calculate the seasonally adjusted growth in sales volume from Quarter 1 to Quarter 4 for Yankee Ltd. Express your answer as a percentage, to the nearest whole %.

[   ]

Should the Sales Manager be paid a bonus? YES/NO *(Delete as appropriate.)*

309 SEB

Seb uses product XYZ and has collected data from the last few months in order to forecast the cost per litre of XYZ in the next few months.

	Apr X3	May X3	Jun X3
Cost per litre of XYZ	£104.55	£107.70	£110.85

Complete the table below to forecast the expected price of product XYZ in July X3 and September X3.

	July X3	September X3
Cost per litre of XYZ		

310 TOAST

The Production Director at Toast has asked for your help and has been given you an equation and information to estimate the cost of a supply for the coming months.

The equation is Y = a + bX, where

X is the time period in quarters

the value for X in quarter 1 of 20X3 is 24 and quarter 2 of 20X3 is 25

Y is the underlying trend of the cost of the supply. The supply is of seasonal nature and can cost more at certain times of the year due to a shortage of supply or excessive demand.

Below are the actual prices paid in each quarter of 20X3 and the seasonal variations.

(a) Calculate the trend figures.

	20X3 Qtr 1	20X3 Qtr 2	20X3 Qtr 3	20X3 Qtr 4
Actual	£3,200	£3,020	£3,320	£3,060
Seasonal variation	+£200	−£80	+£120	−£240
Trend				

KAPLAN PUBLISHING

AAT: APPLIED MANAGEMENT ACCOUNTING

(b) From the above trend figures, determine the value of a and b in the equation Y = a + bX

	£
b	
a	

(c) Using the trend equation, calculate the trend for 20X7 quarter 1 and 3:

	Trend (£)
20X7 Qtr 1	
20X7 Qtr 3	

(d) Assuming the seasonal variation acts as in 20X3, calculate the forecast cost for 20X7 quarter 2 and 4.

	Forecast (£)
20X7 Qtr 2	
20X7 Qtr 4	

(e) If the forecast figures for quarter 1 and 2 of 20X8 are 5,200 and 5,020, express these as an index number with base Qtr 1 20X3.

	Index number (2DP)
20X8 Qtr 1	
20X8 Qtr 2	

311 COAST

The Production Director at Coast has asked for your help and has been given you an equation and information regarding historic costs to help forecast costs in the future.

The equation is Y = a + bX, where

X is the time period in quarters

the value for X in quarter 1 of 20X2 is 10 and quarter 2 of 20X2 is 11

Y is the underlying trend of the cost of the supply. The supply is of seasonal nature and can cost more at certain times of the year due to a shortage of supply or excessive demand.

The trend in prices is an increase of £0.50 per quarter.

Below is an incomplete table showing actual prices paid, amounts purchased, cost per kg and trend figures in each quarter of 20X2.

(a) Calculate missing figures:

	20X2 Qtr 1	20X2 Qtr 2	20X2 Qtr 3	20X2 Qtr 4
Actual paid (£)		418,500		791,000
Quantity purchased (kg)	10,000		11,000	
Cost per kg (£ to 2DP)	44.00			
Seasonal variation (£ to 2DP)	−5.00	−3.00	2.00	6.00
Trend (£ to 2DP)				

(b) If the price in 20X5 Qtr 1 is £50, what would be the index number if the base is 20X2 Qtr 1 to the nearest whole number?

312 DISADVANTAGES

Which of the following are disadvantages of using an expected value technique?

Disadvantage of EVs?

Expected values only provides the most likely result

It ignores attitudes to risk

Only two possible outcomes can be considered

Probabilities are subjective

The answer provided may not exist

313 STATATAC

Statatac Ltd use trend analysis to help their business plan for the future. They have provided the following information about sales volumes for the third quarter of 20X6.

(a) Complete the table below by entering the missing figures. Use the minus signs for negative numbers.

20X6 volume of units ('000)	July	August	September
Trend			100
Seasonal variation	10	5	
Seasonally adjusted sales		100	92

(b) Assuming the trend of the seasonal variations continue as in (a) above, complete the table below to show the projected sales volumes for the last quarter of 20X7. Use minus signs for negative figures.

20X7 volume of units ('000)	October	November	December
Trend			
Seasonal variation	−10	−12	−15
Seasonally adjusted sales			

Flexi-Indexy paid £12 per kilogram (kg) for material in February 20X7, the base month. In October 20X7 the index is expected to be 112.

(c) Forecast the price per kg (to the nearest penny) in October 20X7.

£ ☐

If in February 20X8 the price is now £14.50 per kilogram.

(d) What would the index (with base Feb 20X7) be to the nearest whole number?

☐

314 TEX-MEX-INDEX

Tex-Mex-Index Co started purchasing a material for use in the manufacture of their products in 20X1. The price in 20X1 (the base year) was 4.50 per kg. It is now 20X8, they have incomplete records regarding the prices paid and the price index for the material over the years.

(a) **Complete the table below**

Give index numbers to the nearest whole numbers and prices in £ to 2 decimal places.

Year	Index	Price per kg £
20X2	105	
20X3		4.87
20X4	110	
20X5		4.61
20X6		4.82
20X7	115	

Another company, Dexi's MR Ltd have a table showing the index of prices for a certain commodity over the last five years (base 20X1):

Year	20X3	20X4	20X5	20X6	20X7
Index	105	115	127	140	152

The price was £10 per kg in 20X5.

(b) **Complete the following sentences (to 2 decimal places):**

The percentage increase in price from 20X4 to 20X6 is ☐ %.

The price in 20X7 is £ ☐ per kg.

Trendy Wendy Ltd is a chain of clothes store specialising in summer fashion. They use trend analysis and have forecast their quarterly sales. Unfortunately some of the data has been lost.

(c) **Complete the below table**

20X7 volume of units ('000)	Quarter 1	Quarter 2	Quarter 3	Quarter 4
Trend	100			
Seasonal variation	−50		+90	−60
Seasonally adjusted sales		130		70

DIVISIONAL PERFORMANCE

ROI, RI AND TRANSFER PRICING

315 DUST CO

Dust Co has two divisions, A and B. Each division is currently considering the following separate projects:

	Division A	Division B
Capital required for the project	£32.6 million	£22.2 million
Sales generated by the project	£14.4 million	£8.8 million
Operating profit margin	30%	24%
Cost of capital	10%	10%
Current return on investment of division	15%	9%

Calculate the residual income for each division:

	Residual Income
Division A	
Division B	

If residual income is used as the basis for the investment decision, what decision is each division likely to make?

Place a tick in the boxes in the table below as appropriate.

	Would choose to invest in the project	Would choose not to invest in the project
Division A		
Division B		

316 PRO MO RI

Pro is a division of Mo and is an investment centre. The head office controls finance, HR and IT expenditure but all other decisions are devolved to the local centres.

The statement of financial position for Pro shows net value of all assets and liabilities to be £4,500m. It carries no debt itself although the group has debt liabilities.

The management accounts for income read as follows:

	£m
Revenue	3,500
Cost of sales	1,800
Local administration	250
IT costs	50
Distribution	80
Central administration	30
Interest charges	90
Net profit	1,200

Ignore taxation.

If the cost of capital is 12%, what is the division's residual income (to the nearest £m)?

£ ☐

317 PRO MO ROI

Pro is a division of Mo and is an investment centre. The head office controls finance, HR and IT expenditure but all other decisions are devolved to the local centres.

The statement of financial position for Pro shows net value of all assets and liabilities to be £4,500m at the start of the year and £4,890m at the end. It carries no debt itself although the group has debt liabilities.

The management accounts for income read as follows:

	£m
Revenue	3,500
Cost of sales	1,800
Local administration	250
IT costs	50
Distribution	80
Central administration	30
Interest charges	90
Net profit	1,200

Ignore taxation.

What is the divisional ROI (1 d.p)? (The opening Capital Employed should be used to calculate the ROI).

☐ %

318 DIVISION B

Division B of a company makes units which are then transferred to other divisions. The division has no spare capacity, and sells units externally as well as internally.

Which of the following statement(s) regarding the minimum transfer price that will encourage the divisional manager of B to transfer units to other divisions is/are true?

(1) Any price above variable cost will generate a positive contribution, and will therefore be accepted.

(2) The division will need to give up a unit sold externally in order to make a transfer; this is only worthwhile if the income of a transfer is greater than the net income of an external sale.

A (1) only

B (2) only

C Neither (1) nor (2)

D Both (1) and (2)

PRACTICE QUESTIONS: SECTION 1

319 TM PLC

TM plc makes components which it sells internally to its subsidiary RM Ltd, as well as to its own external market.

The external market price is £24.00 per unit, which yields a contribution of 40% of sales. For external sales, variable costs include £1.50 per unit for distribution costs, which are not incurred on internal sales.

TM plc has sufficient capacity to meet all of the internal and external sales. The objective is to maximise group profit.

At what unit price should the component be transferred to RM Ltd (to 2 decimal places)?

£ _____

320 JB LTD

JB Ltd is a divisionalised organisation comprising a number of divisions, including divisions A and B. Division A makes a single product, which it sells on the external market at a price of £12 per unit. The variable cost of the product is £8 per unit and the fixed cost is £3 per unit. Market demand for the product considerably exceeds Division A's maximum production capacity of 10,000 units per month.

Division B would like to obtain 500 units of the product from Division A. If Division A does transfer some of its production internally rather than sell externally, then the saving in packaging costs would be £1.50 per unit.

What transfer price per unit should Division A quote in order to maximise group profit?

£ _____

321 OXCO

Oxco has two divisions, A and B. Division A makes a component for air conditioning units which it can only sell to Division B. It has no other outlet for sales.

Current information relating to Division A is as follows:

Marginal cost per unit	£100
Transfer price of the component	£165
Total production and sales of the component each year	2,200 units
Specific fixed costs of Division A per year	£10,000

Cold Co has offered to sell the component to Division B for £140 per unit. If Division B accepts this offer, Division A will be shut down.

If Division B accepts Cold Co's offer, what will be the impact on profits per year for the group as a whole?

A Increase of £65,000

B Decrease of £78,000

C Decrease of £88,000

D Increase of £55,000

KAPLAN PUBLISHING 191

AAT: APPLIED MANAGEMENT ACCOUNTING

322 ZIG

Zig plc has three divisions A, B and C, whose performance is assessed on Return on investment.

Forecast data for 20X6 is provided as follows:

	A £	B £	C £
Capital Employed	250,000	350,000	450,000
Profit	47,500	73,500	112,500

Calculate the ROI for each division:

	A	B	C
ROI %			

Three new proposals are being considered:

- A is considering investing £75,000 in order to increase profit by £21,000 each year.

- B is considering selling a machine, forecast to earn a profit of £25,000 in the coming year, for its net book value of £70,000.

- C is considering giving a 2.5% discount for prompt payment. This should reduce debtors by £20,000. C's sales revenue is £500,000 each year and a 50% take up of the offer is expected.

Complete the following table assuming each division proceeds with their respective proposal:

	A	B	C
Revised Capital Employed (£)			
Revised Profit (£)			
Revised ROI (% to 1 dp)			

The managers of each division receive a bonus based on how far above the ROI target they are, comment on the ethical implications and implications for decision making.

323 CTD

CTD has two divisions – FD and TM. FD is an iron foundry division which produces mouldings that have a limited external market and are also transferred to TM division. TM division uses the mouldings to produce a piece of agricultural equipment called the 'TX' which is sold externally. Each TX requires one moulding. Both divisions produce only one type of product.

The performance of each Divisional Manager is evaluated individually on the basis of the residual income (RI) of their division. The company's average annual 12% cost of capital is used to calculate the finance charges. If their own target residual income is achieved, each Divisional Manager is awarded a bonus equal to 5% of the residual income. All bonuses are paid out of Head Office profits.

The following budgeted information is available for the forthcoming year:

	TM division TX per unit	FD division Moulding per unit
External selling price (£)	500	80
Variable production cost (£)	*366	40
Fixed production overheads (£)	60	20
Gross profit (£)	74	20
Variable selling and distribution cost (£)	25	**4
Fixed administration overhead (£)	25	4
Net profit (£)	24	12
Normal capacity (units)	15,000	20,000
Maximum production capacity (units)	15,000	25,000
Sales to external customers (units)	15,000	5,000
Capital employed	£1,500,000	£750,000
Target RI	£105,000	£85,000

* The variable production cost of TX includes the cost of an FD moulding.

** External sales only of the mouldings incur a variable selling and distribution cost of £4 per unit.

FD division currently transfers 15,000 mouldings to TM division at a transfer price equal to the total production cost plus 10%.

The current transfer price is £_____

Fixed costs are absorbed on the basis of normal capacity

AAT: APPLIED MANAGEMENT ACCOUNTING

Complete the below table to calculate the bonus each Divisional Manager would receive under the current transfer pricing policy.

	FD		TM	
	£000	£000	£000	£000
Internal sales				
External sales				
Total sales				
Production – variable costs				
Selling/distribution – variable costs				
Total variable cost				
Contribution				
Production overheads				
Administration overheads				
Net profit				
Interest charge				
Residual income (RI)				
Target RI				
Bonus				

Section 2

ANSWERS TO PRACTICE QUESTIONS

BUDGETING

SOURCES OF INFORMATION

Key answer tips

Make sure you read all the possible options in the 'Sources' column before making your decision.

1 SOURCES (I)

Data	Source
UK interest rates	Bank of England
Competitor prices	Pricing research
UK Economic growth forecasts	UK Treasury, independent economics consultants

2 SOURCES (II)

Data	Source
UK tax rates	HMRC publications
UK house prices	Building society data
Customer tastes	Market research

3 SOURCES (III)

Data	Source
French tax rates	French government
Political party likely to win power	Opinion poll surveys
Customer preferences	Market research

4 SOURCES (IV)

Data	Source
UK economic growth forecasts	UK treasury, independent economics consultants
UK duty rates (tax on alcohol etc.)	HMRC publications
Brazilian import tax rates	Brazilian government

BUDGETARY RESPONSIBILITIES

Key answer tips

Make sure you read all the possible options in the 'Contact' column before making your decision.

5 CONTACTS (I)

Situation	Contact
You want to identify any production constraints	Production planning manager
You want to forecast the cost of labour	Trade union representative
The budget is ready for final approval	Board of directors

6 CONTACTS (II)

Situation	Contact
You want to know the future strategy of the firm	Board of directors
You want to forecast the cost of machinery	Machinery buyers
You want to assess the efficiency of labour	Management accountants

Tutorial note

Any strategic element will involve the Board of Directors of a company.

7 CONTACTS (III)

Situation	Contact
You want to know day to day regional firm policy	Regional manager
You want to forecast sales	Sales team
You want to know idle time last period	Management accountants

ANSWERS TO PRACTICE QUESTIONS: **SECTION 2**

8 CONTACTS (IV)

Situation	Contact
You want to forecast the price of raw materials	Firms' buying department
You want to examine competitors' prices	Other firms' price lists
You want to check the availability of skilled labour	Employment agency

9 THE RIGHT BUDGET

Capital expenditure
New machinery
New delivery van

Marketing
Magazine advertising
Incentives paid to sales staff

Maintenance
Spare parts for production machines
Salaries of repair engineers

Personnel
Salary of HR Manager

Cost of production
Wages of assembly line workers
Raw material usage

10 CUMIN COMPANY

Resource Budget – Material X	Unit	December
Needed for production	kg	5,000
Wastage	kg	102
Total requirement	kg	5,102
Closing inventory	kg	950
Opening inventory	kg	900
Purchases in month	kg	5,152
Cost per kg	£	1
Purchase cost of material X	£	5152.04

AAT: APPLIED MANAGEMENT ACCOUNTING

11 DRAG AND DROP

Capital expenditure
New conveyor belt
Enhancements to production machines

Marketing
Television advertising
Commissions paid to sales staff

IT
Salary of IT manager
Wages of IT engineers

Personnel
Salary of HR Manager

Cost of production
Wages of production line workers

12 ADAM

Capital expenditure
New photocopier
New cars
New building

Marketing
Radio advertising
Market research costs
Internet advertising
Bonuses paid to sales team

Maintenance
Spare parts for production machines
Cost of machinery repairs
Spare parts for old trucks

Personnel
Salary of HR manager
Cost of HR staff

Cost of production
Lighting costs for factory
Raw material usage
Wages of assembly line workers
Cost of heating factory

ANSWERS TO PRACTICE QUESTIONS: SECTION 2

ACCOUNTING TREATMENT

13 ACCOUNTING TREATMENT (I)

• Materials used in the production process	Direct cost
• Administrative wages	Allocate to administrative overheads
• Depreciation of production equipment	Charge to production in a machine hour overhead rate
• Advertising costs	Allocate to marketing overheads
• Rent of a labour intensive production facility	Charge to production in a labour hour overhead rate
• Office stationery	Allocate to administrative overheads
• Idle time pay for production workers	Charge to production in a labour hour overhead rate
• Overtime premium for production workers	Charge to production in a labour hour overhead rate

14 ACCOUNTING TREATMENT (II)

• Materials used in the production process	Direct cost
• Rent of a machine intensive production facility	Charge to production in a machine hour overhead rate
• Office paper	Allocate to administrative overheads
• Basic pay for production workers	Direct cost
• Secretarial wages	Allocate to administrative overheads
• Overtime premium for production workers	Charge to production in a labour hour overhead rate
• Payments to marketing staff	Allocate to marketing overheads

15 ACCOUNTING TREATMENT (III)

• Wood used in the production process	Direct cost
• General postage costs	Allocate to administrative overheads
• Internet advertising costs	Allocate to marketing overheads
• Office stationery	Allocate to administrative overheads
• Chemicals used in the production process	Direct cost
• Idle time pay for production workers	Charge to production in a labour hour overhead rate
• Power costs for machinery	Charge to production in a machine hour overhead rate

INDICES

16 TACO

Sales revenue	Actual Year 1 £	Forecast Year 2 £	Forecast Year 3 £	Forecast Year 4 £	Forecast Year 5 £
At Year 1 prices	120,000	122,400	128,400	128,400	129,600
At expected prices		123,513	130,735	131,902	135,491

17 ARCHER

Sales revenue	Actual Year 1 £	Forecast Year 2 £	Forecast Year 3 £	Forecast Year 4 £	Forecast Year 5 £
At Year 1 prices	275,000	277,292	279,583	281,875	284,167
At expected prices		284,719	299,554	314,593	329,836

18 FLASH

Sales revenue	Actual Year 1 £	Forecast Year 2 £	Forecast Year 3 £	Forecast Year 4 £	Forecast Year 5 £
At Year 1 prices	280,000	287,119	289,492	291,864	294,237
At expected prices		294,809	310,169	325,742	341,525

19 SOPHIE

Sales revenue	Actual Year 1 £	Forecast Year 2 £	Forecast Year 3 £	Forecast Year 4 £	Forecast Year 5 £
At Year 1 prices	280,000	284,746	296,610	301,356	303,729
At expected prices		292,373	317,797	336,335	352,542

PRODUCTION BUDGETS

20 TITANIA

Production (units)	Week 1	Week 2	Week 3	Week 4	Week 5
Opening inventory	20,000	19,800	20,100	21,000	
Good production	64,800	66,300	67,900	70,600	
Sales Volume	65,000	66,000	67,000	70,000	72,000
Closing inventory	19,800	20,100	21,000	21,600	

Rejected Production	2,005	2,051	2,100	2,184
Total manufactured units	66,805	68,351	70,000	72,784

Tutorial note

There are different ways of going about this, and you must find the approach that works best for you. For example, the following method could be applied to tackle this task.

First, fill in the 'Closing Inventory' row. You are told in the question that **'Closing inventory should be 30% of the following week's sales volume'**. So in week 1, closing inventory is 30% of Week 2 sales volume; this means 30% of 66,000 = 19,800. In week 2, closing inventory is 30% of Week 3 sales volume; this means 30% of 67,000 = 20,100. Fill in all four values like this.

Secondly, rewrite all these values you have just calculated for closing inventory as 'opening inventory' for the following week. So closing inventory for week 1 (19800) becomes the opening inventory for week 2. Closing inventory for week 2 (20100) becomes the opening inventory for week 3. Closing inventory for week 3 (21000) becomes the opening inventory for week 4.

Thirdly, calculate the good production for week 1. Good production is equal to the sales volume units PLUS the closing inventory units, but LESS the units that were already there to start the week i.e. the opening inventory units. So, for week 1, we calculate 'Good production' as Sales volume 65,000 units + Closing Inventory 19800 units – opening inventory units 20,000 = 64,800 units. Repeat this for every week.

In the second table, that contains the 'Rejected production' and 'Total manufactured units' rows, you should start with your 'Total manufactured units' answer. The total number of manufactured units represents 100% of the total production. The 'Good Production' you had calculated before (64,800 units) only represents 97% of the total production, as 3% of the total production was faulty. So by dividing 64,800 units by 97, you get 1% of total production, i.e. 668.04 units. Leave this number in you calculator and multiply it by 100: this is your total production of **66,805** units (rounded up). The last number to fill in is that for rejected production, which is always your total production **(66,805)** less your good production of 64800 units = 2,005. Repeat the same approach for every week in the table.

21 PUCK

Production (units)	Week 1	Week 2	Week 3	Week 4	Week 5
Opening inventory	35,000	23,400	23,400	21,000	
Good production	68,400	78,000	75,600	73,000	
Sales Volume	80,000	78,000	78,000	70,000	80,000
Closing inventory	23,400	23,400	21,000	24,000	

	Week 1	Week 2	Week 3	Week 4
Rejected Production	2,850	3,250	3,150	3,042
Total manufactured units	71,250	81,250	78,750	76,042

22 OBERON

Production (units)	Week 1	Week 2	Week 3	Week 4	Week 5
Opening inventory	32,000	23,400	22,500	21,000	
Good production	69,400	77,100	73,500	73,000	
Sales Volume	78,000	78,000	75,000	70,000	80,000
Closing inventory	23,400	22,500	21,000	24,000	

	Week 1	Week 2	Week 3	Week 4
Rejected Production	7,712	8,567	8,167	8,112
Total manufactured units	77,112	85,667	81,667	81,112

23 LYSANDER

Production (units)	Week 1	Week 2	Week 3	Week 4	Week 5
Opening inventory	20,000	19,500	20,100	21,000	
Good production	64,500	65,600	67,900	70,600	
Sales Volume	65,000	65,000	67,000	70,000	72,000
Closing inventory	19,500	20,100	21,000	21,600	

	Week 1	Week 2	Week 3	Week 4
Rejected Production	1,317	1,339	1,386	1,441
Total manufactured units	65,817	66,939	69,286	72,041

24 DEMETRIUS

Production (units)	Week 1	Week 2	Week 3	Week 4	Week 5
Opening inventory	19,000	19,800	20,100	21,000	
Good production	65,800	66,300	67,900	70,600	
Sales Volume	65,000	66,000	67,000	70,000	72,000
Closing inventory	19,800	20,100	21,000	21,600	

	Week 1	Week 2	Week 3	Week 4
Rejected Production	1,343	1,354	1,386	1,441
Total manufactured units	67,143	67,654	69,286	72,041

ANSWERS TO PRACTICE QUESTIONS: **SECTION 2**

25 HERMIA

Production (units)	Week 1	Week 2	Week 3	Week 4	Week 5
Opening inventory	19,000	19,800	20,100	21,000	
Good production	65,800	66,300	67,900	73,000	
Sales Volume	65,000	66,000	67,000	70,000	80,000
Closing inventory	19,800	20,100	21,000	24,000	

	Week 1	Week 2	Week 3	Week 4	Week 5
Rejected Production	2,036	2,051	2,100	2,258	2,035
Total manufactured units	67,836	68,351	70,000	75,258	67,835

26 EVIE

Units of product A	Week 1	Week 2	Week 3	Week 4	Week 5
Opening inventory	1,000	2,000	1,875	1,750	2,000
Production	8,000	7,875	7,375	7,250	
Sub-total	9,000	9,875	9,250	9,000	
Sales	7,000	8,000	7,500	7,000	8,000
Closing inventory	2,000	1,875	1,750	2,000	

27 EGO

Units of Ego	Week 1	Week 2	Week 3	Week 4	Week 5
Opening inventory	2,000	4,000	3,750	3,500	4,000
Production	16,000	15,750	14,750	14,500	
Sub-total	18,000	19,750	18,500	18,000	
Sales	14,000	16,000	15,000	14,000	16,000
Closing inventory	4,000	3,750	3,500	4,000	

28 PRODUCT C

Units of product C	Week 1	Week 2	Week 3	Week 4	Week 5
Opening inventory	500	800	750	700	800
Production	3,800	3,950	3,700	3,600	
Sub-total	4,300	4,750	4,450	4,300	
Sales	3,500	4,000	3,750	3,500	4,000
Closing inventory	800	750	700	800	

29 PRODUCT B

	Month 1	Month 2	Month 3
Required units	90,250	95,000	99,750
Manufactured units	95,000	100,000	105,000

KAPLAN PUBLISHING

30 ROPE

	Month 1	Month 2	Month 3
Required units	180,670	190,980	185,900
Manufactured units	190,179	201,032	195,685

31 CAMELIA

Tutorial note

There are different ways of getting to the right answer but make sure you do not confuse minutes with hours in your calculations.

800 hours of overtime.

Working:

104,000 × 3/60 = 5,200 hrs required.

5,200 − (25 × 176) = 800 hrs overtime needed.

32 SAGE

66,500m

Working:

20,000 items @ 2.5 metres = 50,000 metres.

50,000m × 100/80 (wastage) = 62,500m

Plus 14,000m closing stock less 10,000m = 66,500m

33 BUMBLEBEE

Tutorial note

Remember to round up to the nearest whole unit.

	Month 1	Month 2	Month 3
Required units	18,900	20,150	22,200
Manufactured units	19,286	20,562	22,654

ANSWERS TO PRACTICE QUESTIONS: **SECTION 2**

34 QUALITY CONTROL

There is labour available to make **231,000** units in normal time. Therefore, **13,500** hours of overtime will be needed.

The raw material contract will provide enough material to make **200,000** units. Therefore, **100,000** kg will have to be purchased on the open market.

Quality control can test **216,000** units in the year. It will be necessary to make alternative arrangements for **24,000** units.

35 COMPANY A

There is labour available to make **131,250** units in normal time. Therefore, **10,500** hours of overtime will be needed.

The raw material contract will provide enough material to make **100,000** units. Therefore, **72,000** kg will have to be purchased on the open market.

Quality control can test **120,000** units in the year. It will be necessary to make alternative arrangements for **20,000** units.

36 JONES

There is labour available to make **131,250** units in normal time. Therefore, **15,000** hours of overtime will be needed.

The raw material contract will provide enough material to make **100,000** units. Therefore, **150,000** kg will have to be purchased on the open market.

Quality control can test **144,000** units in the year. It will be necessary to make alternative arrangements for **6,000** units.

37 DONALD

200

Working:

84,000 × 3/60 = 4,200 hrs basic time.

4,200 − (25 × 160) = 200 hrs overtime.

38 THEO

40

Working:

48,000 × 6/60 = 4,800 hrs required.

4,800 − (28 × 170) = 40 hrs overtime needed.

KAPLAN PUBLISHING

MACHINE UTILISATION

39 E, F AND G

Product	Units	Hours per unit	Hours required
E	100	1.0	100
F	230	2.0	460
G	370	3.5	1,295
		Total hours for Department Y	1,855

How many additional machines should be hired? | 3 |

40 ZEE

Product	Units	Hours per unit	Hours required
C	200	0.5	100
D	460	2.0	920
E	740	2.5	1,850
		Total hours for Zee	2,870

How many additional machines should be hired? | 1 |

41 CLAUDIO

Tutorial note

The total number of machine hours available is 100 machines × 80 hours each = 8,000 hours.

For each product A, B and C, hours required = Items × hours per item:

- For A, hours required = 2,000 items × 1.00 hour per item = 2,000 hours.
- For B, hours required = 1,750 items × 2.00 hours per item = 3,500 hours.
- For C, hours required = 610 items × 3.00 hours per item = 1,830 hours.

We have calculated in the above table that the total machine hours required (sum of hours required for products A, B and C) is 7,330 hours.

This represents (7,330 hours/8,000 hours) × 100 = 91.625% of the total number of hours available (we round up to 92%).

ANSWERS TO PRACTICE QUESTIONS: **SECTION 2**

Budgeted machine loading Product	Items	Hours per item	Hours required
A	2,000	1.00	2,000
B	1,750	2.00	3,500
C	610	3.00	1,830
Total machine hours required			7,330
% utilisation			92%

42 DOGBERRY

Budgeted machine loading Product	Items	Hours per item	Hours required
A	120	3.75	450
B	175	1.50	263
C	190	1.50	285
Total machine hours required			998
% utilisation			40%

43 LEONATO

Budgeted machine loading Product	Items	Hours per item	Hours required
A	250	3.00	750
B	1,000	1.00	1,000
C	390	1.50	585
Total machine hours required			2,335
% utilisation			98%

44 BORACHIO

Budgeted machine loading Product	Items	Hours per item	Hours required
A	25	4	100
B	10	2	20
C	40	1.50	60
Total machine hours required			180
% utilisation			90%

CAPACITY CONSTRAINTS

45 GLOUCESTER

Tutorial note

From the question, we have 2,500 kilograms of materials available. As every unit requires 1 kilogram, we therefore have sufficient materials to manufacture 2,500 kilograms/ 1 kilogram per unit = 2,500 units.

420 hours of direct labour available represent 420 × 60 minutes = 25,200 minutes; that is sufficient to produce (before overtime is needed) (25,200/40 minutes of labour per unit) = 630 units.

120 hours of machine time represent 120 × 60 minutes = 7,200 minutes, which is sufficient to produce 7,200/5 minutes per hour = 1,440 units.

Without overtime, the maximum sales volume is (as labour is the limiting factor) 630 units.

With unlimited overtime, the maximum overtime is (as labour is no longer a limiting factor) 1440 units (as machine time becomes the limiting factor then).

Production capacity	Units
Sufficient materials are budgeted to manufacture	2,500
Without overtime, sufficient direct labour is budgeted to manufacture	630
Sufficient machine time is budgeted to manufacture	1,440
Without overtime, the maximum sales volume is	630
With unlimited overtime, the maximum sales volume is	1,440

46 BEDFORD

Production capacity	Units
Sufficient materials are budgeted to manufacture	100
Without overtime, sufficient direct labour is budgeted to manufacture	300
Sufficient machine time is budgeted to manufacture	432
Without overtime, the maximum sales volume is	100
With unlimited overtime, the maximum sales volume is	100

ANSWERS TO PRACTICE QUESTIONS: SECTION 2

WORKING SCHEDULES AND OPERATING BUDGETS

47 WASHINGTON

Materials	Kg	£
Opening inventory	2,200	3,080
Purchases @ £1.50 per kg	82,800	124,200
Sub-total	85,000	127,280
Used	50,000	74,780
Closing inventory	35,000	52,500
Closing inventory to be valued at budgeted purchase price		

Labour	Hours	£
Basic time @ £16 per hour	1,600	25,600
Overtime	400	9,600
Total	2,000	35,200

Production Overhead	Hours	£
Variable @ £2.50 per hour	2,000	5,000
Fixed		165,020
Total		170,020

48 ADAMS

Operating budget	Units	£ per unit	£
Sales revenue	18,000	27.00	486,000

			£
Cost of goods sold			
Opening inventory of finished goods			40,000
Cost of production		£	
Materials		74,780	
Labour		35,200	
Production overhead		170,020	280,000
Closing inventory of finished goods			42,700
Cost of goods sold			277,300
Gross profit/(loss)			208,700
Overheads		£	
Administration		80,000	
Marketing		25,000	105,000
Operating profit/(loss)			103,700

49 JEFFERSON

Materials	Kg	£
Opening inventory	20,000	12,000
Purchases @ £2.00 per kg	97,500	195,000
Sub-total	117,500	207,000
Used	82,500	137,000
Closing inventory	35,000	70,000

Closing inventory to be valued at budgeted purchase price

Labour	Hours	£
Basic time @ £8.00 per hour	2,100	16,800
Overtime	1,200	14,400
Total	3,300	31,200

Production Overheads	Hours	£
Variable @ £2.00 per hour	3,300	6,600
Fixed		155,200
Total		161,800

50 BURR

Operating budget	Units	£ per unit	£
Sales revenue	15,000	30.00	450,000

Cost of goods sold		£
Opening inventory of finished goods		40,000
Cost of production	£	
Materials	137,000	
Labour	31,200	
Production overhead	161,800	330,000
Closing inventory of finished goods		90,000
Cost of goods sold		280,000
Gross profit/(loss)		170,000
Overheads	£	
Administration	55,000	
Marketing	60,000	115,000
Operating profit/(loss)		55,000

51 SINCLAIR LTD

1 (a) Production budget – 4 periods to 21 October 2011

	1	2	3	4	5 (*)
Sales volume	19,400	21,340	23,280	22,310	22,310
Add: closing inventory	4,268	4,656	4,462	4,462	
Less opening inventory	(3,880)	(4,268)	(4,656)	(4,462)	(4,462)
Good production	19,788	21,728	23,086	22,310	
Faulty production (3/97)	612	672	714	690	
Gross production of Doms	20,400	22,400	23,800	23,000	

Notes:

Closing Inventory = 4/20 × next period's sales volumes.

Closing Inventory equals next period's opening inventory.

(*) Period 5 shown to demonstrate calculation of period 4's closing inventory.

(b) Material purchases budget – 3 periods to 23 September 2011

	1	2	3	4
Gross production of Doms	20,400	22,400	23,800	23,000
Material required (3 litres per Dom)	61,200	67,200	71,400	69,000
Add closing inventory	16,800	17,850	17,250	
Less opening inventory	(16,500)	(16,800)	(17,850)	(17,250)
Purchases, in litres	61,500	68,250	70,800	

(c) Cost of purchases

	1	2	3
Purchases, in litres	61,500	68,250	70,800
Cost £8	£8	£8	£8
Total cost in £	492,000	546,000	566,400

(d) Labour budget – 3 periods to 23 September 2011

	1	2	3
Gross production of Doms	20,400	22,400	23,800
Hours (0.5 hours per Dom)	10,200	11,200	11,900
Basic hours (70 workers × 40 hours × 4 weeks)	11,200	11,200	11,200
Overtime (surplus hours)	(1,000)	NIL	700

(e) Cost of wages

	1	2	3
Basic wages (70 workers × 4 weeks × £240)	£67,200	£67,200	£67,200
Overtime (£9 × overtime hours)			£6,300
	£67,200	£67,200	£73,500

2   **MEMO**

To: Production director

From: Management accountant

Date: XX June 2001

Subject: Overtime payments and faulty production

Following our recent meeting to discuss the budgets, you questioned the need for over-time and made the observation that the 3% failure rate may be due to poor working practices on the shop floor.

(a)   **Overtime payments**

There are 700 hours of overtime allowed for in the budget during period 3. There is however a surplus of labour capacity of 1,000 hours in period 1. If we produce an extra 1,400 units in period 1, the overtime hours in period 3 would be avoided.

This would result in a saving of (£9 × 700 hours) = £6,300.

(b)   **Costs incurred in achieving the overtime saving (one only required)**

- Financing costs
- Storage costs.

CASH FLOW FORECASTS

52   WASHINGTON AND ADAMS

Tutorial note

'Sales receipts' is not the same as 'Sales revenue' because even if we have made a sale, it doesn't necessarily mean that we have received the cash for that sale. We need to look at the 'Receivables' movement and this information is given to us in the requirement. Here, we are told that 'Receivables' are expected to decrease by £162,000 over the year. This means that, as well as receiving cash from sales of £486,000 as we calculated in the 'Adams' question, we also have received £162,000 from our debtors.

Therefore, 'Total sales receipts' = £486,000 + £162000 = £648,000.

- 'Payments for materials': the expenditure in the 'Washington' schedule for materials stands at £124,200, but this is not necessarily the amount that has been paid to our suppliers/ creditors in cash. Balance Sheet movements tell us that our creditors (='Payables') will increase by £26,800 over the year, which is decreasing the level of cash paid and increasing our debt to creditors. Therefore, amount of cash paid is £124,200 – £26,800 = £97,400.

- 'Payments for labour' is straightforward, and can be copied down from 'Washington' or 'Adams' a value of £35,200.

- As depreciation is not a cash flow, the depreciation charge of £19,000 must be taken away from the total production overheads of £170,020 calculated in 'Adams', so

- Production overhead cash flows = £170,020 – £19,000 = £151,020.

- 'Other overheads' represent the addition of the marketing and admin overheads given to us in 'Adams' : £80,000 + £25,000 = £105,000.

ANSWERS TO PRACTICE QUESTIONS: SECTION 2

Cash flow forecast	£	
Opening cash balance/(overdraft)		29,650
Sales receipts		648,000
Payments		
Materials	97,400	
Labour	35,200	
Production overhead	151,020	
Other overheads	105,000	
Capital expenditure	50,000	438,620
Closing cash balance/(overdraft)		239,030

53 JEFFERSON AND BURR

Tutorial note

'Payments for materials': in this example, our creditors (= 'Payables') will decrease by £32,600 over the year, which is increasing the level of cash paid and decreasing our debt to creditors.

Cash flow forecast	£	
Opening cash balance/(overdraft)		90,000
Sales receipts		465,000
Payments		
Materials	227,600	
Labour	31,200	
Production overhead	146,800	
Other overheads	115,000	
Capital expenditure	120,000	640,600
Closing cash balance/(overdraft)		–85,600

54 CASH FORECAST FOR MAY

Cash forecast	May
	£
Opening cash balance	−320
Customer receipts	7,810
Payments	
For purchases	6,700
For wages	400
For overheads	540
For capital exp.	0
Total	7,640
Closing cash balance	−150

55 THE LATEST

Cash-flow forecast	£	£
Sales receipts		262,000
Payments		
Materials	111,200	
Labour	41,250	
Other costs	14,400	166,850
Cash-flow forecast		95,150

56 HARVEST FESTIVAL

Cash-flow forecast	£	£
Sales receipts		113,500
Payments		
Materials	32,500	
Labour	26,200	
Other costs	17,350	76,050
Cash-flow forecast		37,450

57 OKTOBERFEST

Cash flow forecast	£	£
Sales receipts		156,800
Payments		
Materials	55,550	
Labour	20,000	
Other costs	22,450	98,000
Cash Flow forecast		58,800

PERIODIC BUDGETS

58 APRIL BUDGETS

	Budget for the year	Budget for April
Units sold	34,000	3,000
Units produced	36,000	3,500
	£	£
Sales	204,000	18,000
Materials used	59,400	5,775
Labour	67,200	6,800
Variable production overhead	54,000	5,250
Fixed overhead	3,600	300

Working:

Budgeted annual labour hours = 36,000 × 6 mins ÷ 60 = 3,600 hours

Standard variable overhead rate per hour = £54,000/3,600 = £15/hr

April labour hours = 3,500 × 6/60 = 350 hours

April variable overhead = 350 × 15 = £5,250

59 ROSE

	Budget for the year	Budget for May
Units sold	68,000	6,000
Units produced	72,000	7,000
	£	£
Sales	1,408,000	124,235
Materials used	720,000	70,000
Labour	264,000	27,000
Variable production overhead	96,000	9,333
Fixed overhead	3,600	300

Working:

Budgeted annual labour hours = 72,000 × 10 mins ÷ 60 = 12,000 hours

Standard variable overhead rate per hour = £96,000/12,000 = £8/hr

May labour hours = 7,000 × 10/60 = 1166.67 hours

May variable overhead = 1166.67 × 8 = £9,333

AAT: APPLIED MANAGEMENT ACCOUNTING

60 SALES AND COSTS

	Budget for the year	Budget for June
Units sold	120,000	11,000
Units produced	110,000	10,000
	£	£
Sales	1,649,000	151,158
Materials used	1,155,000	105,000
Labour	95,500	9,000
Variable production overhead	55,000	5,000
Fixed overhead	3,600	300

ALTERNATIVE SCENARIOS

61 MADISON

Operating budget	First draft	Alternative scenario
Sales price per unit (£)	15.00	15.75
Sales volume	75,000	69,000
		£
Sales revenue	1,125,000	1,086,750
Costs		
Material	131,250	120,750
Labour	187,500	172,500
Energy	44,000	43,200
Depreciation	62,400	56,160
Total	425,150	392,610
Gross Profit	699,850	694,140
Increase/(decrease) in gross profit		−5,710

Tutorial note

First, you can calculate a selling price increase from £15.00 to £15.00 × (1 + 5%) = £15.75.

The decrease in sales volume can be calculated as 75,000 units in the first draft × (1–8%) = 69,000 units. By multiplying these two numbers together, we then get sales revenue in the alternative scenario of £1,086,750.

Material costs are variable, as we are told in the question. With the first draft numbers we can calculate that the material cost per unit is £131,250/75,000 units, i.e. £1.75 per unit. We apply this to the alternative scenario volumes of 69,000 units and get a new material cost of £120,750.

Likewise, labour costs are variable, as we are told in the question. With the first draft numbers we can calculate that the labour cost per unit is £187,500/75,000 units, i.e. £2.50 per unit. We apply this to the alternative scenario volumes of 69,000 units and get a new labour cost of £172,500.

In the first draft, energy costs currently stand at £44,000. This £44,000 amount includes a rise of 10%. Before this rise of 10% was incorporated in the calculation, we had an energy cost of £44,000/(1–10%), i.e. £44,000/90% so £40,000. In the alternative scenario we may then increase this starting amount of £40,000 by the revised increase of 8% and get a new energy cost of £40,000 × (1 + 8%) = £43,200.

Depreciation is the trickiest number to calculate in this task. It is a stepped cost and in the first draft we had 75,000 units/8,000 units = 9.375 steps of 8,000 units. We must round this up to 10 steps. If 10 steps incurred a depreciation expense of £62,400 in the first draft, it means that each 'step' incurs a depreciation expense of £62,400/10 steps = £6,240. So, in the alternative scenario where we have 69,000 units, we have 69,000 units/8,000 units per step = 8.625 steps. We must round this up to 9 steps, and 9 × £6,240 = £56,160.

62 MONROE

Operating budget	First draft	Alternative scenario
Sales price per unit (£)	20.00	21.00
Sales volume	6,200	6,076
		£
Sales revenue	124,000	127,596
Costs		
Material	4,650	4,557
Labour	12,400	12,152
Energy	33,000	30,900
Depreciation	14,000	14,000
Total	64,050	61,609
Gross Profit	59,950	65,987
Increase/(decrease) in gross profit		6,037

SALES REVENUE AND COSTS FORECASTS

63 INCOME FORECAST (I)

Tutorial note

When deflating a revenue (i.e. stripping the effect of inflation on forecasts), ensure you divide (not multiply) the inflated number with the increase percentage given in the question.

$$\frac{£4,284,000 \text{ forecast for next year, including 2\% increase}}{1+2\% \text{ increase}} = £4,200,000$$

64 INCOME FORECAST (II)

The forecast should be revised to **£7,200,000**

65 INCOME FORECAST (III)

The forecast should be revised to **£800,000**

66 ENERGY COSTS

The energy budget should be **£143,820**

67 ELECTRICITY COSTS

The energy budget should be **£197,600**

$$\frac{£212,160 \text{ forecast for next year, including 2\% increase}}{1+2\% \text{ increase}} = £208,000 \text{ before the increase.}$$

After the reduction, we have £208,000 × (1 – 5%) = £197,600.

The 4% increase in gas and electricity tariffs remains and no changes in calculations are needed.

68 FIXED OVERHEADS AND HIGH-LOW

The amount of fixed overheads is £187,000

	£
Total cost of 18,500 hours	251,750
Total cost of 17,000 hours	246,500
Variable cost of 1,500 hours	5,250

ANSWERS TO PRACTICE QUESTIONS: SECTION 2

Variable cost per machine hour = £5,250/1,500 machine hours = £3.50.

	£
Total cost of 17,000 hours	246,500
Less variable cost of 17,000 hours (× £3.50)	59,500
Balance = fixed costs	187,000

69 FLUTE

The answer is **B: £30**.

Variable cost per unit = (400,000 − 250,000)/(10,000 − 5,000) = 150,000/5,000 = £30

70 DISCOUNTS ONE

£35,255.50

Litres	Cost per litre	Total £
1,000	× 2.50 × .99	2,475
2,000	× 2.50 × .98	4,900
4,000	× 2.50 × .96	9,600
8,000	× 2.50 × .95	19,000
15,000		35,975
		× .98
		35,255.50

71 DISCOUNTS TWO

£23,310.00

kg	Cost per litre	Total £
2,000	× 3.00 × .99	5,940
1,000	× 3.00 × .98	2,940
1,000	× 3.00 × .97	2,910
4,000	× 3.00 × .96	11,520
8,000		**23,310.00**

KAPLAN PUBLISHING

72 HIGH – LOW

	Units	£
High	13,100	69,750
Low	11,150	60,000
	1,950	9,750

Variable cost = £9,750/1,950 = £5 per unit

Total costs = Fixed cost + Variable cost

£69,750 = FC + (13,100 units × £5)

FC = £4,250 (in total)

73 HILOW

	Units	£
High	460	5,000
Low	410	4,500
	50	500

Variable cost = £500/50 = £10 per unit

Total costs = Fixed cost + Variable cost

£5,000 = FC + (460 units × £10)

FC = £400 (in total)

74 STEPPED

£458,750 – £418,750 = £40,000 of which £25,000 is the step up. Therefore only £15,000 is the total variable cost.

Change in output = 29,000 – 25,000 = 4,000 units.

Variable cost per unit = £15,000/4,000 units = £3.75

75 STEEPLE

£21,000 – £15,000 = £6,000 of which £5,000 is the step up. Therefore only £1,000 is the total variable cost.

Change in output = 2,400 – 2,000 = 400 units.

Variable cost per unit = £1,000/400 units = £2.50

ANSWERS TO PRACTICE QUESTIONS: SECTION 2

76 PEN

First remove the effect of the discount, it will only have been applied to the higher level (24,000 units).

This means the cost for 15,000 is £0.50 per unit more than the total cost for 24,000 units.

To make the total cost figures comparable, we need to increase the cost of the higher level by £0.50 per unit. 24,000 × £0.50 = £12,000

So without the discount the cost for 24,000 units would've been 158,000 + 12,000 = 170,000.

£170,000 – £125,000 = £45,000.

Change in output = 24,000 – 15,000 = 9,000 units.

Variable cost per unit (before the discount) = £45,000/9,000 units = £5.00

Total costs = Fixed cost + Variable cost

Using the low level, £125,000 = FC + (15,000 units × £5)

FC = £50,000 (in total)

Forecasting for 25,000 units:

The discount will be applied as it is greater than 23,000 units. So the variable cost per unit is £5.00 – £0.50 = £4.50

TC = FC + (units × VC/unit)

TC = £50,000 + (25,000 × £4.50)

TC = £162,500

77 POPPY

£48,750 – £38,750 = £10,000 of which £2,500 is the step up. Therefore only £7,500 is the caused by the variable cost.

(We can ignore the bulk buy discount of 16% at this stage as both activity levels are below the level at which it becomes relevant.)

Change in output = 34,000 – 28,000 = 6,000 units.

Variable cost per unit (before the discount) = £7,500/6,000 units = £1.25

Fixed cost before the step up:

TC = FC + (units × VC/unit)

Using the lower level of activity

£38,750 = FC + (28,000 × £1.25)

The Fixed cost before the step up = £3,750

Forecasting for 40,000 units

FC = £3,750 + £2,500 = £6,250

VC/unit = £1.25 × 0.84 = £1.05

TC = £6,250 + (40,000 × £1.05) = £48,250

WRITTEN TASKS

78 NOSEY

To	Chief executive	Date	(Today)
From	Budget accountant	Subject	Review of operating statement

(a) Reasons for variances

I have reviewed the results for May 2009. Profit in the month was £1,933,900 driven by a 10% price improvement over budget and increased volume. After flexing the original budget to allow for the increased volume we are reporting adverse expense variances of £109,700.

The most significant adverse expense variance is labour. I would expect this cost variance to be adverse because increased workloads tend to create high overtime costs and this appears to be the case here.

Material costs were above budget despite the reduction in the chemical costs during the month. We need to investigate whether working overtime has resulted in the staff being tired which may have led to higher levels of material wastage. It may be preferable to employ additional staff instead.

Marketing costs were £16,800 over budget, no doubt due to the costs of the advertising campaign, and this seems to be money well spent.

The administration overspend is worrying and needs to be investigated. It could have been a one-off. Alternatively, perhaps there are variable costs such as overtime or bonus that should not have been budgeted as fixed costs.

(b) Three steps to motivate managers to achieve budgets

Maintaining motivated managers is an important aspect of setting and achieving budgets.

To do this, managers should be involved in the planning process so that budgets are not set at unachievable levels.

Proper lines of communication should be established so that managers can be kept informed and understand the part they have to play in achieving the budgets.

The establishment of performance targets that are challenging and lead to acceptable rewards, such as salary increases or bonuses, is another way of keeping managers motivated.

ANSWERS TO PRACTICE QUESTIONS: SECTION 2

79 CM LTD

To	Chief executive	Date	(Today)
From	Budget accountant	Subject	Review of operating statement

(a) **Examine the planning assumptions and calculations in the proposed budget and identify any weaknesses.**

The draft budget is based on the assumption of 10% growth in sales volume. No justification is offered for this round figure assumption. I suggest that we need to review recent trends in CM Ltd's products; look at the potential for the anticipated new products and estimate the likely additional business generated from our own customers. With only 50 current products, this should not be difficult.

The assumption that sales revenue will only grow relative to sales volume is probably pessimistic. Although we are told prices can never be raised, new products should command a healthy margin when launched, particularly as they are patent protected.

All costs have been increased by 12.5% in the draft budget (2.5% for inflation and 10% for growth). There is no reason why fixed costs should increase by more than an appropriate rate for inflation. Each line of costs needs to be considered carefully according to its cost type (variable, fixed, etc.) and its own cost pressures.

In particular, agreement is required about the management bonus. This has been accrued at £21,000 for 2016 and, in effect, budgeted at £23,625 for 2017. This has not yet been approved.

(b) **Explain how costs and profitability should be managed in an organisation that manufactures multiple products.**

In a multi-product manufacturing business, it is essential that costs and profitability are reviewed by product. Therefore, a costing system needs to be in place.

A standard costing system has particular advantages in that it is based on calculations of what the costs should be – called standard costs. This is useful for control as variances from these standards can be reported and investigated.

The standard cost of each product can be compared with its selling price to identify profitability.

Standard costs can be calculated for planned new products to inform price setting.

(c) **Give your opinion, with reasons, on how well the budget would motivate managers to create sustainable, profitable growth.**

Budgetary control can be a powerful tool to encourage managers and staff to create sustainable, profitable growth. To do this, budgets need to be stretching but achievable.

The proposed CM Ltd budget has been prepared by its own directors who have a vested interest, in the form of the management bonus, in ensuring that it is easy to achieve. They have not provided sufficient supporting data to enable us to verify that the sales volume and pricing assumptions are stretching.

Increasing all costs, fixed and variable, by 12.5% cannot be justified and creates significant budgetary slack.

I do not believe that this draft budget would motivate CM Ltd to create sustainable, profitable growth.

80 CONTROLLABILITY

| To | Chief executive | Date | (Today) |
| From | Assistant Management Accountant | Subject | Review of variances |

(a) Performance of production manager and sales manager

- The production manager Jon McRae seems to have been operating in a well performing department in February (before the move to cotton).

- In a traditional sense, the production manager has seriously overspent in March following the move to cotton. He/she has a net variance against his department of £3,200 in the month of March.

- The sales manager seems to have missed his targets in February, but the change to cotton certainly helped him achieve a huge favourable variance in March.

- The move to a better quality material (but more expensive) can partly or wholly explain the adverse material variance in March for Jon McRae, but a higher quality has certainly contributed to the increased sales of clothes (reflected in a favourable sales variance in March).

- The adverse material usage variance may be the result of more waste as the workers get used to using cotton rather than nylon.

(b) Controllability of variances in R&T and the fairness of the bonus scheme

- No adjustment to the standards has been made between the two months to allow for the change to cotton.

- Variances have to be allocated to one individual. In R&T, the good sales variances have been allocated to the sales manager, when in truth, the Production Manager's decision to use cotton appears to have been the driver of business success.

- Under out-of-date standards, Jon Mc Rae has no chance of making a bonus as the price of cotton is totally out of his control.

- The system does not appear to be fair.

ANSWERS TO PRACTICE QUESTIONS: SECTION 2

81 FRANKA

To	Chief executive	Date	(Today)
From	Budget accountant	Subject	Review of operating statement

(a) Key variances and reasons for increase in the actual profit

There are three significant adverse variances, relating to revenue, materials and labour. The adverse variance on revenue shows that the actual selling price of the product was less than planned. In addition, it would appear that either the unit material and unit labour costs were greater than planned or the material usage and labour productivity were adverse compared to the budget.

There are three favourable variances: power, depreciation and marketing. The reduced cost of electricity arose from decisions by the supplier and not from the introduction of performance-related pay. The favourable variance on marketing might not be in the company's best interest as demand may fall without advertising support. Finally, depreciation is a non-cash item and any change is more likely to reflect a policy change rather than any enhanced performance by senior managers. Hence the increase in actual profit is unlikely to be due to the introduction of performance-related pay.

(b) FOUR general conditions necessary for performance-related pay to successfully lead to improved performance in organisations

1. Budgets need to be consistent with the objectives of the whole organisation.

2. Managers must feel that the objectives are achievable but they should also provide a challenge.

3. The level of rewards – both financial and non-financial – should be sufficient to help motivate managers.

4. The actual results should not be capable of being manipulated.

82 LABOUR COSTS

To Production director   **Date** (Today)
From Budget accountant   **Subject** Direct labour budget

(a) Budget submission

I attach the proposed direct labour budget for next year for your consideration and approval.

The agreed production plan indicates an increase in volume to 1,650,000 units next year. No change in productivity has been assumed. Therefore the staffing level needs to increase by 23 to 81.

The manager of human resources estimates that average pay will increase by 5% next year to £31,500.

Please let me know if you need any further information.

(b) Performance indicators

There is a range of useful measures to monitor cost, efficiency, effectiveness and employee satisfaction. Staff hours and output data should be available on a daily basis. Labour rates are reviewed periodically. However employee satisfaction is probably best canvassed once or twice a year. I recommend that we conduct a weekly review of performance based on:

- Minutes per unit
- Hours of overtime
- Percentage of good output (or similar quality measure)
- Average hourly rate

We should also commission a confidential employee satisfaction and involvement questionnaire.

ANSWERS TO PRACTICE QUESTIONS: SECTION 2

83 DIEGO

| To | Production director | Date | (Today) |
| From | Budget accountant | Subject | Direct labour budget |

(a) Budget submission

I attach the proposed direct labour budget for next year for your consideration and approval.

As you know, the tough economic climate has impacted the company's sales and there is a need for productivity to increase as profits are squeezed.

The agreed production plan indicates a 21% decrease in volume to 950,000 units next year. An increase in productivity has been assumed as the minutes per unit should fall from 6 to 5.4. The increased productivity, the decreased production volume and an assumed increase in annual hours per staff member enables the staffing level to fall by 21 to 46.

The manager of human resources estimates that average pay will decrease by approximately 3% next year to £34,000.

Please let me know if you need any further information.

(b) Performance indicators

There is a range of useful measures to monitor how well the company is doing in financial terms. These include the calculation of:

- Net profit margin
- Gross profit margin
- Return on capital employed
- Asset turnover.

84 DRAFT BUDGET

To	Production director	Date	(Today)
From	Budget accountant	Subject	Direct labour budget

(a) Budget submission

I attach the proposed direct labour budget for next year for your consideration and approval.

The agreed production plan indicates an increase in volume to 1,500,000 units next year. An increase in productivity has been assumed. The staffing level needs to increase by 8 to 52.

The manager of human resources estimates that average pay will increase by approximately 6% next year to £36,000. This is due to labour shortages.

Please let me know if you need any further information.

(b) Performance indicators

There is a range of useful measures to monitor cost, efficiency, effectiveness and employee satisfaction. Staff hours and output data should be available on a daily basis. Labour rates are reviewed periodically. However employee satisfaction is probably best canvassed once or twice a year. I recommend that we conduct a weekly review of performance based on:

- Minutes per unit.
- Hours of overtime.
- Percentage of good output (or similar quality measure).
- Average hourly rate.

We should also commission a confidential employee satisfaction and involvement questionnaire.

MONTHLY OPERATING REPORTS AND VARIANCE CALCULATIONS

85 OS

Monthly operating statement

	Flexed budget	Actual	Variance Fav/(Adv)
Volume	72,000		
	£	£	£
Revenue	3,240,000	3,312,000	72,000
Costs			
Material	864,000	836,000	28,000
Labour	504,000	509,000	(5,000)
Distribution	18,000	19,500	(1,500)
Energy	205,000	201,250	3,750
Equipment hire (*)	40,000	42,000	(2,000)
Depreciation	212,000	206,000	6,000
Marketing	268,000	255,000	13,000
Administration	184,000	190,000	(6,000)
Total	2,295,000	2,258,750	36,250
Operating profit	945,000	1,053,250	108,250

(*) Note in stepped equipment hire costs

In the fixed budget, we have 76,000 units and equipment hire costs of £48,000. Each 'step' is made up of 15,000 units.

$$\frac{76,000 \text{ units}}{15,000 \text{ units}} = 5.06 \text{ steps, so 6 steps}$$

$$\frac{\text{Cost } £48,000}{6 \text{ steps}} = £8,000 \text{ per step}$$

In the **flexed** budget, we have 72,000 units.

$$\frac{72,000 \text{ units}}{15,000 \text{ units}} = 4.8 \text{ steps, so 5 steps}$$

5 × £8,000 = **£40,000** flexed equipment hire costs.

86 OS2

Monthly operating statement

	Volume	80,000		
		Flexed budget	Actual	Variance Fav/(Adv)
		£	£	£
Revenue		3,600,000	3,520,000	(80,000)
Costs				
Material		960,000	945,000	15,000
Labour		560,000	570,000	(10,000)
Distribution		20,000	19,500	500
Energy		225,000	219,250	5,750
Equipment hire		48,000	50,000	(2,000)
Depreciation		212,000	215,000	(3,000)
Marketing		268,000	253,000	15,000
Administration		184,000	166,000	18,000
Total		2,477,000	2,437,750	39,250
Operating profit		1,123,000	1,082,250	(40,750)

87 OS3

Monthly operating statement

	Volume	110,000		
		Flexed budget	Actual	Variance Fav/(Adv)
		£	£	£
Revenue		2,200,000	2,255,000	55,000
Costs				
Material		440,000	425,000	15,000
Labour		165,000	149,000	16,000
Distribution		11,000	12,500	(1,500)
Energy		106,000	110,250	(4,250)
Equipment hire		25,000	32,000	(7,000)
Depreciation		145,000	148,000	(3,000)
Marketing		260,000	255,000	5,000
Administration		172,000	181,000	(9,000)
Total		1,324,000	1,312,750	11,250
Operating profit		876,000	942,250	66,250

ANSWERS TO PRACTICE QUESTIONS: SECTION 2

BUDGET REVISION AND VARIANCE ANALYSIS

88 LAPEL

Units made	50,000	60,000	70,000
Costs:	£	£	£
Variable costs:			
Direct materials	5,250	6,300	7,350
Direct labour	2,250	2,700	3,150
Overheads	11,100	13,320	15,540
Fixed costs:			
Indirect labour	9,200	9,200	9,200
Overheads	15,600	15,600	15,600
Total cost	43,400	47,120	50,840
Cost per unit	0.868	0.785	0.726

	A (£)	B (£)	Total (£)
Selling price per unit	1.50	1.20	
Less: variable costs per unit			
Direct materials	0.20	0.25	
Direct labour	0.12	0.14	
Variable overheads	0.15	0.19	
Contribution per unit	1.03	0.62	
Sales volume (units)	300,000	500,000	
Total contribution	309,000	310,000	619,000
Less: fixed costs			264,020
Budgeted profit			354,980

89 SLUSH

Litres made	10,000	14,000	18,000
Costs:	£	£	£
Variable costs:			
Direct materials	1,200	1,680	2,160
Direct labour	1,000	1,400	1,800
Overheads	1,600	2,240	2,880
Fixed costs:			
Indirect labour	700	700	700
Overheads	1,600	1,600	1,600
Total cost	6,100	7,620	9,140
Cost per litre	0.61	0.54	0.51

90 THREE MONTHS

Use the two levels of production above 1,100 units per month for the high/low analysis as at these levels fixed costs are the same, so the only change in cost is caused by increase in output multiplied by the variable cost per unit.

Units	Total cost (£)
1,400	68,200
1,200	66,600
200	1,600

This gives a variable cost per unit = (£1,600 ÷ 200) = £8

Now use one of the output levels used to calculate the fixed cost after the step up.

Total fixed cost (above 1,100 units) = [£68,200 – (1,400 × £8)] = £57,000

From this, to work out the fixed cost before the step up: £57,000 – £6,000 = £51,000.

Now work out the total cost for 1,000 units

Total cost (1,000 units) = £51,000 + (1,000 × £8) = £59,000

ANSWERS TO PRACTICE QUESTIONS: SECTION 2

91 EASTERN BUS COMPANY

Likely miles	10,000	12,000	14,000
	£	£	£
Sales revenue	100,000	120,000	140,000
Variable costs:			
Fuel	8,000	9,600	11,200
Drivers' wages and associated costs	5,000	6,000	7,000
Overheads	6,000	7,200	8,400
Fixed costs:			
Indirect labour	10,600	10,600	10,600
Overheads	25,850	25,850	25,850
Total cost	55,450	59,250	63,050
Total profit	44,550	60,750	76,950
Profit per mile	4.455	5.063	5.496

92 ST DAVIDS

(a) **The material total variance**

This is the difference between what 1,000 units should have cost and what they did cost.

1,000 units should have cost (× £100)	£100,000	
1,000 units did cost	£98,631	
Material total variance	£1,369	F

The variance is **favourable** because the unit cost less than they should have cost.

Now, we can break down the material total variance into its two constituent parts: the material price variance and the material usage variance.

(b) **The material price variance**

This is the difference between what 11,700 kgs should have cost and what 11,700 kgs did cost.

11,700 kgs of Y should have cost (× £10)	£117,000	
11,700 did cost	£98,631	
Material Y price variance	£18,369	(F)

The variance is **favourable** because the material cost is less than it should have been.

AAT: APPLIED MANAGEMENT ACCOUNTING

(c) **The material usage variance**

This is the difference between how many kilograms of Y should have been used to produce 1,000 units of X and how many kilograms were used, valued at the standard cost per kilogram.

1,000 units should have used (×10 kgs)	10,000 kgs
1,000 units did use	11,700 kgs
Usage variance, in kilograms	1,700 kgs (A)
	× £10
Usage variance in £	£17,000 A

The variance is **adverse** because more material was used than should have been used.

93 EASTER FUN

Raw material cost statement	£
Standard raw material cost of production	130,000
Variance (adverse shown as negative)	£ FAV/ – ADV
Material price	22,000
Material usage	–4,000
Material cost	18,000

Standard raw material cost of production

The standard Raw Material cost of production is the standard cost of actual production. In other terms, it is how much actual production should have cost, according to standards.

The 'Activity Data' table tells us that the standard cost of one item produced is $\frac{£126,000}{63,000 \text{ items}}$

That is £2 per item. Therefore, the actual production of 65,000 items should have cost 65,000 × £2 = £130,000.

Material price variance

Formula:

Actual quantity purchased/used × Actual price
V
Actual quantity purchased/used × Standard price

Then:	£
33,500 kgs	112,000
33,500 × £4.00	134,000
	———
Materials price variance	22,000 F

ANSWERS TO PRACTICE QUESTIONS: SECTION 2

Alternative method

We could use what we call the **Did** and **Should** method to work out the answer.

33,500 kgs **did cost**	£112,000
33,500 kgs **should have cost** @ £4.00 per kg	**£134,000**
Variance	£22,000 F

The variance is **favourable** because the kilograms of material were cheaper than expected.

Material usage variance

Formula:

Actual quantity used × Standard price

V

Standard quantity used for actual production × Standard price

Then: £

33,500 kgs × £4.00   134,000
65,000 items × 0.5 kgs per item × £4.00   130,000
                                                                         ————

Materials usage variance   £4,000 A

Alternative method

We could use what we call the **Did** and **Should** method to work out the answer.

65,000 items produced should have used 65,000 × 0.5 kgs per item	32,500 kgs
65,000 items did use	**33,500 kgs**
Variance	1,000 kgs A

1,000 kgs A × £4.00 = £4,000 Adverse variance.

The variance is **adverse** because we used more kilograms than expected.

94 ANNIVERSARY

Raw material cost statement	£
Standard raw material cost of production	12,500
Variance (adverse shown as negative)	£ FAV/ – ADV
Material price	–2,000
Material usage	–500
Material cost	–2,500

Standard raw material cost of production

The standard raw material cost of production is the standard cost of actual production. In other terms, it is how much actual production should have cost, according to standards.

The 'Activity Data' table tells us that the standard cost of one item produced is $\dfrac{£12,000}{1,200 \text{ items}}$

That is £10 per item. Therefore, the actual production of 1,250 items should have cost 1,250 × £10 = £12,500.

KAPLAN PUBLISHING

Material price variance

Formula:

Actual quantity purchased/used × Actual price

V

Actual quantity purchased/used × Standard price

Then:	£
1,300 kgs	15,000
1,300 × £10.00	13,000
Materials price variance	2,000 A

Alternative method

We could use what we call the **Did** and **Should** method to work out the answer.

1,300 kgs **did cost**	£15,000
1,300 kgs **should have cost** @ £10.00 per kg	**£13,000**
Variance	£2,000 A

The variance is **adverse** because the kilograms of material were more expensive than expected.

Material usage variance

Formula:

Actual quantity used × Standard price

V

Standard quantity used for actual production × Standard price

Then:	£
1,300 kgs × £10.00	13,000
1,250 items × 1 kg per item × £10.00	12,500
Materials usage variance	£500 A

Alternative method

We could use what we call the **Did** and **Should** method to work out the answer.

1,250 items produced should have used 1,250 × 1 kgs per item	1,250 kgs
1,250 items did use	**1,300 kgs**
Variance	50 kgs A

50 kgs A × £10.00 = £500 Adverse variance.

The variance is **adverse** because we used more kilograms than expected.

95 APPLES AND PEARS

Raw material cost statement	£
Standard raw material cost of production	68,460
Variance (adverse shown as negative)	£ FAV/ – ADV
Material price	–11,250
Material usage	–3,540
Material cost	–14,790

Standard raw material cost of production

The standard raw material cost of production is the standard cost of actual production. In other terms, it is how much actual production should have cost, according to standards.

The 'Activity Data' table tells us that the standard cost of one item produced $\frac{£65,520}{78,000 \text{ items}}$

That is £0.84 per item. Therefore, the actual production of 81,500 items should have cost 81,500 × £0.84 = £68,460.

Material price variance

Formula:

Actual quantity purchased/used × Actual price
V
Actual quantity purchased/used × Standard price

Then:	£
120,000 kgs	83,250
120,000 × £0.60	72,000
Materials price variance	11,250 A

Alternative method

We could use what we call the **Did** and **Should** method to work out the answer.

120,000 kgs **did cost**	83,200	
120,000 kgs **should have cost** @ £0.60 per kg	**£72,000**	
Variance	£11,250	A

The variance is **adverse** because the kilograms of material were more expensive than expected.

Material usage variance

Formula:

Actual quantity used × Standard price

V

Standard quantity used for actual production × Standard price

Then: £
120,000 kgs × £0.60   72,000 ⎫
81,500 × 1.4 kg per item × £0.60   68,460 ⎭

Materials usage variance   £3,540 A

Alternative method

We could use what we call the **Did** and **Should** method to work out the answer.

81,500 items produced should have used 81,500 × 1.4 kgs per item	114,100 kgs
81,500 items did use	**120,000 kgs**
Variance	5,900 kgs A

5,900 kgs A × £0.60 = £3,540 Adverse variance.

The variance is **adverse** because we used more kilograms than expected.

96 INDEPENDENCE DAY

Raw material cost statement	£
Standard raw material cost of production	52,200
Variance (adverse shown as negative)	£ FAV/ – ADV
Material price	4,000
Material usage	–7,800
Material cost	–3,800

Standard raw material cost of production

The standard raw material cost of production is the standard cost of actual production. In other terms, it is how much actual production should have cost, according to standards.

The 'Activity Data' table tells us that the standard cost of one item produce $\frac{£50,400}{126,000 \text{ items}}$

That is £0.40 per item. Therefore, the actual production of 130,500 items should have cost 130,500 × £0.40 = £52,200.

Material price variance

Formula:

Actual quantity purchased/used × Actual price
V
Actual quantity purchased/used × Standard price

Then:	£
120,000 kgs	56,000
120,000 × £0.50	60,000
Materials price variance	4,000 F

Alternative method

We could use what we call the **Did** and **Should** method to work out the answer.

120,000 kgs **did cost**	£56,000
120,000 kgs **should have cost** @ £0.50 per kg	**£60,000**
Variance	£4,000 F

The variance is **favourable** because the kilograms of material were less expensive than expected.

Material usage variance

Formula:

Actual quantity used × Standard price
V
Standard quantity used for actual production × Standard price

Then:	£
120,000 kgs × £0.50	60,000
130,500 items × 0.8 kg per item × £0.50	52,200
Materials usage variance	£7,800 A

Alternative method

We could use what we call the **Did** and **Should** method to work out the answer.

130,500 items produced should have used 130,500 × 0.8 kgs per item	104,400 kgs
130,500 items did use	**120,000 kgs**
Variance	15,600 kgs A

15,600 kgs A × £0.50 = £7,800 Adverse variance.

The variance is **adverse** because we used more kilograms than expected.

97 AUGUST

Raw material cost statement	£
Standard raw material cost of production	9,300
Variance (adverse shown as negative)	£ FAV/ – ADV
Material price	–210
Material usage	300
Material cost	90

Standard raw material cost of production

The standard raw material cost of production is the standard cost of actual production. In other terms, it is how much actual production should have cost, according to standards.

The 'Activity Data' table tells us that the standard cost of one item produced is $\frac{£9,000}{1,500 \text{ items}}$

That is £6.00 per item. Therefore, the actual production of 1,550 items should have cost 1,550 × £6.00 = £9,300.

Material price variance

Formula:

Actual quantity purchased/used × Actual price
V
Actual quantity purchased/used × Standard price

Then:	£
4,500 kgs	9,210 ⎫
4,500 × £2.00	9,000 ⎭
Materials price variance	210 A

Alternative method

We could use what we call the **Did** and **Should** method to work out the answer.

4,500 kgs **did cost**	£9,210	
4,500 kgs **should have cost** @ £2.00 per kg	**£9,000**	
Variance	£210	A

The variance is **adverse** because the kilograms of material were more expensive than expected.

ANSWERS TO PRACTICE QUESTIONS: SECTION 2

Material usage variance

Formula:

Actual quantity used × Standard price

V

Standard quantity used for actual production × Standard price

Then: £

4,500 kgs × £2   9,000 ⎫
1,550 items × 3 kg per item × £2   9,300 ⎭

Materials usage variance   £300 F

Alternative method

We could use what we call the **Did** and **Should** method to work out the answer.

1,550 items produced should have used 1,550 × 3 kgs per item	4,650 kgs
1,550 items did use	**4,500 kgs**
Variance	150 kgs F

150 kgs F × £2.00 = £300 favourable variance.

The variance is **favourable** because we used fewer kilograms than expected.

98 BIRTHDAY

Direct labour cost statement	£
Standard direct labour cost of production	165,000
Variance (adverse shown as negative)	–3,000
Labour rate	–8,000
Labour efficiency	5,000
Labour cost	–3,000

Workings:

From the question, standard direct labour time per unit =

$$\frac{\text{Budgeted hours}}{\text{Budgeted number of items produced}}$$

Standard direct labour time per unit = $\frac{7{,}500 \text{ hours}}{10{,}000 \text{ units}}$

So standard direct labour time per unit = 0.75 hours, or 45 minutes.

We also need to work the standard direct labour cost per hour.

From the question, standard direct labour cost per hour = $\frac{\text{Budgeted cost in £}}{\text{Budgeted number of hours}}$

Therefore standard direct labour cost per hour = $\frac{£150{,}000}{7{,}500 \text{ hours}}$

Standard direct labour cost per hour = £20

KAPLAN PUBLISHING   241

Standard direct labour cost of production
11,000 units × 0.75 hrs × £20 per hour   £165,000
Actual cost of labour, as per question   £168,000
Variance   £3,000   A

Labour rate variance

Formula:

Actual labour hours paid × Actual rate
V
Actual labour hours paid × Standard rate

Then: £
8,000 hours   168,000 ⎫
8,000 hours × £20   160,000 ⎭

Labour rate variance   8,000 A

Alternative method

We could use what we call the **Did** and **Should** method to work out the answer.

8,000 hours **did cost**   £168,000
8,000 hours **should have cost** @ £20 per hour   £160,000
Variance   £8,000   A

The variance is **favourable** because the average hourly rate was lower than expected.

Labour efficiency variance

Formula:

Actual hours worked × Standard rate
V
Standard hours worked for actual production × Standard rate

Then: £
8,000 hours × £20   160,000
11,000 units × 0.75 hours × £20 per hour   165,000

Labour efficiency variance   £5,000 F

We can use the **Did** and **Should** method to calculate the labour efficiency also.

11,000 units **did use**   8,000 hours
11,000 units **should have used** @ 0.75 hours per unit 8,250 hours
                                                       250 hours
Multiplied by the standard (expected) rate   × £20 per hour
Variance is   £5,000

The variance is **favourable** because we used less direct labour than expected to make 11,000 units.

ANSWERS TO PRACTICE QUESTIONS: SECTION 2

99 VALENTINE

Direct labour cost statement	£
Standard direct labour cost of production	589,000
Variance (adverse shown as negative)	−7,412
Labour rate	1,043
Labour efficiency	−8,455
Labour cost	−7,412

Workings:

From the question, standard direct labour time per unit =

$$\text{Standard direct labour time per unit} = \frac{\text{Budgeted hours}}{\text{Budgeted number of items produced}}$$

$$\text{Standard direct labour time per unit} = \frac{64{,}500 \text{ hours}}{6{,}450 \text{ units}}$$

So standard direct labour time per unit = 10 hours.

We also need to work the standard direct labour cost per hour.

From the question, standard direct labour cost per hour = $\frac{\text{Budgeted cost in £}}{\text{Budgeted number of hours}}$

Therefore standard direct labour cost per hour = $\frac{£612{,}750}{64{,}500 \text{ hours}}$

Standard direct labour cost per hour = £9.50

Standard direct labour cost of production
6,200 units × 10 hours × £9.50 per hour   £589,000
Actual cost of labour, as per question   £596,412
Variance   **£7,412   A**

Labour rate variance

Formula:

Actual labour hours paid × Actual rate
V
Actual labour hours paid × Standard rate

Then: £
62,890 hours   596,412
62,890 hours × £9.50   597,455
                          ———————
Labour rate variance   1,043 F

KAPLAN PUBLISHING

AAT: APPLIED MANAGEMENT ACCOUNTING

Alternative method

We could use what we call the **Did** and **Should** method to work out the answer.

62,890 hours **did cost**	£596,412
62,890 hours **should have cost** @ £9.50 per hour	**£597,455**
Variance	£1,043 F

The variance is **favourable** because the average hourly rate was lower than expected.

Labour efficiency variance

Formula:

Actual hours worked × Standard rate

V

Standard hours worked for actual production × Standard rate

Then:	£
62,890 hours × £9.50	597,455
6,200 units × 10 hours × £9.50 per hour	589,000
Labour efficiency variance	£8,455 A

We can use the **Did** and **Should** method to calculate the labour efficiency also.

6,200 units **did use**	62,890 hours
6,200 units **should have used** @ 10 hours per unit	**62,000 hours**
	890 hours
Multiplied by the standard (expected) rate	× £9.50 per hour
Variance is:	£8,455

The variance is **adverse** because we used more direct labour than expected to make 6,200 units.

100 TRINITY

	Flexed budget	Actual	Variance
Volume sold	28,800	28,800	
	£000	£000	%
Revenue	4,320	3,877	−10.25
Direct materials	252	212	15.87
Direct labour	1,260	912	27.62
Variable overheads	641	448	30.11
Fixed overheads	300	325	−8.33
Profit from operations	1,867	1,980	6.05

ANSWERS TO PRACTICE QUESTIONS: SECTION 2

STANDARD COSTING AND VARIANCES

STANDARD COSTING

101 BUDGIE

(a) The standard quantity of labour per unit is 30 minutes (1,750/3,500 × 60 minutes)

(b) The budgeted quantity of materials needed to produce 3,000 units of A is 6,000 litres (7,000/3,500 × 3,000)

(c) The budgeted labour hours to produce 3,600 units of A is 1,800 hours (1,750/3,500 × 3,600)

(d) The budgeted labour cost to produce 3,600 units of A is £16,200 (£15,750/3,500 × 3,600)

(e) The budgeted overhead absorption rate is £10 (£35,000/3,500)

(f) The fixed overheads were over absorbed by £1,675

Absorption rate = £43,500/4,000 units	£10.875
	£
Actual overheads	44,000
Absorbed overheads 4,200 × £10.875	45,675
Over absorbed	1,675

102 CARROT

(a) The standard quantity of labour per unit is 1.5 minutes (250/10,000 × 60 minutes)

(b) The budgeted quantity of materials needed to produce 9,950 units of B is 3,980 kg (4,000/10,000 × 9,950)

(c) The budgeted labour hours to produce 9,950 units of B is 248.75 hours (250/10,000 × 9,950)

(d) The budgeted labour cost to produce 9,950 units of B is £2,487.50 (£2,500/10,000 × 9,950)

(e) The budgeted overhead absorption rate is £0.30 (£3,000/10,000)

(f) The fixed overheads were over absorbed by £287

Absorption rate = £2,900/9,000 units	£0.322
	£
Actual overheads	3,000
Absorbed overheads 10,200 × £0.322	3,287
Over absorbed	287

103 RABBIT

(a) The standard quantity of labour per unit is 60 minutes (12,500/12,500 × 60)

(b) The budgeted quantity of materials needed to produce 12,000 units of A is 24,000 litres (25,000/12,500 × 12,000)

(c) The budgeted labour hours to produce 12,600 units of A is 12,600 hours (12,500/12,500 × 12,600)

(d) The budgeted labour cost to produce 12,600 units of A is £126,000 (£125,000/12,500 × 12,600)

(e) The budgeted overhead absorption rate is £6 (£75,000/12,500)

(f) The fixed overheads were over absorbed by £2,800

Absorption rate = £78,000/13,000 units	£6
	£
Actual overheads	74,000
Absorbed overheads 12,800 × £6	76,800
Over absorbed	2,800

104 BELLS

1 box of Bells	Quantity	Cost per unit	Total cost
Material	16 kg	1.50	24
Labour	3 hrs	9.00	27
Fixed overheads	1 (accept 3 hrs)	60 (20 per hr)	60
Total			111

105 TEA BAGS

1,000 tea bags		Quantity (Units)	Unit price £	Total cost £
Loose tea	Kilograms	3	5	15
Tea bags	Bags	1000	0.006	6
Direct labour	Hours	0.2	10	2
Fixed production overheads	Hours	0.2	50	10
				33

ANSWERS TO PRACTICE QUESTIONS: SECTION 2

106 GEM

1 unit of Gem	Quantity	Cost per unit	Total cost
Material	5.25	7	36.75
Labour	3.5	3	10.5
Fixed overheads	3.5	15	52.5
Total			99.75

It takes a manufacturing department 750,000 hours to produce 250,000 units of Pearl. The standard hours per unit are **3 hours**.

107 BESPOKE SUIT

1 bespoke suit	Quantity	Cost per unit	Total cost
Material	4.50	48	216
Labour	40	15	600
Fixed overheads	40	10	400
Total			1,216

108 GARDEN SHEDS

1 Shed	Quantity	Cost per unit	Total cost
Material	90	6.50	585
Labour	5	10	50
Fixed overheads	5	20	100
Total			735

109 PERFORMANCE

1000 bulbs	Quantity	Cost per unit	Total cost
Material	40	5	£200.00
Labour	2	7	£14.00
Fixed overheads	2	15	£30.00
Total			£244.00

The standard quantity is 1,500/1,000 = **1.5 kg**.

110 DISCO

The standard machine time required for a disc is **5** hours.

111 HARRY

The standard labour time required for a unit is 2,000/500 = **4** hours.

KAPLAN PUBLISHING

AAT: APPLIED MANAGEMENT ACCOUNTING

112 OSCAR

The standard machine time required for a widget is 0.0025 hours.

113 PIZZA

The standard quantity of flour for a pizza is **0.20** kilograms.

300,000 kg/1,500,000 pizzas

114 SETTING BUDGETS

Actual results should always be compared to flexed budgets.

Correct answer is **A**

115 STANDARD

Ideal standards are demotivating since they expect perfect performance at all times which is not humanly possible.

Correct answer is **D**

116 BASIC

Correct answer is **C**, by definition.

117 SAPPHIRE

Correct answer is 290,000 kg

145,000 units × 2 kg = 290,000 kg

SALES VARIANCES

118 GREEN

(Budgeted quantity − Actual quantity) × standard profit per unit

(1,000 − 900) × (£50 − £39) = £1,100

119 PURPLE

The standard contribution per unit is £(50 − 4 − 16 − 10 − 1) = £19.

Sales volume variance

= (Budgeted sales volume − actual sales volume) × Standard contribution per unit

= (3,000 − 3,500) × £19

= £9,500

Correct answer **A**

ANSWERS TO PRACTICE QUESTIONS: SECTION 2

120 ORANGE

Sales volume variance

= (Budgeted sales volume – actual sales volume) × Standard profit per unit

= (10,000 – 9,800) × £5

= £1,000 A

Correct answer **C**

121 Z LTD 1

Correct answer **D**

Sales price variance

	£
Actual units did sell for (642 × £465)	298,530
Actual units should sell for (£500)	321,000
Sales price variance	22,470 (A)

122 Z LTD 2

Correct answer **C**

Sales volume contribution variance

	Units	
Actual quantity sold	642	
Budget quantity sold	600	
Sales volume variance in units	42	(F)
× Std contribution per unit (25% × £500)	× £125	
	£5,250	(F)

123 PQR LTD

The favourable sales volume profit variance for the period was **£20,000**.

Sales volume profit variance

Budgeted sales volume (units)	100,000	
Actual sales volume (units)	110,000	
	10,000	F
Standard profit per unit (£10 – £8)	£2	
	£20,000	F

124 AUDIT

The favourable sales price variance is **£17,400**

Sales price variance

	£
Actual output did sell for	365,400
Actual output should sell for (58 × £6,000)	348,000
Sales price variance	17,400 (F)

125 MAUVE

When using a marginal costing system, the sales volume variance will be based on the standard contribution per unit.

The volume variance is 5,000 units, and the total value = 5,000 × 20 = £100,000

Correct answer **B**

MATERIAL VARIANCES

126 MAT (1)

AQ × AP

1,000 × £5 = £5,000

AQ × SP

1,000 × £5.50 = £5,500   Price variance = £500 F

SQ × SP

200 × 6 × £5.50 = £6,600   Usage variance = £1,100 F

			£
Budgeted/Standard cost of materials for actual production			6,600
Variances	Favourable	Adverse	
Direct materials price	500		
Direct materials usage	1,100		
Total variance	1,600		1,600
Actual cost of materials for actual production			5,000

ANSWERS TO PRACTICE QUESTIONS: SECTION 2

127 MAT (2)

AQ × AP

12,000 × £4 = £48,000

AQ × SP

12,000 × £4.50 = £54,000   Price variance = £6,000 F

SQ × SP

2,000 × 5 × £4.50 = £45,000   Usage variance = £9,000 A

			£
Budgeted/Standard cost of materials for actual production			45,000
Variances	**Favourable**	**Adverse**	
Direct materials price	6,000		
Direct materials usage		9,000	
Total variance	6,000	9,000	3,000
Actual cost of materials for actual production			48,000

128 SMITH

AQ × SP

29,000 × 0.27 = £7,830

SQ × SP   Usage variance £108 F

9,800 × 3 × 0.27 = £7,938

129 MATERIAL

AQ × AP

60,000 × ? = £720,000

AQ × SP

60,000 × £11 = £660,000

Price variance is £60,000 A

130 MOUSE

AQ × AP

AQ × SP

SQ × SP

2,450,000 units × 0.03 × £0.75 = £55,125

(W1) Standard quantity = 60,000 kg/2,000,000 = 0.03 kg per bottle

Correct answer **C**

131 RAW MATERIALS

AQ used × SP

2,300 kg × £0.75 = £1,725

SQ × SP

1,200 × 2kg × £0.75 = £1,800

Usage variance = £75 F

Correct answer is **D**

132 ALPHA

AQ × AP

10,000 × ? = £55,000

AQ × SP

10,000 × £5 = £50,000

Price variance = £5,000 A

Correct answer is **B**

133 BETA

AQ × AP

5,000 × ? = £27,500

AQ × SP

5,000 × £5 = £25,000

Price variance = £2,500 A

Correct answer is **C**

ANSWERS TO PRACTICE QUESTIONS: SECTION 2

134 DELTA

AQ × SP

10,000 × (£28,000/8,000 kg) = £35,000

SQ × SP

1,000 units × 8 kg × £3.50 = £28,000

Usage variance = £7,000 A

Correct answer is **A**

LABOUR VARIANCES

135 LAB (1)

AH × AR

12,000 × £8 = £96,000

AH × SR

12,000 × £8.50 = £102,000   Rate variance = £6,000 F

SH × SR

2,000 × 5 × £8.50 = £85,000   Efficiency variance = £17,000 A

			£
Budgeted/Standard cost of labour for actual production			85,000
Variances	**Favourable**	**Adverse**	
Direct labour rate	6,000		
Direct labour efficiency		17,000	
Total variance	6,000	17,000	11,000
Actual cost of labour for actual production			96,000

136 LAB (2)

AH × AR

22,000 × £10 = £220,000

AH × SR

22,000 × £9.80 = £215,600   Rate variance = £4,400 A

SH × SR

21,000 × 1 × £9.80 = £205,800   Efficiency variance = £9,800 A

			£
Budgeted/Standard cost of labour for actual production			205,800
Variances	**Favourable**	**Adverse**	
Direct labour rate		4,400	
Direct labour efficiency		9,800	
Total variance		14,200	14,200
Actual cost of labour for actual production			220,000

137 BEALE

AH × AR

340 × ? = £5,440

AH × SR   Labour rate variance = £340 A

340 × £15 = £5,100

138 MY

A unit takes 0.5 hours (3,000 hours/6,000 units).

7,000 units × 0.5 hours = 3,500 hours

3,500 hours × £7 = £24,500

Correct answer is £24,500.

139 GOSSIP

140,000 units × (60,000/120,000) hours × £14 = £980,000

Correct answer is **£980,000.**

140 HIT

11,000 units × (8,000/10,000) hours × £10 = £88,000

Correct answer is **£88,000.**

ANSWERS TO PRACTICE QUESTIONS: **SECTION 2**

141 JOY

AH × AR

3,400 × ? = £53,140

AH × SR

3,400 × £15 = £51,000

Labour rate variance = £2,140 A

Correct answer is **C**

142 LEMON

AH × SR

7,000 × £9 = £63,000

SH × SR

1,000 × 6 hours × £9 = £54,000

Labour efficiency variance = £9,000 A

Correct answer is **D**

143 MUFFIN

AH × SR

16,000 × £12 = £192,000

SH × SR

10,000 × 1.5 hours × £12 = £180,000

Labour efficiency variance = £12,000 A

Correct answer is **D**

144 JAYRO

Variance		
	£	A/F
Direct material usage variance	Nil	N/A
Direct material price	1,100	A
Direct labour efficiency variance	4,400	A

145 DIVISION

W1 Standard cost of production: 0.2ltrs × 6,000 units × (£2/0.2ltrs) = **£12,000**

11,110/£10.10 = 1,100 litres actually used.

AQ × SP = 1,100 × £10 = 11,000

Price variance = 11,110 – 11,000 = **£110 A**

Usage variance = 11,000 – 12,000 = **£1,000 F**

W2 Standard labour cost of production: 0.8 × 6,000 units × (£4/0.8hrs) = **£24,000**

AH × SR = 4,500 × £5 = £22,500

Labour rate variance = 25,000 – 22,500 = **£2,500 A**

Efficiency variance = 22,500 – 24,000 = **£1,500 F**

Variance		£	A/F
Actual cost of materials		**11,110**	
Direct material price variance		110	A
Direct material usage variance		1,000	F
Standard material cost of production	W1	**12,000**	
Actual cost of labour		25,000	
Direct labour rate variance		2,500	A
Direct labour efficiency variance		1,500	F
Standard labour cost of production	W2	24,000	

146 NIGHT

W1 Standard cost of production: 1ltr × 900 units × (£20/1ltr) = **£18,000**

AQ × SP = 950 × £20 = 19,000

Price variance = 19,100 – 19,000 = **£100 A**

Usage variance = 19,000 – 18,000 = **£1,000 A**

W2 Standard labour cost of production: 4hrs × 900 units × (£40/4hrs) = **£36,000**

AH × SR = 3,950 × £10 = £39,500

Labour rate variance = 38,095 – 39,500 = **£1,405 F**

Efficiency variance = 39,500 – 36,000 = **£3,500 A**

Variance		£	A/F
Actual cost of materials		**19,100**	
Direct material usage variance		1,000	A
Direct material total variance		1,100	A
Standard material cost of production	W1	**18,000**	
Actual cost of labour		38,095	
Direct labour rate variance		1,405	F
Direct labour efficiency variance		3,500	A
Standard labour cost of production	W2	36,000	

ANSWERS TO PRACTICE QUESTIONS: **SECTION 2**

147 HINDER

The price variance will be favourable (buying at a lower price) but the usage variance will be adverse (more waste).

The correct answer is **C**

148 LABOUR VARIANCE RATIOS

Labour Activity ratio = $\dfrac{3{,}502}{3{,}630} \times 100 =$ **96.5%**

Labour Efficiency ratio = $\dfrac{3{,}502}{3{,}471} \times 100 =$ **100.9%**

Idle time ratio = $\dfrac{3{,}710 - 3{,}471}{3{,}710} \times 100 =$ **6.4%**

149 LAB VAR RATIOS

Labour Activity ratio = $\dfrac{30{,}502}{29{,}470} \times 100 =$ **103.5%**

Labour Efficiency ratio = $\dfrac{30{,}502}{31{,}630} \times 100 =$ **96.4%**

Idle time ratio = $\dfrac{32{,}000 - 31{,}630}{32{,}000} \times 100 =$ **1.2%**

150 LABOUR

Better quality material might enable workers to work more quickly as there might be less wastage and hence rework.

151 TIDLE

AHp × AR

5,200 × £7.50 = £39,000

Rate variance = **£2,600 A**

AHp × SR

5,200 × £7 = £36,400

Idle time variance = **£2,100 A**

AHw × SR

4,900 × £7 = £34,300

Efficiency variance = **£1,575 F**

AP × SH × SR

41,000 × (5,000 / 40,000) × £7 = £35,875

Total variance = **£3,125 A**

152 BRIDLE

AHp × AR

5,200 × £? = £36,000

                                                          Rate variance = **£400 F**

AHp × SR

5,200 × £7 = £36,400

                                                     Idle time variance = **£700 A**

AHw × SR

5,100 × £7 = £35,700

                                                     Efficiency variance = **£175 F**

AP × SH × SR

4,100 × (5,000 / 4,000) × £7 = £35,875

153 SIDLE

AP × SH × SR = standard cost of labour for actual production = 9,000 pots × (5,000 hrs/10,000 pots) × £10 = **£45,000**

Actual labour cost for actual production = 5,100 hours × £9.61 = **£49,011**

AHw = 5,100 − 200 = 4,900 hours

AHp × AR

5,100 × £9.61 = £49,011

                                                     Rate variance = **£1,989 F**

AHp × SR

5,100 × £10 = £51,000

                                                   Idle time variance = **£2,000 A**

AHw × SR

4,900 × £10 = £49,000

                                                   Efficiency variance = **£4,000 A**

AP × SH × SR

9,000 × 0.5 hrs × £10 = £45,000

		£
Standard labour cost for actual production		**45,000**
Variances	Favourable / adverse / No variance	
Labour rate variance	Favourable	1,989
Idle time variance	Adverse	2,000
Labour efficiency variance	Adverse	4,000
Actual labour cost from actual production		**49,011**

ANSWERS TO PRACTICE QUESTIONS: SECTION 2

VARIABLE OVERHEAD VARIANCES

154 VAR (1)

AH × AR

12,000 × £5 = £60,000

AH × SR

12,000 × £5.50 = £66,000   Expenditure variance = £6,000 F

SH × SR

2,000 × 5 × £5.50 = £55,000   Efficiency variance = £11,000 A

			£
Budgeted/Standard cost of variable overheads for actual production			55,000
Variances	**Favourable**	**Adverse**	
Variable overhead expenditure	6,000		
Variable overhead efficiency		11,000	
Total variance	6,000	11,000	5,000
Actual cost of variable overheads for actual production			60,000

155 JIF

AH × AR

3,400 × ? = £53,140

AH × SR

3,400 × £15 = £51,000

Variable overhead expenditure variance = £2,140 A

156 CALLUM

AH × SR

10,000 × £5 = £50,000

SH × SR

10,000 × 1.2 hours × £5 = £60,000

Labour efficiency variance = £10,000 F

157 VALERIE (1)

AH × AR

23,400 × ? = £103,140

AH × SR

23,400 × £5 = £117,000

Variable overhead expenditure variance = £13,860 F

Correct answer is **A**

158 VALERIE (2)

AH × SR

23,400 × £5 = £117,000

SH × SR

11,000 × 2 hours × £5 = £110,000

Variable overhead efficiency variance = £7,000 A

Correct answer is **C**

159 SHIRLEY

AH × AR

10,000 × ? = £55,800

AH × SR

10,000 × £5 = £50,000

Variable overhead expenditure variance = **£5,800 A**

AH × SR

10,000 × £5 = £50,000

SH × SR

11,000 × 0.9 hours × £5 = £49,500

Variable overhead efficiency variance = **£500 A**

FIXED OVERHEAD VARIANCES

160 OVERHEAD

Actual expenditure = £25,000

Budgeted expenditure = £20,000

Expenditure variance = £5,000 A

Budgeted expenditure = £20,000

SQ × SP

12,000 units × £2 per unit = £24,000

Volume variance = £4,000 F

The fixed overhead volume variance is **4,000 F**

The fixed overhead expenditure variance is **5,000 A**

161 FRANK

Actual expenditure £900,000

Budgeted expenditure £800,000

£100,000 A

Budgeted expenditure £800,000

AP × SR

42,000 × (£800,000/40,000 units) = £840,000

£40,000 F

The fixed overhead volume variance is **40,000 F**

The fixed overhead expenditure variance is **100,000 A**

162 TRUMPET

Budgeted production = 14,000/1.75hrs per unit = **8,000** units

Actual expenditure £209,000

Budgeted expenditure 8,000 × £25 = £200,000

Expenditure variance **£9,000 A**

Budgeted expenditure £200,000

AP × SR

6,000 × £25 = £150,000

Volume variance **£50,000 A**

163 FLOPPY

Actual expenditure £1,750,000

Budgeted expenditure 100,000 units × £15 = £1,500,000

Expenditure variance = **£250,000 A**

Budgeted expenditure £1,500,000

Actual production × Standard rate

110,000 units × 2 hrs × £7.50 = £1,650,000

Volume variance = **£150,000 F**

164 FIX (1)

Actual fixed overheads = £450,000

Budgeted fixed overheads = £400,000   Fixed overhead expenditure variance = £50,000 A

SQ × SR   21,000 × £20 = £420,000   Fixed overhead volume variance = £20,000 F

			£
Budgeted/Standard fixed cost for actual production			420,000
Variances	Favourable	Adverse	
Fixed overhead expenditure		50,000	
Fixed overhead volume	20,000		
Total variance	20,000	50,000	30,000
Actual fixed cost for actual production			450,000

165 FIX (2)

Actual fixed overheads = £245,000

Budgeted fixed overheads = £250,000

Fixed overhead expenditure variance = 5,000 F

SQ × SR   2,100 × £125 = £262,500   Fixed overhead volume variance = £12,500 F

			£
Budgeted/Standard fixed cost for actual production			262,500
Variances	Favourable	Adverse	
Fixed overhead expenditure	5,000		
Fixed overhead volume	12,500		
Total variance	17,500		17,500
Actual fixed cost for actual production			245,000

ANSWERS TO PRACTICE QUESTIONS: SECTION 2

WRITTEN TASKS

166 ARTETA

To:	Junior accounting technician	Subject:	Material variances
From:	AAT Technician	Date:	Today

Total direct material variance

The total direct material variance compares the flexed budget for materials with the actual cost incurred. The flexed budget is the budgeted cost of materials for the actual production level – 11,000 units in this example. It is incorrect to calculate the variance as £33,500 – £30,000 = £3,500 as you will not be comparing like with like in terms of activity level.

The flexing of the budget calculates the quantity of materials which are expected to be used in actual production. Therefore, the expected usage of materials to produce 11,000 units is 15,000 kg/10,000 units × 11,000 units = 16,500 kg. The expected cost would be 16,500 kg × the standard price per kg of £2 (£30,000/15,000 kg) = £33,000.

This flexed budget can now be compared with the actual costs to produce a total material variance of £500 (£33,500 – £33,000).

This variance is adverse because the actual cost was greater than the flexed budgeted cost

This total variance can now be split into two elements:

- The variance due to the price being different from that expected – called the material price variance

- The variance due to the quantity of material used being different from that expected – called the material usage variance.

The expected price was £2 per kg and therefore the expected cost of 16,000 kg would be 16,000 × £2 = £32,000.

The price variance can now be calculated by comparing the actual cost of £33,500 with the expected cost of £32,000. This gives a variance of £1,500 which is adverse because the actual cost is greater than the expected cost.

The material usage variance is calculated by taking the quantity of materials which would be expected to be used to produce the actual volume of production. In this case 11,000 units were produced and the expected quantity of material for each unit was 1.5 kg (15,000 kg/10,000 units). Therefore, to produce 11,000 units requires 11,000 × 1.5 kg = 16,500 kg. Comparing this to the actual quantity used (only 16,000 kg) produces a variance of 500 kg. This needs to be valued at the expected cost of £2 per kg giving a favourable variance of £1,000.

The usage variance is always valued at standard cost (expected cost or budgeted cost) because the price variance has already been isolated, If both variances have been calculated correctly they should reconcile back to the total materials variance. In this example:

Price variance 1,500 A + Usage variance 1000 F = Total variance 500 A

KAPLAN PUBLISHING

167 MERTESACKER

To:	Junior accounting technician	**Subject:**	Labour variances
From:	AAT Technician	**Date:**	Today

Total direct labour variance

The total direct labour variance compares the flexed budget for labour with the actual cost incurred. The flexed budget is the budgeted cost of labour for the actual production level – 95 units in this example. It is incorrect to calculate the variance as £31,500 – £30,000 = £1,500 as you will not be comparing like with like in terms of activity level.

The flexing of the budget calculates the amount of labour hours which are expected to be used in actual production. Therefore, the expected hours to produce 95 units is 1,500 hours/100 units × 95 units = 1,425 hours. The expected cost would be 1,425 hours × the standard rate per hour of £20 (£30,000/1,500 hrs) = £28,500.

This flexed budget can now be compared with the actual costs to produce a total labour variance of £3,000 (£28,500 – £31,500).

This variance is adverse because the actual cost was greater than the flexed budgeted cost.

This total variance can now be split into two elements:

- The variance due to the rate being different from that expected – called the labour rate variance

- The variance due to the hours of labour used being different from that expected – called the labour efficiency variance.

The expected rate was £20 per hour and therefore the expected cost of 1,600 hours would be 1,600 × £20 = £32,000.

The rate variance can now be calculated by comparing the actual cost of £31,500 with the expected cost of £32,000. This gives a variance of £500 which is favourable because the actual cost is less than the expected cost.

The labour efficiency variance is calculated by taking the hours of labour which would be expected to be used to produce the actual volume of production. In this case 95 units were produced and the expected labour hours for each unit were 15 hours (1,500 hrs/100 units). Therefore, to produce 95 units requires 95 × 15 hrs = 1,425 hrs. Comparing this to the actual hours used (1,600 hours) produces a variance of 175 hrs. This needs to be valued at the expected rate of £20 per hour giving an adverse variance of £3,500.

The efficiency variance is always valued at standard rate (expected rate or budgeted rate) because the rate variance has already been isolated. If both variances have been calculated correctly they should reconcile back to the total labour variance. In this example:

Rate variance 500 F + Efficiency variance 3,500 A = Total variance 3,000 A

ANSWERS TO PRACTICE QUESTIONS: SECTION 2

168 TOP DOG

To:	Managing Director	Subject:	Analysis of variances
From:	AAT student	Date:	1 May 2012

Direct materials price variance – £1,152 A

The direct material price variance is adverse which means that Top Dog has spent more on materials than expected. i.e. the material cost per kilogram was higher than expected.

This may have arisen due to the purchaser buying better quality materials which were more expensive.

The purchaser might want to consider other suppliers in the future so as to reduce the price. (Alternatively, they may want to update their standard for the increased price if it is going to be permanent.)

Direct materials usage variance – £4,080 F

The direct material usage variance is favourable which means that Top Dog has used fewer materials than expected during production.

This may have arisen due to better quality materials being bought which reduced the possible wastage, or it may have enabled the workers to work more quickly. i.e. less rework.

The material price and usage variance are often linked in that a price increase (adverse variance) will often lead to a usage decrease (favourable variance) and vice versa.

Top Dog has overspent on materials by £1,152 but then used fewer materials by £4,080. This leads to a possible net saving of £2,928. Top dog may want to consider continuing this strategy. They should investigate whether it is possible every period.

The wage rate may have risen with inflation which would cause the adverse variance. (Or more experienced staff could have been used who are paid a higher rate.)

Labour rate variance – £1,008 A

The labour rate variance is adverse which means that Top Dog has spent more on wages than expected. i.e. the wage rate was higher than expected.

If the wage rate rose due to inflation, and this was to remain stable, Top Dog may wish to revise their standard. Alternatively, if more experienced staff were used they may want to look at this variance in conjunction with the labour efficiency variance (less efficient) which might mean that the more experienced staff are not worth the extra cost. On the other hand, linking it to the favourable material usage variance also, overall Top Dog is slightly better off by employing more expensive, more experienced staff.

Labour efficiency variance – £2,880 A

The labour efficiency variance is adverse which means that Top Dog has spent longer on production than expected.

This could be due to a machine breakdown, where idle time might be included in the efficiency variance. (Or expensive staff may have been used who were not familiar with Top Dog's processes and therefore took longer.)

If the inefficiency was due to a machine breakdown and idle time, then maintenance of the machines might need to be improved.

KAPLAN PUBLISHING

Fixed overhead expenditure variance – £14,192 F

The fixed overhead expenditure variance is favourable which means that Top Dog has actually spent less on fixed overheads than budgeted.

Fixed overheads might include rent of the factory. The rent may have been reduced by the landlord.

Future negotiations with their landlord might secure further low rents.

Fixed overhead volume variance – £8,000 A

The fixed overhead volume variance is adverse which means that Top Dog has under absorbed their fixed overhead.

This has arisen due to actual production being only 2,400 units whereas the budget was to produce 2,500 units.

Training of the workforce may be necessary to improve the speed of output. Alternatively, a customer may have been lost and production was scaled down during the period since fewer barrels were required.

Note: Only one reason was required for each variance. Several have been given in this answer to aid learning.

169 O'DOUZIE

(a) Descriptions of the standards:

Tutorial note – this is pure knowledge and so a well prepared candidate should have no problem with a requirement like this.

Attainable standards

This type of standard is based on an improved level of activity (higher) and cost (lower).

It is designed to have some allowance for wastage and inefficiencies.

Ideal standards

This type of standard is based on perfect operating conditions.

The standard would allow no inefficiencies, stoppages or losses. Ultimately it is not realistically possible to achieve.

Basic standards

This type of standard has not been revised over a long period of time. It is likely to be the time/cost when the organisation was set up or activity commenced.

The standard will be of limited value as it is often out of date.

It can be useful to see how much the process has improved over a long period of time.

(b) Types of variances arising and impact on employee behaviour.

Tutorial note – this is a mix of knowledge and an opportunity to apply it to the scenario given, discuss the impact on employee behaviour, using examples specific to O'Douzie.

Attainable standards

Variances under this type of standard could be favourable, adverse or there could even be no variance at all.

A significant variance either way would be a sign that it is worth investigating to find out why the process deviated from the target set.

The levels set are deemed achievable and should motivate. It is realistic but challenging and should help O'Douzie get the best out of its workers.

Ideal standards

All the variances are likely to be adverse, no variance would be a sign of perfection, it is virtually impossible to achieve a favourable variance.

The idea is that it helps the organisation strive for machines and employees working at optimal efficiency at all times. This can be demotivating as no matter how efficiently the employees work they are assessed against something that is incredibly unlikely to happen.

It could lead to employees behaving in a dysfunctional manner by trying to achieve the target to the detriment of the company. For example it could be the staff not cooking the scones for long enough to achieve an efficiency target, the result being undercooked scones that would tarnish the O'Douzie reputation either through poor quality or potentially customers becoming ill, or both.

Basic standards

Variances for price, rate or cost will be adverse, as inflation generally leads to cost increases overtime, leading to actual costs being higher than the historic standards they are being compared to. For O'Douzie inflation has led to price increases of around 10% since they set up the organisation.

In terms of impact on behaviour, as with ideal standards this is likely to cause motivation issues for anyone being judged against these basic variances. It could lead to a lack of faith in the budgeting process if it is considered to be out of date.

Basic standards for usage of materials or efficiency type variances are likely to lead to favourable variances as the staff are likely to become better at the process of making scones over a period of time and be able to work more quickly than they originally could. Also any investment in new technology by O'Douzie is likely to lead to equipment that operates more quickly.

In terms of impact on behaviour, at first this may lead to positive motivation as recognition of an improvement, but overtime it is likely to lead to a loss of motivation as the target is too easy to hit and so workers do not need to try to achieve the target.

(c) **Tutorial note** – the requirement asks for calculations to support your recommendations so some of the marks available will be for illustrating your discussion with some calculations.

Ingredients

Flour/butter

Normal wastage should be incorporated into the material standards, for flour the 10% wastage of the input appears to be reasonable and so would give a better standard that was more achievable. The same can be said of the 5% wastage of input for butter.

In terms of calculations, the current figures represent what is required in a batch of scones, therefore it represents 90% (for flour) and 95% (for butter) of the amount that should be put in, to allow for the wastage.

Assuming that the standard costs per kg are reasonable then this would change the flour and butter standard cost per batch as follows:

Flour – £1.08 is 90% of input, so the input figure and cost to use is £1.20 (£1.08/0.90)

Butter – £2.09 is 95% of input, so the input figure and cost to use is £2.20 (£2.09/0.95)

Milk

Milk is already an attainable standard so no adjustment needs to be made.

Dried fruit

The current standard is out of date and the changes in quantity (a reduction of 8%) and price (an increase of 6%) should be reflected in the standard costs card.

£1.25 × 0.92 × 1.06 = £1.219 or £1.22.

Labour

The current standard is out of date and the changes in time taken (a reduction of 14%) and the rate paid (an increase of 10%) should be reflected in the standard cost card.

£5.00 × 0.86 × 1.10 = £4.73

Overall

The total prime cost would now be:

£1.20 + £2.20 + £0.50 + £1.22 + £4.73 = £9.85

ANSWERS TO PRACTICE QUESTIONS: SECTION 2

170 DIXON

To:	Production Director	**Subject:**	Variances
From:	Accounting Technician	**Date:**	XX/XX/20XX

TR13 price variance

The TR13 price variance is likely to be favourable.

This is due to a reduction in price of 10% during the month, resulting in the actual price being lower than the standard price.

The quality of the latest batch of TR13 is higher than expected even though the price is lower, which may lead to a favourable TR13 usage variance.

TR13 usage variance

The TR13 usage variance is likely to be favourable.

The purchase of a higher quality product would usually be expected to result in less wastage, and therefore the actual quantity used would be lower than the standard usage.

The usage and price variances are often linked when a higher priced and therefore higher quality product may reduce wastage costs, however in this case the higher quality is probably due to the advances in production of TR13 and so is unlikely to be linked with the TR13 price variance.

Also employees may be demotivated by the lack of pay rise but the new material usage control policy recently implemented should keep material usage favourable.

Direct labour efficiency variance

The direct labour efficiency variance is likely to be adverse, with each unit taking more hours to manufacture than expected. Efficiency will be affected by the demotivation caused by the suspension of the pay rise.

In addition the cancelled order means that production will be lower by 33% during the month and there is likely to be idle time for employees which will have an adverse effect on the labour efficiency.

Fixed overhead expenditure variance

The fixed overhead expenditure variance is likely to be adverse, due to costs of resetting the machine and the repair of the defective machine. Therefore the actual fixed overheads will be higher than expected.

Fixed overhead volume variance

The fixed overhead volume variance is likely to be adverse because the actual volume produced is likely to be 33% lower than the forecast volume due to the cancellation of the order for 500 units. Therefore overheads are likely to be under-absorbed.

171 GRIPPIT (2)

(a) (i) Standard labour rate per hour

£4,800, budgeted cost/600, budgeted labour hours = **£8 per hour**

(ii) Standard labour hours for actual production

600hours/200 tonnes × 210 tonnes = **630 hours**

(iii) Budgeted cost per tonne of Crumb

£94,800 total budgeted cost/200 tonnes, the budgeted output = **£474**

(iv) Budgeted overhead absorption rate per tonne

£90,000, fixed overheads/200 tonnes, the budgeted output = **£450**

(v) Overheads absorbed into actual production

210 units produced × £450, the absorption rate = **£94,500**

(vi) The total standard cost of actual production

£474 (94,800/200 tonnes), standard cost per tonne × 210 tonnes

Actual output = **£99,540**

(b) (i) Direct labour rate variance

AH × AR

600 hrs × = £5,100

AH × SR

600 hrs × £8 = £4,800

(Standard rate = £4,800/600 hrs = £8)

=> **£300 (A)**

(ii) Direct labour efficiency variance

AH × SR

600 hrs × £8 = £4,800

SH × SR

210 tonnes × 3 × £8 = £5,040

(Standard hours per tonne = 600 hrs/200 tonnes = 3 hrs per tonne)

=> **£240 (F)**

(iii) Fixed overhead expenditure variance

Actual expenditure £95,000

Budgeted expenditure £90,000

=> **£5,000 (A)**

(iv) Fixed overhead volume variance

Budgeted expenditure £90,000

AP × SH × SR

210 tonnes × 3 hrs × £150 per hr = £94,500

£4,500 (F)

(c)

To:	Finance Director	Subject:	Reason for variances
From:	AAT student	Date:	16 June 2008

(i) **Direct labour rate variance**

The variance was £300 adverse. The actual cost of labour was £8.50 compared to the expected cost of £8. The Production Director has stated that a 25p per hour pay rise was awarded after the standard had been set, this therefore accounts for half of the variance. The other half of the variance must have been caused by some other reason such as overtime.

(ii) **Direct labour efficiency variance**

The variance was £240 favourable. The software upgrade is said to reduce the standard time to 2.7 hours per tonne, the actual labour time was 2.86 hours per tonne (actual hours of 600/ actual output of 210). Therefore the expected efficiency reduction was not achieved. The upgrade has improved efficiency but perhaps it will take time for the full 10% effect to be realised. There may be initial teething problems.

(iii) **Fixed overhead expenditure variance**

The variance was £5,000 adverse. The IT upgrade cost £120,000 for a 2-year licence which equates to £5,000 per month. Therefore the £5,000 expenditure variance is due to this upgrade.

(iv) **Fixed overhead volume variance**

This variance was £4,500 favourable. The expected volume of output was 200 tonnes, while the actual output was 210 tonnes. This could be due to the software upgrade improving labour efficiency which in turn produced more output per hour and hence increased the volume.

AAT: APPLIED MANAGEMENT ACCOUNTING

172 VARIANCE ETHICS

Ethical issues

The bonus structure at Variance Ltd could lead to problems with the production manager's integrity and objectivity.

The objectivity issue is caused by the self interest in the bonus, that the manager may make decision to ensure favourable labour variances to the detriment of Variance Ltd as a whole.

Integrity issues could be around the way he/she manages the employees, the materials usage variance does not impact the bonus so he/she could unfairly treat staff who are considerate of material waste to encourage speed.

Goal congruence issues

In terms of goal congruence, the ultimate aim should be the long term success of Variance Ltd.

The way the bonus is currently structured the manager will not be worried about the material price variance, the £6,000 adverse variance, could be an overspend on materials to get superior quality for the workers so they can do their work quicker.

Similarly, the £10,000 adverse materials usage variance could be because the manager encourages speed and a favourable labour efficiency variance over good use of the quality materials purchased.

173 WOODEN SPOON

(a)

To:	Manager	Subject:	Standard setting at Wooden Spoon
From:	Accounting Technician	Date:	24/3/20X7

(i) **Types of standard**

Wood and treatment – the volumes appear to be based on a basic standard as they have remained unchanged since the company began.

There have been changes in design over the years which have not been reflected in the standard.

The standard appears to be too easy to achieve.

Labour – It appears the labour time is based on an ideal standard as it is based on no wastage, but the rate is based on a basic standard.

It appears unlikely that anyone could achieve this standard.

(ii) **Behavioural implications**

Note – as you've been asked to evaluate try to include positive and negatives for each standard used.

Wood and treatment

The positive here is that a comparison to the standard will give an indication as to how much material efficiency has improved over the years at Wooden Spoon, but the management are already aware of this so it is not that meaningful.

The negative is that given the standard is far too easy to achieve now, the workers will not have anything to strive for, as they could be inefficient based on current expectations and still post a favourable variance against this standard.

It is out of date and needs to be revised.

Labour

The positive of an ideal standard is that it could encourage workers to improve as they aim to achieve the target set.

The negative and more likely response in a situation like this, where on average 4% of time is non-productive during a year, is that a worker will feel that the standard time is unachievable and become demotivated.

The labour efficiency variance will have been adverse every single year that wooden spoon have used this standard and they could well have lost good employees who felt criticised in spite of working hard.

The labour rate variance would suffer similar issues to the materials usage based on the basic standard, which will compensate somewhat for the adverse labour efficiency variance when consulting the total variance.

Overall – the standards being used currently are not really suitable and need to be revised.

(iii) **Revised standards and justification**

Wood and treatment

They can produce 15% more spoons per batch than originally expected, so £3.45 will make 1.15 wooden spoons.

So the cost for one wooden spoon would now be: £3.45/1.15 = £3.00

Treatment: £0.46/1.15 = £0.40

Labour

An attainable standard would be more motivating and would include an allowance for non-productive time. If on average last year 4% of time was non-productive then it would be reasonable to assume that the productive time makes up 96% of the time allowed meaning that the new standard labour cost would be:

£4.80 × 100/96 = £5.00

This then needs to be adjusted for the higher wages:

£5.00 × 1.1 = £5.50

Overall prime cost would now be: 3.00 + 0.40 + 5.50 + 2.50 = £11.40

(assuming variable overhead varies with labour time: 2.40 × 100/96 = 2.50)

AAT: APPLIED MANAGEMENT ACCOUNTING

(b) **Goal Congruence**

The issue highlights the problem with too much focus on financial measures.

Manager v business – the manager's decision while helping them achieve their bonus could have an adverse impact on the overall business should the delayed maintenance result in any machinery malfunction stopping production or even injuring an employee.

Short v long term – the manager is making a decision that will help hit a short term financial target, but through stoppages/delays could harm the long term survival of the business by failing to fulfil an order.

Ethics

The bonus creates a self-interest threat for the manager, which could impact their objectivity. The manager stands to benefit personally from actions they take which could have a detrimental impact on the business overall and potentially the health of the people working there.

174 FOODRINK

(a) (i) Standard price of materials per kilogram

£5,400/450 = **£12 per kg**

(ii) Standard usage of materials for actual production

9,900 × (450/9,000) = **495 kgs**

(iii) Standard labour rate per hour

4,500/300 = **£15**

(iv) Standard labour hours for actual production

9,900 × (300/9,000) = **330 hours**

(v) Budgeted overhead absorption rate per unit

18,000/9,000 = **£2**

(vi) Overheads absorbed into actual production

9,900 × £2 = **£19,800**

(b) (i) Direct material price variance

AQ × AP

5,014 ×   = £6,534

AQ × SP

594 × £12 = £7,128

= **£594 (F)**

(ii) Direct material usage variance

AQ × SP

5,014 × £12 = £7,128

SQ × SP

9,900 × (450/9,000) × £12 = £5,940

= **£1,188 (A)**

(iii) Direct labour rate variance

AH × AR

325 ×   = £4,225

AH × SR

325 × £15 = £4,875

= **£650 (F)**

(iv) Direct labour efficiency variance

AH × SR

325 × £15 = £4,875

SH × SR

9,900 × 300/9,000 × £15 = £4,950

= **£75 (F)**

(v) Fixed overhead expenditure variance

Actual expenditure £19,000

Budgeted expenditure £18,000

= **£1,000 A**

(vi) Fixed overhead volume variance

Budgeted expenditure £18,000

AP × SR

9,900 × (18,000/9,000) = £19,800

= **£1,800 (F)**

OPERATIONAL CONTROL

IMPACT OF TECHNOLOGY

175 CLOUD

A, B and C

Cloud technology allows pay as you go computing charged based on what a company actually needs and is therefore cost efficient.

Cloud computing allows frequent upgrades making it scalable.

Cloud computing supports remote working increasing flexibility

176 REMOTE SERVERS

A

This describes the basic idea of cloud computing.

177 RISE OF THE MACHINES

C

This is a description of artificial intelligence.

178 RELIABILITY

D

By definition. Veracity considers the reliability of the data being received.

179 UNDERSTANDABLE

D

Improving the layout and ease of understanding is one of the main benefits of effective data visualisation.

180 VISUALISATION

A

The graphic produced will only be as accurate as the original data. Visualisation does not improve this accuracy

181 BIG DATA

B

The new technology is driving an expansion beyond sample-based testing to include analysis of entire populations of audit-relevant data, using intelligent analytics to deliver a higher quality of audit evidence and more relevant business insights.

Whilst statement D is correct, it has more relevance to the management accounting function than internal audit.

Statements A and C are false.

182 STATEMENTS

B, C and E

Option A is incorrect in that big data does not refer to any specific financial amount. Option D is also incorrect. Big data can indeed come from many sources, but this is too narrow a definition. Big data refers to the large volume of data, the many sources of data and the many types of data.

ANSWERS TO PRACTICE QUESTIONS: SECTION 2

ACTIVITY BASED COSTING

183 CAT

Machine hour absorption rate $= \dfrac{£10,430+£5,250+£3,600+£2,100+£4,620}{(120\times4)+(100\times3)+(80\times2)+(120\times3)}$

$= \dfrac{26,000}{1,300} = £20\text{/machine hour}$

The total costs for each product are:

	A	B	C	D
	£	£	£	£
Direct materials	40	50	30	60
Direct labour	28	21	14	21
Production overhead	80	60	40	60
Per unit	148	131	84	141
Total	17,760	13,100	6,720	16,920

Cost driver rates

Machine dept costs = 10,430/1,300 = (m/c hour basis)	£8.023/hr
Set up costs = 5,250/21 =	£250/run
Stores receiving = 3,600/80 =	£45/requisition
Inspection/quality control = 2,100/21 =	£100/run
Material handling despatch = 4,620/42 =	£110/order

Total costs	A	B	C	D
	£	£	£	£
Direct materials	4,800	5,000	2,400	7,200
Direct labour	3,360	2,100	1,120	2,520
Machine dept costs	3,851	2,407	1,284	2,888
Set up costs	1,500	1,250	1,000	1,500
Stores receiving	900	900	900	900
Inspection/quality control	600	500	400	600
Materials handling despatch	1,320	1,100	880	1,320
	16,331	13,257	7,984	16,928

KAPLAN PUBLISHING

184 SMASH-HIT

Cost centre	Machining	Finishing	Packing
Production overhead	£160,000	£65,000	£35,000
Direct labour hours	25,000	12,500	6,500
Recovery rate per labour hour	£6.40	£5.20	£5.38

Production cost of one unit of 'Heman 3'

	£
Direct labour 2.7 hours × £7/hour	18.90
Direct material	38.00
Production overhead	
Machining 1.5 hrs × £6.40/hr	9.60
Finishing 1.0 hrs × £5.20/hr	5.20
Packing 0.2 hrs × £5.38/hr	1.08
Production cost	72.78

Selling price of one unit of 'Heman 3'

	£
Production cost	72.78
Add: 15% for selling, admin and distribution	10.92
	83.70
Add: 10% to cover profit	8.37
Selling price	92.07

Cost driver rates

Activity	Cost pool	Cost driver volume	Cost driver rate
Process set up	£80,000	200 set-ups	£400 per set up
Material procurement	£20,000	100 purchase orders	£200 per order
Maintenance	£25,000	20 maintenance plans	£1,250 per maintenance plan
Material handing	£50,000	4,000 material movements	£12.50 per material movement
Quality control	£45,000	500 inspections	£90 per inspection
Order processing	£40,000	600 customers	£66.67 per customer

Overhead chargeable to batch of 500 units of 'Heman 3'

	£
6 set ups × £400 per set up	2,400
6 purchase orders × £200 per order	1,200
2 maintenance plans × £1,250 per plan	2,500
150 material movements × £12.50 per material movement	1,875
75 inspections × £90 per inspection	6,750
10 sales customers × £66.67 per customer	667
	15,392

Tutorial note

At this point it is useful to calculate the overhead cost per unit:

$15,392 / 750 = £20.52$)

Production cost of one unit of Herman 3	£
Direct labour 2.7 hours × £7	18.90
Direct material	38.00
Production and other overhead	20.52
Production cost	77.42

KAPLAN PUBLISHING

185 ABC LTD

(a) OAR = (£80,000 + £40,000)/((5 × 1000) + (7 × 5000)) = £120,000/40,000hrs = £3/hr

DEF = £3 × 5,000 = £15,000

GHI = £3 × 35,000 = £105,000

	DEF (£)	GHI (£)
Fixed overheads	15,000	105,000

(b) Cost driver rates:

Special parts = £40,000/400 = £100 per part;

machine set ups = £80,000/200 = £400 per set up

DEF: special parts = £100 × 300 = £30,000; machine set ups = £400 × 150 = £60,000

GHI: special parts = £100 × 100 = £10,000; machine set ups = £400 × 50 = £20,000

	£	DEF (£)	GHI (£)
Cost driver rate – special parts handling	100		
Cost driver rate – machine set ups	400		
Total special parts		30,000	10,000
Total machine set ups		60,000	20,000

(c) **DEF**

Absorption cost = £15,000/1,000 = £15 per unit; Unit cost = £8 + £25 + £15 = £48

ABC cost = £90,000/1,000 = £90 per unit; Unit cost = £8 + £25 + £90 = £123 per unit

GHI

Absorption cost = £105,000/5,000 = £21 per unit; Unit cost = £12 + £35 + £21 = £68

ABC cost = £30,000/5,000 = £6 per unit; Unit cost = £12 + £35 + £6 = £53 per unit

	DEF	GHI
Total unit cost – Absorption costing	48.00	68.00
Total unit cost – ABC	123.00	53.00

(d) Benefits from using technology for operational control processes

> One of the most common benefits of using technology in any form is that it can increase the speed at which a task is completed, this would mean that information is with decision makers more quickly and allow them to action any insights more quickly.
>
> Technology can also completely replace human involvement in time consuming repetitive processes, this can free up employee and management time to focus on critical areas, thus improving the control of these critical areas.
>
> Considering ABC Ltd and their transition to ABC costing, there is a lot more detail involved in the data required for ABC and using appropriate technology could speed up the production and improve the accuracy of this data, thus could mean more accurate and quicker calculation of cost driver rates.

186 FOUR LIONS LTD

(a) OAR = (£180,000 + £140,000)/((3 × 20,000) + (4 × 10,000)) = £3.20/hr

Lion = £3.20 × 60,000 = £192,000

Pride = £3.20 × 40,000 = £128,000

	Lion (£)	Pride (£)
Fixed overheads	192,000	128,000

(b) Cost driver rates:

Material movements = £180,000/2500 = £72 per movement; quality control = £140,000/100 = £1,400 per quality inspection

Lion: material movements = £72 × 2,000 = £144,000; quality control = £1,400 × 15 = £21,000

Pride: material movements = £72 × 500 = £36,000; quality control = £1,400 × 85 = £119,000

	£	Lion (£)	Pride (£)
Cost driver rate – material movements	72		
Cost driver rate – quality control	1,400		
Total material movements		144,000	36,000
Total quality control		21,000	119,000

(c) **Lion**

Absorption cost per unit = £192,000/20,000 = £9.60; Unit cost = 12 + 16 + 9.60 = 37.60

ABC cost per unit = £165,000/20,000 = £8.25; Unit cost = 12 + 16 + 8.25 = 36.25

Pride

Absorption cost per unit = £128,000/10,000 = £12.80; Unit cost = 20 + 24 + 12.80 = 56.80

ABC cost per unit = £155,000/10,000 = £15.50; Unit cost = 20 + 24 + 15.50 = 59.50

AAT: APPLIED MANAGEMENT ACCOUNTING

	Lion	Pride
Total unit cost – Absorption costing	37.60	56.80
Total unit cost – ABC	36.25	59.50

(d)

> Activity Based Costing works on the premise that the volume of activities create costs and not the volume of production, so this provides a more accurate cost per unit
>
> This more accurate cost per unit can lead to better information about pricing, sales strategy and performance management
>
> ABC should provide Four Lions better insight into what causes (drives) overhead costs.
>
> Overhead costs can be a significant proportion of total costs, and the management of Four Lions will be able to understand the drivers of overhead costs allowing them to manage the business properly.
>
> ABC can be applied to all overhead costs, not just production overheads, so it could lead to savings elsewhere for Four Lions.
>
> Research, production and sales effort at Four Lions can be directed towards those products and services which ABC has identified as offering the highest sales margins.

187 RVI

(a) OAR = (£300,000 + £500,000)/((2 × 1,000) + (1.5 × 2,000)) = £160 per surgeon hour

A = £160 × 2,000 hrs = £320,000; B = £160 × 3,000 hrs = £480,000

	A (£)	B (£)
Fixed overheads	320,000	480,000

(b) Cost driver rates:

Nursing costs = £300,000/6,000hrs = £50 per hour

Remedial costs = £500,000/5,000 visit = £100 per visit

A: nursing costs = £50 × 2,000 = £100,000; remedial costs = £100 × 2,000 = £200,000

B: nursing costs = £50 × 4,000 = £200,000; remedial costs = £100 × 3,000 = £300,000

	£	A (£)	B (£)
Cost driver rate – nurse costs	50		
Cost driver rate – remedial costs	100		
Total nursing costs		100,000	200,000
Total remedial costs		200,000	300,000

(c) **A:**

Absorption cost per procedure = £320,000/1,000 = £320; Procedure cost = £275 + £320 = £595

ABC cost per unit = £300,000/1,000 = £300; Procedure cost = £275 + £300 = £575

B:

Absorption cost per procedure = 480,000/2,000 = £240; Procedure cost = £235 + £240 = 475

ABC cost per unit = £500,000/2,000 = £250; Procedure cost = £235 + £250 = £485

	A	B
Total procedure cost – Absorption costing	595	475
Total procedure cost – ABC	575	485

(d)

> RVI must consider if the overhead costs are primarily volume related or if the overhead is a small proportion of the overall cost, if it is ABC will be of limited benefit.
>
> RVI could have difficulty allocating all overhead costs to specific activities.
>
> RVI may find that in some cases the choice of both activities and cost drivers might be inappropriate.
>
> RVI will have to take time to train staff and management how the costing exercise works.
>
> The benefits obtained from ABC might not justify the costs.

188 ABC STATEMENTS (I)

A cost **driver** is any factor that causes a change in the cost of an activity

VPS manufactures touch screens, the most likely cost driver for the cost pool called 'quality control' is number of **inspections**.

189 ABC STATEMENTS (II)

A cost **pool** is an activity which consumes resources and for which overhead costs are identified and allocated.

F supplies pharmaceutical drugs, the most likely cost driver for the cost pool 'invoice processing costs' is the number of **invoices processed**.

AAT: APPLIED MANAGEMENT ACCOUNTING

LIFE CYCLE COSTING

190 NPV

Year	0	1	2	3	4
Cash flow	(40,000)	15,200	14,900	13,585	11,255
DF	1.000	0.909	0.826	0.751	0.683
PV	(40,000)	13,817	12,307	10,202	7,687
				NPV	£4,013

The proposal **SHOULD** go ahead.

191 DAFFY

Year	0	1	2	3	4	5
Cash flow	(£120,000)	(£8,000)	(£8,000)	(£8,000)	(£8,000)	£12,000
DF	1.000	0.909	0.826	0.751	0.683	0.621
PV	(£120,000)	(£7,272)	(£6,608)	(£6,008)	(£5,464)	£7,452
NPV	(£137,900)					

Year	0	1	2	3	4
Lease costs	(£25,000)	(£25,000)	(£25,000)	(£25,000)	(£25,000)
DF	1.000	0.909	0.826	0.751	0.683
PV	(£25,000)	(£22,725)	(£20,650)	(£18,775)	(£17,075)
NPV	(£104,225)				

Based on the calculations it is best to LEASE the machines. This saves £33,675.

192 LIFECYCLE COSTING

Year	0	1	2	3	4
Cash flow	(30,000)	(2,500)	(2,500)	(2,500)	3,000
DF at 5%	1.000	0.952	0.907	0.864	0.823
Present value	(30,000)	(2,380)	(2,268)	(2,160)	2,469
NPV	(34,339)				

Year	0	1	2	3	4
Cash flow	(8,500)	(8,500)	(8,500)	(8,500)	–
DF at 5%	1.000	0.952	0.907	0.864	0.823
Present value	(8,500)	(8,092)	(7,710)	(7,344)	–
NPV	(31,646)				

Based on the above calculations, it would be best to **LEASE** the machine, because it saves **£2,693** (£34,339 – £31,646).

ANSWERS TO PRACTICE QUESTIONS: SECTION 2

193 HOULTER

Year	0	1	2	3	4	5
Cash flow ('000)	(£300)	(£30)	(£30)	(£30)	(£30)	£20
DF	1.000	0.952	0.907	0.864	0.823	0.784
PV	(£300)	(£28.56)	(£27.21)	(£25.92)	(£24.69)	£15.68
NPV (£000)	(£390.70)					

Year	1	2	3	4	5
Labour savings in '000 (3 × 5,000 × £7 per year)	£105	£105	£105	£105	£105
DF	0.952	0.907	0.864	0.823	0.784
PV (£000)	£99.960	£95.235	£90.720	£86.415	£82.320
NPV (£000)	£454.650				

Investing in the new machine saves **£63,950** and is therefore financially beneficial.

194 YANKEE (1)

Year	0	1	2	3	4	5
Cash flow	(£1,500,000)	(£150,000)	(£150,000)	(£150,000)	(£150,000)	£100,000
DF	1.000	0.909	0.826	0.751	0.683	0.621
PV	(£1,500,000)	(£136,350)	(£123,900)	(£112,650)	(£102,450)	£62,100
NPV	(£1,913,250)					

Year	0	1	2	3	4
Lease costs	(£450,000)	(£450,000)	(£450,000)	(£450,000)	(£450,000)
DF	1.000	0.909	0.826	0.751	0.683
PV	(£450,000)	(£409,050)	(£371,700)	(£337,950)	(£307,350)
NPV	(£1,876,050)				

Based on the calculations it is best to **LEASE** the machine, to save **£37,200**.

195 BUDGE

£000

Year	0	1	2	3	4	5
Cash flow	(£600)	(£45)	(£45)	(£45)	(£45)	£175
DF	1.000	0.909	0.826	0.751	0.683	0.621
PV	(£600)	(£41)	(£37)	(£34)	(£31)	£109
NPV	(£634)					

AAT: APPLIED MANAGEMENT ACCOUNTING

£000

Year	0	1	2	3	4
Lease costs	(£135)	(£135)	(£135)	(£135)	(£135)
DF	1.000	0.909	0.826	0.751	0.683
PV	(£135)	(£123)	(£112)	(£101)	(£92)
NPV	(£563)				

Based on the calculations it is best to **LEASE** the machine because it saves **£71,000**.

196 LIFE CYCLE STATEMENTS (I)

Lifecycle costing is a concept which traces all costs to a product over its complete lifecycle, from design through to **cessation**.

One of the benefits that adopting lifecycle costing could bring is to improve decision-making and **cost** control.

197 LIFE CYCLE STATEMENTS (II)

Life cycle costing recognises that for many products there are significant costs committed by decisions in the **early** stages of its lifecycle.

One of the benefits of life cycle costing is the visibility of all costs is increased, rather than just costs relating to one period. This facilitates better **decision-making**.

198 ABITFIT CO

(a) The total life cycle cost is all the costs across the products life added together

	£
Research and development costs	250,000
Marketing costs = 500,000 + 1,000,000 + 250,000	1,750,000
Administration costs = 150,000 + 300,000 + 600,000	1,050,000
Total variable production cost = (£55 × 150,000) + (£52 × 250,000)	21,250,000
Fixed production cost = 600,000 + 900,000	1,500,000
Total variable sales and distribution cost = (£10 × 150,000) + (£12 × 250,000)	4,500,000
Fixed sales and distribution costs	400,000
Total costs	30,700,000

The life cycle cost per unit is then the total cost divided by the total number of units:

Life cycle cost per unit = £30,700,000/400,000 = £76.75

(b) Changing costs throughout the life of a product

> **Intro**
>
> At this stage the R&D cost (to create the product) and marketing (to create awareness of the product) will be the most significant. Looking at Abitfit in Yr1 almost 90% of the costs are from these two areas.
>
> **Growth**
>
> Marketing expense is still vital at this stage, but production costs will also be increasing in significance. Looking at Abitfit marketing costs doubled in the second year.

ANSWERS TO PRACTICE QUESTIONS: SECTION 2

> **Maturity**
>
> Here production costs will be the most significant, although there will be economies of scale and learning effects that will reduce the costs. Looking at Abitfit the production cost per unit falls from £55 per unit to £52 per unit.
>
> **Decline**
>
> As sales and production start to fall a company could lose some of the economies of scale at this stage. There are likely to costs associated with decommissioning/clean up at the end of the products life. Looking at Abitfit the increase in administration costs could be associated with the decommissioning/clean-up.

(c) Data visualisation

> Data visualisation is a technique to assist with communication of large or complex data or information.
>
> **Decision making ability**
>
> Abitfit operate in technologically advanced market that is likely to change rapidly and being able to understand market related data will help the decision making process
>
> **Understanding**
>
> At the heart of data visualisation is the idea of being able to display and make sense of data quickly and easily. Some of the concepts behind life cycle costing can be difficult and displaying the data in a simple form could assist with the communication.
>
> **Improving performance**
>
> As Abitfit learns from the various products that it makes, it will be able to improve the forecasts about costs, sales and length of products life cycles so it will be able to produce more accurate life cycle cost analysis.

199 LCC PLC

(a) The total life cycle cost is all the costs across the products life added together

	£
Research and development costs	500,000
Marketing and administration costs = 450,000 + 750,000 + 800,000 + 350,000	2,350,000
Total variable production cost = (£28 × 200,000) + (£25 × 250,000) + (£20 × 100,000)	13,850,000
Fixed production cost = 200,000 + 300,000 + 400,000	900,000
Total variable sales and distribution cost = (£18 × 200,000) + (£16 × 250,000) + (£18 × 100,000)	9,400,000
Fixed sales and distribution costs	450,000
Total costs	27,450,000

The life cycle cost per unit is then the total cost divided by the total number of units:

Life cycle cost per unit = £27,450,000/550,000 = 49.91

(b)

> **Production costs**
>
> One of the key areas likely to experience this change is the production cost. During the growth phase production costs are likely to be variable and increase in line with production, but in the maturity phase due to economies of scale like bulk buying and the learning effect the production costs may remain fairly constant regardless of the production levels.
>
> Then moving into decline they may well revert back to variable as economies of scale are lost.

(c)

> Life cycle costing is the accumulation of costs throughout a products life, from inception to abandonment. It can often highlight costs that have previously been overlooked and also can lead to greater focus on costs in the design phase.
>
> This can aid ethical considerations by highlighting the costs associated with the clean-up/decommissioning of a product or site that could lead to more environmentally friendly practices throughout the life of the product reducing the final clean-up cost.
>
> The focus of cost in the design phase could also have benefits as companies give careful consideration to the resources or amount of resources required for a product and features/processes that consume significant resources/costs but add little value could be removed.

TARGET COSTING

200 TARGET COSTING

	£
Selling price	10
Profit margin at 20%	(2)
Total costs	8
Fixed costs	(1.50)
Material cost	(2)
Maximum labour cost	4.50
Target cost per hour (£4.50/4.5 hours)	1

Extra labour cost = £0.20 × 4.5 hours = £0.90

New total cost = £2 + £4.50 + £0.90 + £1.50 = £8.90

Profit = £10 − £8.90 = £1.10

Profit margin = 11%

If labour cost increases by £0.90, material costs will need to fall by £0.90, for the margin to remain the same.

Therefore material costs will need to fall by £0.90/£2 = 45%

ANSWERS TO PRACTICE QUESTIONS: SECTION 2

201 HOLDER

	£
Sales price per unit	£50.00
Profit margin (20% of sales)	£10.00
Total costs	£40.00
Fixed cost per unit	£15.50
Labour cost per unit	£4.00
Maximum material cost per unit	£20.50
Target cost per kilogram	£102.50

The discount should **ACCEPTED** because the £120 reduces to **£102** which is **BELOW** the target cost.

The minimum percentage discount needed to achieve the target cost is **14.6%**.

202 AKEA

	£
Sales price per sofa	1,500
Profit margin @ 30%	(450)
Total costs	1,050
Fixed cost per sofa	(140)
Labour cost per sofa 8 hrs × £25	(200)
Wooden frame and stuffing material	(110)
Maximum leather cost per sofa	600
Target cost per square metre (£600/8m)	75

Akea's leather supplier quotes a list price of £100 per square metre for the grade of leather Akea needs. However, Akea has managed to negotiate a discount of 15% on this price. The discount should be **REJECTED** because the £100 reduces to **£85** which is **ABOVE** the target cost.

The minimum percentage discount needed to achieve the target cost is **25%** (£25/£100)

203 SHORTY

	£
Sales price per unit	150.00
Profit margin	(37.50)
Total costs	112.50
Fixed cost per unit	(40.00)
Labour cost per unit	(40.00)
Maximum rubber cost per unit	32.50
Target cost per kg	6.50

The discount should be REJECTED because the £10 reduces to £7.50 which is ABOVE the target cost.

The minimum percentage discount needed to achieve the target cost is **35%** (£3.50/£10)

204 LONG

	£
Sales price per unit	250.00
Profit margin	(87.50)
Total costs	162.50
Fixed cost per unit	(20.00)
Material cost per unit	(110.00)
Maximum labour cost per unit	32.50
Target cost per labour hour	16.25

The discount should be REJECTED because the £20 reduces to £17 which is ABOVE the target cost.

The minimum percentage discount needed to achieve the target cost is **18.75%** (£3.75/£20)

205 GRIPPIT (1)

	£
Selling price	25.00
Profit margin at 30%	(7.50)
Target cost	17.50

206 SHOCK

	£
Selling price	95
Profit margin at 20%	(19)
Target cost	76

207 TRICKY (II)

	£
Selling price	205.00
Profit margin at 10%	(20.50)
Target cost	184.50

ANSWERS TO PRACTICE QUESTIONS: **SECTION 2**

208 TC ETHICS

To:	TC Colleague	**Subject:**	Ethics and Target Costing
From:	AAT Student	**Date:**	Today

Labour

Reducing the skill level of labour used is fine from a product cost point of view; a key consideration is how the current grade of labour will be used in future. If they are to be made redundant, that could not only cost the company more in the short term, but also have a detrimental effect on the long term success of the workforce.

Then there is the impact on the members of staff made redundant, which could impact the morale of those that remain, while the job losses could have an adverse impact on the local community.

Another consideration is that the product should not lose any value to the customer, value analysis is about reducing cost without reducing the value of the product to the consumer.

If TC are putting pressure on the managers, or awarding a bonus linked to achieving the target cost then their objectivity may be compromised and make a decision which is not goal congruent with the long term company aims.

Material

A consideration is confidentiality, should TC disclose to the public the change in materials. The material could be unethically sourced. Another issue would be around the quality of the material and the impact on the final product. As with the labour, if the end product is inferior then the customer should be informed, if there is no adverse impact on the product or the health of the consumer from using the product then TC do not need to disclose it to the customer.

209 TARGET COSTING STATEMENTS (I)

To calculate the target cost, subtract the **target profit** from the target price.

If there is a cost gap, attempts will be made to close the gap. Techniques such as value engineering and value **analysis** may be used to help close the gap.

210 TARGET COSTING STATEMENTS (II)

The cost gap is the difference between the **target cost** and the estimated product cost per unit.

Target costing works the opposite to **traditional pricing** techniques in that it starts by setting a competitive selling price first.

211 FORMAT

	Sales price £4	Sales price £5
Target total production cost per unit	£4 × 80% = £3.20	£5 × 80% = £4.00
Target fixed production cost per unit	£3.20 – £1.20 = £2.00	£4.00 – £1.30 = £2.70
Total target fixed production cost	£2.00 × 50,000 = £100,000	£2.70 × 45,000 = £121,500

Format should set the price at £5 to achieve the target profit margin.

212 MR WYNN

(a)

	Workings	£
Profit per unit	45% × 500 =	225
Target cost per unit	500 – 225 =	275

(b)

	Workings	£
Bought in material	(£100 × 25% × 90%) + (£100 × 75% × 40%)	52.50
Direct labour	W1	15.63
Machining costs	2 × 20 = 40	40.00
Quality costs	((8,000 × 5%) × 40)/8,000	2.00
Remedial work	((8,000 × 15%) × £40)/8,000	6.00
Initial design costs	400,000/8,000	50.00
Sales and Marketing costs	£1,000,000/8,000	125.00
Estimated lifetime cost per unit		291.13

W1

First 1,000:

40/60hrs × 1,000 units @ £30 per hour = £20,000

Rest: 8,000 – 1,000 = 7,000 units

30/60hrs × 7,000 units @ £30 per hour = £105,000

Labour cost = 20,000 + 105,000 = £125,000

(c) There is a cost gap of **£16.13** per unit as it stands.

(d) Value engineering

Material

Mr Wynn could see if he can negotiate discounts on the lower grade materials as well as the luxury materials.

Labour

Mr Wynn could look into training the workers to try to speed up the familiarisation or to decrease the time below the 30 minutes.

Machine costs

Mr Wynn should look into different machines that could do the work faster than the 2 hours it currently takes, or cheaper than the current cost of £20 per hour.

Quality costs

The additional training could reduce the need for inspections below the current 5% level.

Remedial work

Training could also help reduce the amount of remedial work required as the workers may become more proficient with the materials/processes used.

Sales and marketing

Mr Wynn could look into alternative marketing tools or distribution networks that could reduce the cost below current expectation of £1 million for the 2 year period.

(e) Four benefits of data analytics

Cost control

The production of a wedding dress and associated accessories can be a complex process and analysis of cost data can help control throughout the dress manufacture through improved information.

Inventory management

Mr Wynn could be able to make more accurate purchasing decisions based on the most popular fabrics and materials reducing the need to stock a variety of materials, saving both space and reducing costs.

Sales analysis

Mr Wynn should be able to look into the different styles and designs that are the most popular at a particular time, allowing him to make better design decisions.

Predictive analysis

Over time, Mr Wynn may be able to identify sales patterns that develop when one fashion or trend ends and a new one starts. This may allow him to anticipate the next popular styles and designs before they are widely known.

Note: Other valid points can gain credit as long as they are specific to Mr Wynn's business and are explained sufficiently.

213 TOPCAT

(a)

		£
Total anticipated sales revenue	30,000 × 25	750,000.00
Target total net profit	750,000 × 20%	150,000.00
Target total costs	750,000 – 150,000	600,000.00
Target cost per unit	600,000/30,000	20.00

(b)

		£
Total lifecycle costs	150 + 35 + 300 + 100 + 75 =	660,000.00
Lifecycle cost per unit	660,000/30,000	22.00

If a margin of 20% is required, the new product **should not be** introduced.

(c)

		£
Reduced selling price per unit	25 – 0.50	24.50
Target net profit per unit	24.50 × 20%	4.90
Target total cost per unit	24.50 × 80%	19.60
Expected variable manufacturing cost per unit	£300,000/30,000 units	10.00
Target fixed costs per unit	19.60 – 10	9.60

To the nearest whole unit, the required sales volume is **37,500** units.

Total life cycle fixed costs = 150,000 + 35,000 + 100,000 + 75,000 = £360,000

Units required to produce to have a fixed cost per unit of 9.60 = 360,000/9.60 = 37,500 units

(d)

> **Value engineering**
>
> Value engineering is a philosophy of designing products which meet customer needs at the lowest cost while assuring the required standard of quality and reliability.
>
> **Value analysis**
>
> Value analysis relates to existing products. A company may sell a product with a feature that they discover adds no value to the customer, but incurs cost to include in the product. Using value analysis they would remove this feature, thus saving money, without harming the value of the product to the customer.
>
> **Ethics**
>
> Focus on reducing cost while good for the profitability of the company, careful thought must be given to maintaining the value of the end product to the customer. The whole point of target costing is that costs are reduced without reducing the performance of the product, it certainly should not compromise the safety of the workers or the consumers. Consideration must be given to suppliers too, pushing the supplier to provide components at a cheaper price could lead to poor working conditions at the supplier or even put them out of business.

214 CELSIUS

	Sales price £22	Sales price £20
Target total production cost per unit	£22 × 75% = £16.50	£20 × 75% = £15
Target fixed production cost per unit	£16.50 – £10.50 = £6.00	£15 – £9.20 = £5.80
Total target fixed production cost	£6.00 × 18,000 = £108,000	£5.80 × 20,000 = £116,000

Celsius should set the price at £20 to achieve the target profit margin.

SHORT TERM DECISION MAKING TECHNIQUES

RELEVANT COSTING

215 MATERIAL D

The material is in regular use by the organisation and so would be replaced if it is used on the special order. The material is readily available at a price of £3.24 per kg.

Therefore the relevant cost of the material is 1,250 kgs × £3.24 = **£4,050**

216 H LTD

Replacement material cost saved (4 kg @ £5.00)	£20.00
Less further processing cost (£0.75 × 5 kg)	£3.75
Value of M in current use, for each unit made	£16.25

Therefore opportunity cost of using M on the job being tendered for =

£16.25/5 kg = **£3.25 per kg**.

217 LABOUR

Labour is in short supply so there is an opportunity cost. The contribution from Contract Z will still be earned but will be delayed. The relevant cost is therefore the wages earned plus the penalty fee.

(£15 × 100) + (£1,000) = **£2,500**

AAT: APPLIED MANAGEMENT ACCOUNTING

218 NEW CONTRACT

D

A bad debt provision is an accounting entry and is not a cash flow. It is therefore not relevant for decision making.

The other elements would all be relevant to the decision.

219 K LTD

The relevant cost of the 2,000 kg of material J to be included in the quotation is £16,000

Since material J is in regular use and is readily available in the market, its relevant cost is the replacement price of £8/kg.

So 2,000 kgs × £8/kg = £16,000

220 CONSULTANT

It is cheaper to hire the external consultant for £4,500 rather than pay the £5,000 bonus to the existing junior consultant. The consultant's salary is not a relevant cost as the consultant will still be paid even if the project does not proceed.

The relevant cost to be used in preparing the quotation is: £4,500.

221 RELEVANT COST

D

Opportunity costs are concerned with identifying the value of any benefit forgone as the result of choosing one course of action in preference to another. They will always be relevant for decision making purposes.

222 LIQUID

The relevant cost of using the material is £460

As the material is not regularly used in the business the inventory should be used. This will be valued at the forgone revenue of £4 per litre, giving a value for the inventory of: 40 litres × £4 = £160.

The remaining material needs to be purchased at a cost of £15 per litres, giving a value of: (60 litres − 40 litres) × £15 = £300.

This give a total relevant cost = £160 + £300 = £460.

223 SKILLED LABOUR

The relevant cost of labour is £900

Existing staff are fully employed and cannot be used. The cost of the labour will be the cost of the agency work = 20 × £45 = £900

ANSWERS TO PRACTICE QUESTIONS: SECTION 2

224 NORTH EAST CONTRACT

		North-east contract
		£
Materials:		
(1)	In inventory at original cost, Material X	19,440
(2)	In inventory at original cost, Material Y	60,800
(3)	Not yet ordered – current cost, Material X	60,000
(4)	Labour – hired locally	86,000
(5)	Site management	34,000
(6)	Staff accommodation and travel for site management	6,800
(7)	Plant on site – depreciation	0
(8)	Interest on capital, 8%	0
Total local contract costs		267,040
(9)	Headquarters costs allocated at rate of 5% on total contract costs	0
Contract price		288,000
Benefit based on relevant cost principles		20,960

Notes:

(1) Material X can be used in place of another material which the company uses. The value of material X for this purpose is 90% × £21,600 = £19,440. If the company undertakes the North-east contract it will not be able to obtain this saving. This is an opportunity cost.

(2) The original cost of material Y is a sunk cost and is therefore not relevant. If the material was to be sold now its value would be 30,400 × 2 × 85% = £51,680, i.e. twice the purchase price less 15%, however, if the material is kept it can be used on other contracts, thus saving the company from future purchases. The second option is the better. The relevant cost of material Y is 2 × 30,400 = £60,800. If the company uses material Y on the north east contract, it will eventually have to buy an extra £60,800 of Y for use on other contracts.

(3) The future cost of material X not yet ordered is relevant.

(4) As the labour is to be sub-contracted it is a variable cost and is relevant.

(5) Site management is a specific fixed cost and therefore will only be incurred if the contract is undertaken and is therefore relevant.

(6) It is assumed that the staff accommodation and travel is specific to the contracts and will only be incurred if the contract is undertaken.

(7) The depreciation on plant is not a cash flow. It is therefore not relevant.

(8) It is assumed that the notional interest has no cash flow implications.

(9) It is assumed that the HQ costs are not specific to particular contracts.

LIMITING FACTORS AND OTHER TYPES OF DECISION

225 LF

	L	F
	£	£
Selling price per unit	100	200
Material cost per unit	(40)	(60)
Labour cost per unit	(16)	(64)
Contribution per unit	44	76
Contribution per limiting factor	22	9.50
Rank	1	2
Optimal production plan in units (W1)	100	75

(W1) 100 units of L × 2 hours = 200 hours, leaving 600 hours for F. At 8 hrs per F this produces 75 F.

The revised production plan would be 88 units of L and 78 units of F. (W2)

(W2) (78 × 2 hours) + (78 × 8 hours) = 780 hours

20 hours spare to make more L, at 2 hours each = 10 more L (78 + 10 = 88)

226 BQ

	B	Q
	£	£
Selling price per unit	100	150
Material cost per unit	(40)	(60)
Labour cost per unit	(16)	(30)
Contribution per unit	44	60
Contribution per limiting factor	11	10
Rank	1	2
Optimal production plan in units (W1)	100	58

(W1) 100 units of B × 4 kg = 400 kg, leaving 350 kg for Q. At 6 kg per Q this produces 58 Q.

The revised production plan would be 90 units of B and 65 units of Q. (W2)

(W2) (65 × 4 kg) + (65 × 6 kg) = 650 kg

100 kg spare to make more B, at 4 kg each = 25 more B (65 + 25 = 90)

ANSWERS TO PRACTICE QUESTIONS: SECTION 2

227 LEARN

	A	B
The contribution per unit	25	35
The contribution per kg	8.33	8.75

B should be made first and **A** should be made second.

	A	B
Production in units	1,600	1,800 (1,800 × 4 = 7,200)
	(12,000 – 7,200 = 4,800 left)	
Total contribution	1,600 × 25 = 40,000	1,800 × 35 = 63,000

Should Learn purchase the additional material? **YES** (The additional cost per kilogram is less than the contribution earned per kilogram.)

228 FROME

	A	B
The contribution per unit	50	35
The contribution per hour	16.67	14

A should be made first and **B** should be made second.

	A	B
Production in units	200	160
	(200 × 3 = 600 hours)	(1,000 hours – 600 hours = 400 hours)
		(400/2.5 hours each = 160)
Total contribution	200 × 50 = 10,000	160 × 35 = 5,600

Should Learn purchase the additional hours? **NO** (The additional cost per hour is more than the contribution earned per hour.)

229 US

£	A1	A2
Sales revenue	2,800,000	3,000,000
Variable costs	(1,500,0000	(1,620,000)
Fixed production overheads	(450,000)	(400,000)
Fixed selling & distribution overheads	(200,000)	(200,000)
Depreciation	(110,000)	(150,000)
Redundancy costs	(20,000)	(40,000)
Expected annual profit	520,000	590,000

The expected return on investment for each machine, to the nearest whole %, is:

A1   **47%** (520,000/1,100,000 × 100)

A2   **39%** (590,000/1,500,000 × 100)

US should buy machine **A1** (as it has a higher expected return on investment).

230 CHATTY

Workings:

	I	A	IN
	£	£	£
Selling price	100	200	50
Direct materials (£5 per kg)	10	7.50	15
Specialist labour (£10 per hour)	20	30	5
Unskilled labour (£8 per hour)	16	12	4
Variable overhead (£2 per machine hour)	10	12	2
Special component cost to buy in		65	
Contribution per unit	44	73.50	24
Contribution per machine hour	8.80	12.25	24
Ranking	3	2	1

Product	Units	Hrs/unit	Hrs used	Hrs left
IN	6,000	1	6,000	24,000
A	2,000	6	12,000	12,000
I	2,400	5	12,000	–

	I	A	IN
Contribution per unit (£ to 2DP)	44.00	73.50	24.00
Contribution per machine hour (£ to 2DP)	8.80	12.25	24.00
Optimum production plan (units)	2,400	2,000	6,000

There is no change for I & IN, but the estimated cost to make the special component is £15.50 cheaper than buying it in so the contribution per unit of A is now:

73.50 + 15.50 = £89

It takes 2 machine hours to make the special component so it would now take in total 8 machine hours to make a unit of A (2 hours for the special component plus 6 hours normally), so the contribution per machine hour is now:

89/8 = 11.125

The ranking doesn't change, but the production plan would now be:

Product	Units	Hrs/unit	Hrs used	Hrs left
IN	6,000	1	6,000	24,000
A	2,000	8	16,000	8,000
I	1,600	5	8,000	–

	I	A	IN
Contribution per unit (£ to 2DP)	44.00	89.00	24.00
Contribution per machine hour (£ to 2DP)	8.80	11.13	24.00
Optimum production plan (units)	1,600	2,000	6,000

Workings:

Original profit

	Units	Contribution per unit £	Total £
IN	6,000	24	144,000
A	2,000	73.5	147,000
I	2,400	44	105,600
Total contribution			396,600
Less fixed cost			(200,000)
Profit			196,600

Revised profit

	Units	Contribution per unit £	Total £
IN	6,000	24	144,000
A	2,000	89	178,000
I	1,600	44	70,400
Total contribution			392,400
Less fixed cost			(200,000)
Profit			192,400

If Chatty base their decision solely on profit maximisation they would **buy in** the special component.

The difference in profit between the two options is **£4,200**

Considerations could include:

Quality – the quality of either making or buying the component may be superior, doing the cheapest option could compromise the quality of the special component and therefore product A, which would be an issue as it commands a premium price.

Use of spare capacity – Chatty has an abundance of both specialist labour and materials, what will they do with this, could the decision they make lead to redundancies. The staff could be on fixed wages and therefore be paid for idle time.

Impact on customers – in house production would reduce availability of machine hours to make product I, therefore disappointing customers who would like to buy I.

Ethics – would decision be considered fair to customers/staff if it is purely financially driven either deliberately reducing the quality or putting jobs at risk.

231 GRAFTERS

	Current cost per year £	Cost per year with machinery £
Oak costs	60,000,000	60,600,000
Craftsmen cost	1,100,000	330,000
Tool replacement cost	200,000	100,000
Other variable overheads	50,000	40,000
Rental cost	–	100,000
Total cost	61,350,000	61,170,000

On financial grounds, grafters **should** agree to rent the machinery.

Other factors:

Quality – The machinery may compromise the quality of the product, it already leads to increased materials cost which suggests an increase in wastage.

Morale of workforce – those that remain will not have the same loyalty to Grafters.

Reliability of machinery – if the machines breakdown, with a reduced workforce Grafters may struggle to meet customer orders on time.

Reliability of estimates – approached by Machinery Co, they may not know the full extent of the work and veracity of the savings they suggest.

Ethical

Integrity – not mentioning change, trading on reputation of handcrafted even though it is not transparent and many people will continue to buy under the assumption the item is handcrafted.

Integrity – Hiding change in viewing gallery is another example of not being open and honest with their customers.

Professional behaviour – with so many of the workforce being made redundant, it seems difficult to believe that those that remain will be happy with their positions and the level of work they do may well drop.

Approach

The saving is £180,000 which is a relatively small amount (less than 1%) of the total costs.

Once committed and dependent on the machinery the cost could rise.

Familiarity threat given that the FD has a previous relationship with Machinery Co, which may lead to his/her trusting that their machines are going to save them all these costs even if they are actually substandard.

Bonus

A bonus based on one financial measure is very short term.

The finance directors objectivity will be compromised as they stand to benefit from the decision so may not act in the best interests of the company.

232 CCV

(a)

	M	D	C	L	Total
Number of batches	1,000	1,500	2,000	500	5,000
Number of machine setups	4,000	1,500	2,000	3,000	10,500

Workings:

Number of batches: M = 50,000/50 = 1,000; D = 75,000/50 = 1,500; C = 100,000/50 = 2,000; L = 25,000/50 = 500

Number of machine set ups: M = 1,000 × 4 = 4,000; D = 1,500 × 1 = 1,500; C = 2,000 × 1 = 2,000; L = 500 × 6 = 3,000

	£
Cost driver rate – per set up	57

Working: 598,500/10,500 = £57

(b)

	M	D	C	L	Total
	£000	£000	£000	£000	£000
Sales revenue	1,600	1,875	2,750	2,080	8,305
Direct material	200	825	1,000	900	2,925
Direct labour	400	900	1,200	600	3,100
Product specific overhead	200	20	10	421.5	651.5
Machine set up costs	228	85.5	114	171	598.5
General factory costs					100
Profit/(loss)	572	44.5	426	(12.5)	930

Workings:

M = 4,000 × 57 = 228,000; D = 1,500 × 57 = 85,500; C = 2,000 × 57 = 114,000; L = 3,000 × 57 = 171,000

The profit statement shows that Product L is now loss making and therefore from a financial perspective it should be discontinued as this would increase the company's profits by £12,500.

This is in contrast to the original profit statement which showed that products M and L were profitable and products D and C were loss making.

Products M, D and C should be continued because they all have a positive profit. The discontinuance of product L will release resources that were previously used by that product. If there is sufficient demand for products M, D, or C then CCV may be able to increase its output of these other products and increase its profits by even more than £12,500.

Value Analysis is a technique that improves the processes of production so as to achieve a reduction in cost without compromising the quality or usefulness of the product.

CCV would need to compare its products with those provided by its competitors to see if their products offer features that are not found in the products of their competitors. CCV would then have to determine whether these features are important to their customers. If they are not important then these features could be removed without affecting the value of the product.

Alternatively, CCV should review the design of its products as it may be able to produce them using different, lower cost, materials without affecting the customer's perception of the product. This would enable CCV to reduce its costs and thereby increase its profit.

233 WHITLEY

	LS £	ES £	AS £
Incremental revenue	11,100	8,750	6,600
Incremental costs	8,480	8,625	7,650
Net benefit/(loss)	2,620	125	(1,050)

Workings:

Incremental revenue

LS:

Rev from L = 6,000 units @ £4 = 24,000

Rev from LS = (6,000 × 0.9) × £6.50 = 35,100

Incremental rev = 35,100 – 24,000 = 11,100

ES:

Rev from E = 5,000 units @ £5 = 25,000

Rev from ES = (5,000 × 0.9) × £7.50 = 33,750

Incremental rev = 33,750 – 25,000 = 8,750

AS:

Rev from A = 4,000 units @ £6 = 24,000

Rev from AS = (4,000 × 0.9) × £8.50 = 30,600

Incremental rev = 30,600 – 24,000 = 6,600

Incremental costs

LS = (6,000 × 0.9) × 1.20 + 2,000 = 8,480

ES = (5,000 × 0.9) × 1.75 + 750 = 8,625

AS = (4,000 × 0.9) × 1.50 + 2,250 = 7,+650

On financial grounds Whitley should process L further.

On financial grounds Whitley should process E further.

On financial grounds Whitley should not process A further.

ANSWERS TO PRACTICE QUESTIONS: **SECTION 2**

Sales independent, i.e. but not producing AS will there still be a demand for LS & ES. Or by not producing L & E will customers still want A

Demand, there may not be a demand in the market place for all the output at the prices specified and so Whitley may not be able to sell everything they make.

Impact on customers, some customer may be upset that the product they normally buy is no longer made.

LINEAR PROGRAMMING

234 LINEAR PROGRAMMING

B

Linear programming assumes that products are infinitely divisible and that parts of units can be produced and sold.

The other statements are true.

235 LP CONSTRAINT

D

If, say, X = 400, Y would = 800. The only equation that satisfies these numbers is the correct answer.

236 SIMULTANEOUS EQUATIONS

The optimal production plan will have to be determined by using a simultaneous equations technique.

If the Material X function: $A + 2B \leq 9{,}000$ is multiplied by 3:

Material X: $3A + 6B = 27{,}000$

Now we can deduct the Material Y function to remove one of the unknowns:

Material Y: $3A + B = 12{,}000$

$3A - 3A + 6B - B = 27{,}000 - 12{,}000$

$5B = 15{,}000$

$B = 3{,}000$

Substituting this into the Material Y function gives:

$3A + (1 \times 3{,}000) = 12{,}000$

$3A = 9{,}000$

$A = 3{,}000$

Therefore the optimum production plan is 3,000 units of A and 3,000 units of B.

Substituting this production plan into the contribution function gives:

Contribution = $6 \times 3{,}000 + 4 \times 3{,}000$ = **£30,000**

AAT: APPLIED MANAGEMENT ACCOUNTING

237 UNSKILLED LABOUR

A

Each unit of A (X) requires 5 hours of skilled labour so the equation must contain 5X. Each unit of B (Y) requires 1 hour of skilled labour so the equation must contain 1Y.

238 LIMITATIONS

	Limitation?
Linear relationships must exist	✓
There can only be two products	✓
There can only be two scarce resources	
All variables must be completely divisible	✓
A computer must be used to find the optimal point	

Linear programming can cope with any number of constraints and the solution does not always need to be solved by a computer.

239 JRL

B

This should be based on contribution per unit:

	J	L
	£/unit	£/unit
Selling price	115	120
Direct material A (£10 per kg)	20	10
Direct material B (£6 per kg)	12	24
Skilled labour (£14 per hour)	28	21
Variable overhead (£4 per machine hour)	14	18
Contribution	41	47

And the iso-contribution line is: 41J + 47L

240 LP GRAPH

The maximum amount of Material A available is 2,000 kgs

The line crosses the horizontal axis at coordinates T = 0 and R = 1,000. If each unit of R takes 2 kgs of Material A, then there must be 2,000 kgs of Material A available.

ANSWERS TO PRACTICE QUESTIONS: SECTION 2

241 LPG CO

The optimal production plan will have to be determined by using a simultaneous equations technique.

If the Material X function: A + 2B ≤ 8,000 is multiplied by 2

Material X: 2A + 4B = 16,000

Now we can deduct the Material Y function to remove one of the unknowns:

Material Y: 2A + B = 13,000

2A − 2A + 4B − B = 16,000 − 13,000:

3B = 3,000

B = 1,000

Substituting this into Material Y function gives:

2A + (1 × 1,000) = 13,000

2A = 12,000

A = 6,000

Therefore the optimum production plan is 6,000 units of A and 1,000 units of B.

Substituting this production plan into the contribution function gives:

Contribution = 12 × 6,000 + 8 × 1,000 = **£80,000**

242 PRODUCT B

The maximum number of units of Product B which can be produced is 60 units.

If all of the resources have less than or equal to constraints then the feasible region cannot exceed the lowest of the lines on the diagram. This means that the maximum number of units of Product B that can be produced can be no higher than where this line meets the vertical axis which is at 60 units

243 PRODUCT Y

The number of units of Product Y produced in order to maximise contribution (to the nearest whole unit) is 8,000 units.

The optimal production plan will have to be determined by using a simultaneous equations technique.

If the unskilled labour function: 2X + 5Y ≤ 50,000 is multiplied by 3:

Unskilled labour: 6X + 15Y ≤ 150,000

Deducting Skilled labour: 6X + 4Y ≤ 62,000 from the unskilled labour function, gives:

6X − 6X + 15Y − 4Y = 150,000 − 62,000

11Y = 88,000

Y = 8,000

244 B CHEMICALS

Formulation of LP problem

Let x = the gallons of Super petrol produced

y = the gallons of Regular petrol produced each day; and

C = the total contribution

The company needs to maximise an objective function **C = 0.25x + 0.1y**

Subject to constraints:

supply of heavy crude	**0.7x + 0.5y ≤ 5,000 (1)**
supply of light crude	**0.5x + 0.7y ≤ 6,000 (2)**
market conditions rearranging giving	x ≥ 2/3 (x + y) 3x ≥ 2x + 2y **x ≥ 2y (3)**
Non negativity	**x, y ≥ 0 (4)**

You were not required to draw the graph but this is what the graph would look like:

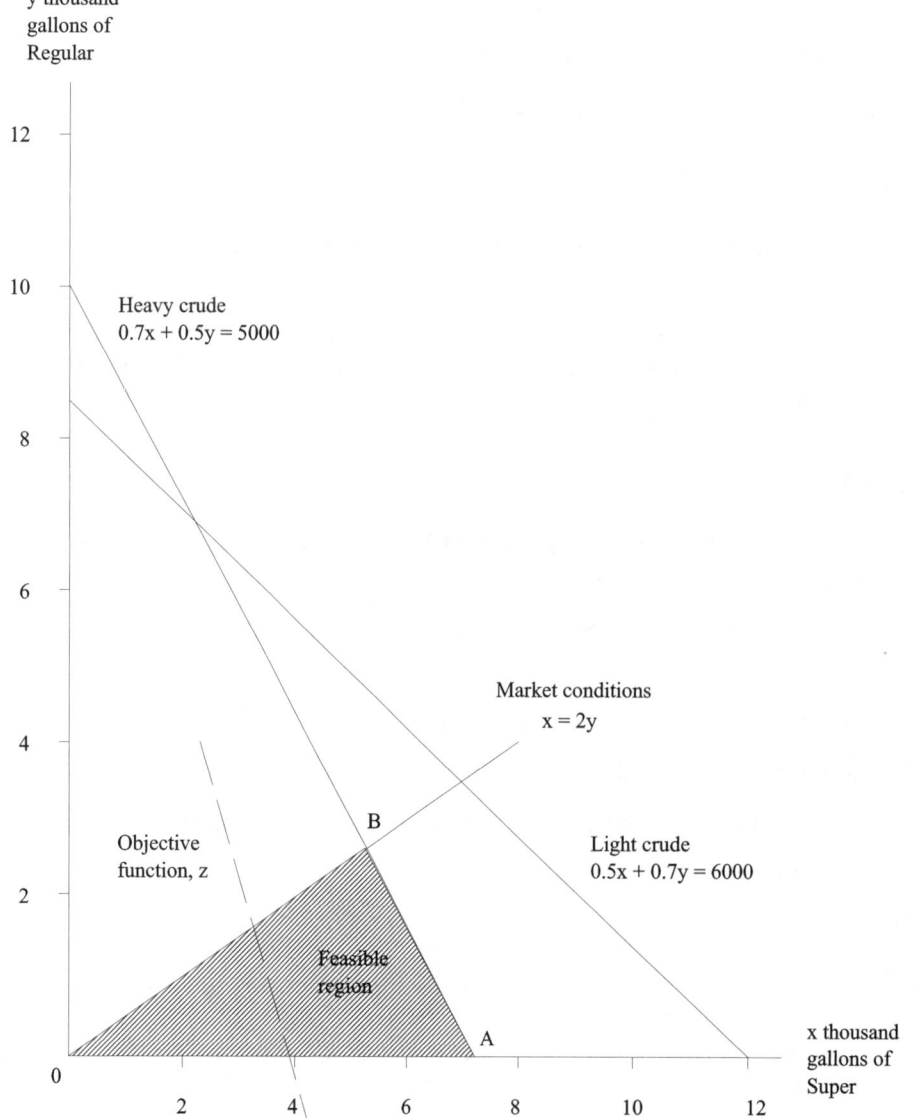

ANSWERS TO PRACTICE QUESTIONS: SECTION 2

Note: the objective function is also shown.

Optimal production plan

As we know that we must make at least 2/3 super, it must be at the end of the heavy crude constraint where regular is zero.

0.7x + 0.5y = 5,000

Therefore:

y = 0 and **x = 7,142.85**.

Contribution

The optimal production policy involves producing no Regular petrol and 7,142.85 gallons of Super petrol. The contribution that this generates is:

7,142.85 × £0.25 = **£1,785.71 per day**.

LONG TERM DECISION MAKING

PAYBACK, ARR, NPV AND IRR

245 JUMP

Appraisal method	Recommendation
Payback period	Reject as more than 3 years
Net present value	Accept as positive
Internal Rate of Return	Accept as greater than cost of capital
Overall	Accept as per most important investment criterion

246 TRUCK TRANSPORT

(a) For the first investment Truck Transport should invest in option **1** as it has the **shortest payback period**

For the second investment Truck Transport should invest in option **4** as it has the **highest NPV**

(b)

Statement	True	False
Payback method uses profits from a project to determine the payback period		✓
If the IRR is less than the cost of capital for a project, then it should be undertaken		✓
The IRR method uses discounted cash flows	✓	
Projects with a negative NPV should be rejected	✓	

247 CARTCYCLE

(a)

	Year 0 £000	Year 1 £000	Year 2 £000	Year 3 £000
Capital expenditure	−1,620			
Sales income		756	1,008	1,440
Operating costs		−216	−270	−342
Net cash flows	−1,620	540	738	1,098
PV factors	1.0000	0.8696	0.7561	0.6575
Discounted cash flows	−1,620	470	558	722
Net present value	130			

The net present value is **positive**

(b)

Year	Cash flow £000	Cumulative cash flow £000
0	(1,620)	(1,620)
1	540	(1,080)
2	738	(342)
3	1,098	756

The payback period is **2** years and **4** months.

Months = 342/1,098 × 12 = 3.7 months

248 AQUARIUS

(a)

	Year 0 £000	Year 1 £000	Year 2 £000	Year 3 £000
Capital expenditure	−1,200			
Sales income		530	570	710
Operating costs		−140	−160	−170
Net cash flows	−1,200	390	410	540
PV factors	1.0000	0.8696	0.7561	0.6575
Discounted cash flows	−1,200	339	310	355
Net present value	−196			

The net present value is **negative**

ANSWERS TO PRACTICE QUESTIONS: SECTION 2

(b)

Year	Cash flow £000	Cumulative cash flow £000
0	(1,200)	(1,200)
1	390	(810)
2	410	(400)
3	540	140

The payback period is **2** years and **9** months.

Months = 400/540 × 12 = 8.9 months

249 GRAPE LTD

(a)

	Year 0 £000	Year 1 £000	Year 2 £000	Year 3 £000
Capital expenditure	−500			
Sales income		280	330	370
Operating costs		−100	−120	−140
Net cash flows	−500	180	210	230
PV factors		1.0000	0.909	0.826	0.751
Discounted cash flows	−500	164	173	173
Net present value	10			

The net present value is **positive**

(b)　D

(c)

Year	Cash flow £000	Cumulative cash flow £000
0	(500)	(500)
1	180	(320)
2	210	(110)
3	230	120

The payback period is **2** years and **6** months.

Months = 110/230 × 12 = 5.7 months

250 BARTRUM LTD

Machine A

	Year 0 £000	Year 1 £000	Year 2 £000	Year 3 £000
Capital expenditure	−1,085			
Net cash flows	−1,085	−200	−200	−200
PV factors	1.0000	0.8696	0.7561	0.6575
Discounted cash flows	−1,085	−174	−151	−132
Net present cost	−1,542			

Machine B

	Year 0 £000	Year 1 £000	Year 2 £000	Year 3 £000
Capital expenditure	−1,200			
Net cash flows	−1,200	−150	−160	−170
PV factors	1.0000	0.8696	0.7561	0.6575
Discounted cash flows	−1,200	−130	−121	−112
Net present cost	−1,563			

Bartrum should invest in **Machine A**

251 CPL

Van type P

	Year 0 £000	Year 1 £000	Year 2 £000	Year 3 £000
Capital expenditure	−600			
Disposal				150
Net cash flows	−600	−275	−290	−165
PV factors	1.0000	0.8621	0.7432	0.6407
Discounted cash flows	−600	−237	−216	−106
Net present cost	−1,159			

Van type R

	Year 0 £000	Year 1 £000	Year 2 £000	Year 3 £000
Capital expenditure/disposal	−750			170
Net cash flows	−750	−345	−365	−220
PV factors	1.0000	0.8621	0.7432	0.6407
Discounted cash flows	−750	−297	−271	−141
Net present cost	−1,459			

CPL should invest in **Van type P**

ANSWERS TO PRACTICE QUESTIONS: SECTION 2

252 GLOBE LTD

(a) No

(b) Yes

(c) £ Nil

253 MIXING MACHINE

> **REPORT**
>
> **To:** The Chief Accountant
>
> **From:** AAT student
>
> **Subject:** Investment appraisal
>
> **Date:** 3 December 20X2
>
> The payback period of 2.4 years is *within* the company's policy of 3 years, and on this criterion the investment *should go* ahead.
>
> The NPV is *negative* and on this criterion the investment *should not go* ahead.
>
> The IRR, at 14%, is *below* the company's 16% cost of capital and on this criterion the investment *should not go* ahead.
>
> Overall the investment *should not* proceed because the *NPV* is the dominant criterion.

254 A COMPANY

14%

$$10 + \frac{£17,706}{(£17,706 - -£4,317)} \times (15 - 10) = 14\%$$

OR BY APPROXIMATION

NPV at 10% = £17,706

NPV at 15% = –£4,317

Change in discount rate = 5% and change in NPV = £22,023

Therefore 1% = £22,023/5 = £4,405

The NPV at 15% is –£4,317 therefore to get to a zero return the IRR is approximately 14%

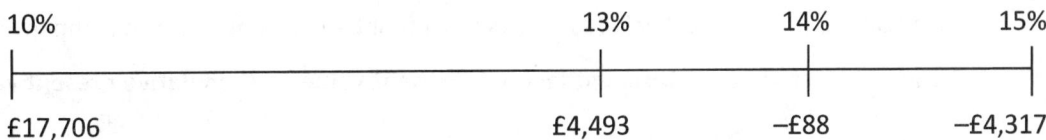

10%		13%	14%	15%
£17,706		£4,493	–£88	–£4,317

KAPLAN PUBLISHING

255 EDUCATION AUTHORITY

C

Year	Cash	20%	PV
	£		£
0	(75,000)		(75,000)
1	25,000	0.833	20,825
2	25,000	0.694	17,350
3	25,000	0.579	14,475
4	25,000	0.482	12,050
5	25,000	0.402	10,050
			(250)

$$\text{IRR} = 15 + \frac{8,800}{8,800 - (250)} \times 5$$

$$\text{IRR} = 15 + \frac{8,800}{9,050} \times 5$$

IRR = 19.86% therefore **20%** to the nearest 1%

OR BY APPROXIMATION

NPV at 15% = £8,800

NPV at 20% = –£250

Change in discount rate = 5% and change in NPV = £9,050

Therefore 1% = £9,050 ÷ 5 = £1,810

The NPV at 20% is –£250 therefore the discount rate to the nearest 1% is 20%

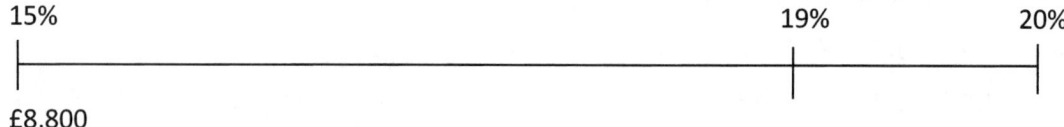

256 DPP

Year 5

To work out discounted payback, cash flows must first be discounted at the company rate.

Year	Cash flow	Discount factor	Present value	Cumulative present value
	£		£	£
0	(100,000)	1	(100,000)	(100,000)
1	40,000	0.909	36,360	(63,640)
2	20,000	0.826	16,520	(47,120)
3	30,000	0.751	22,530	(24,590)
4	5,000	0.683	3,415	(21,175)
5	40,000	0.621	24,840	3,665

Discounted payback occurs in year 5.

257 STATEMENTS

C and D

The true statements are 'the payback method is based on the project's cash flows' and 'a requirement for early payback can increase a company's liquidity'.

The payback method is based on cash flows whereas the ARR method is based on accounting profit. ARR looks at the project's entire life whereas payback may not. Neither method is related to the cost of capital.

258 INK CO

C

Annual operating cash flow = £729,000

Annual depreciation = £1,800,000/4 = £450,000

Annual profit = operating cash flows – depreciation = £729,000 – £450,000 = £279,000

Average investment = (£1,800,000 + 0)/2 = £900,000

ARR = £279,000/£900,000 × 100 = 31%

PERFORMANCE INDICATORS

CALCULATIONS

259 TEES R US

	Actual	Budgeted
Cost of tea pickers as a % of turnover	16.76%	13.33%
Cost of tea processor operators as a % of turnover	4.44%	4.44%
Cost of seeds and fertilizer as a % of turnover	9.52%	6.67%
Gross profit margin	61.65%	70.22%
Operating profit margin	4.51%	25.78%
Return on capital employed	3.79%	24.37%
Net asset turnover	0.84	0.95

260 PARTY

	Party	Topical
Selling price per unit	7.50	10.00
Material cost per unit	2.00	1.50
Labour cost per unit	1.25	1.00
Fixed cost per unit	1.00	1.36
Gross profit margin	43.33%	61.36%
Net profit margin	18.33%	7.95%
Advertising cost as % of turnover	5.56%	45.45%
Return on capital employed	16.50%	20.59%

261 FUDGE

	Fudge	Stubbed
Selling price per unit (£)	0.500	0.606
Material cost per unit (£)	0.078	0.091
Labour cost per unit (£)	0.109	0.076
Fixed production cost per unit (£)	0.047	0.015
Gross profit margin	53.125%	70.000%
Net profit margin	15.625%	27.500%
Advertising cost as % of turnover	18.750%	25.000%
Return on capital employed	5.000%	9.167%

262 DEJAVU

	Budgeted	Actual
Selling price per unit	2.75	3.00
Material cost per unit	0.50	0.55
Labour cost per hour	75.00	75.00
Fixed production cost per labour hour	375.00	394.74
Gross profit margin	49.09%	51.92%
Net profit margin	23.55%	26.08%
Direct materials cost as % of turnover	18.18%	18.33%

ANSWERS TO PRACTICE QUESTIONS: SECTION 2

263 GRANSDEN

	North	South
Gross profit margin	40.74%	37.17%
Operating profit margin	18.75%	18.00%
Wages and salaries as a percentage of turnover	7.41%	6.28%
Inventory turnover in days	91.25	121.67
Receivable collection period in days	45.63	89.34
Payable days	57.03	26.61
Return on capital employed	30.00%	18.09%

264 REVENUE

4 × £950,000 = £3,800,000

265 OPERATING PROFIT

ROCE = Operating profit/Net assets × 100%

25% = Operating profit/£480,000 × 100%

Operating profit = £120,000

266 GROSS PROFIT

Gross profit margin = Gross profit/Sales revenue × 100

30 = Gross profit/£1,000,000 × 100

Gross profit = £300,000

267 INVENTORY

Inventory days = Inventory/Purchases x 365

73 = Inventory/£600,000 × 365

73/365 × £600,000 = Inventory

£120,000 = inventory

268 RECEIVABLES

Receivable days = Receivables/Sales revenue × 365

90 = £400,000/Sales revenue × 365

Sales revenue = £1,622,222

KAPLAN PUBLISHING

269 VALUE ADDED

Value added = Sales revenue − Cost of materials used and bought in services

Value added = £850,000 − £300,000 − £200,000

Value added = £350,000

270 PAYABLES

Payable days = Payables/Cost of sales x 365

75 = Payables/£700,000 × 365

Payables = £143,836

271 BACKWARDS

Rec balance:

Rec days = Receivables/Revenue × 360

30 days = Receivables/30,000 × 360

(30 × 30,000)/360 = Receivables

£2,500 = Receivables

Pay balance:

Pay days = Payables/Cost of sales × 360

GP Margin = 30% so Cost of sales = 70% of revenue

48 days = Payables/(30,000 × 70%) × 360

(48 × 30,000 × 70%)/360 = Payables

£2,800 = Payables

272 REVERSE

Sales Revenue

Rec days = Receivables/Revenue × 360

45 days = 25,000/Revenue × 360

Revenue = (25,000 × 360)/45

Revenue = 200,000

Cost of sales

Pay days = Payables/Cost of sales × 360

64 days = 18,000/Cost of sales × 360

Cost of sales = (18,000 × 360)/64

Cost of sales = 101,250

Expenses

80,000/2 = 40,000

Fixed = 40,000 × 1.05 = 42,000

Variables = 40,000 × 1.02 = £40,800

Expenses = 42,000 + 40,800 = 82,800

ANSWERS TO PRACTICE QUESTIONS: SECTION 2

	£
Sales revenue	200,000
Cost of sales	101,250
Gross profit	98,750
Expenses	82,800
Net profit	15,950

WRITTEN TASKS

273 PAS

(a)

	Year 1	Year 2
Revenue growth (%)		25.8
Gross profit margin (%)	51.4	41.3
Net profit margin (%)	–3.7	3.4

(b)

Report

To:	Polina	Subject:	Financial performance of PAS
From:	Accounting Technician	Date:	Today

Revenue

Almost £2.9 million revenue in the first year of a new business seems very good, but to have revenue growth in the second year of almost 26% in a competitive market place appears to be a fantastic performance by PAS.

Revenue growth can come from growing sales volume, increasing the selling price or a combination of the two; it would be interesting to know how PAS have achieved this growth.

Gross profit

A first year gross profit margin of over 50% looks like an excellent start to business for PAS, the high percentage appears to back up the premium image that PAS are trying to achieve.

Gross profit growth of only 1.2% in the second year is slightly disappointing after such strong sales revenue growth, it suggests that either PAS has bought sales by discounting the prices or that there are cost control issues to consider.

The gross profit margin falling to 41.3% backs up this concern, and it would be interesting to be able to find out why the gross profit margin has fallen so much.

Net profit

A loss in year one is disappointing, but as PAS seem to be taking a long term view it is not unexpected. Especially as some initial set up costs such as the website and marketing costs are so high as predicted by Polina, if these were at the level of year 2 in year 1 then PAS would have returned a very healthy net profit.

The profit, even though it is small in year 2 is very encouraging. If the initial costs continue to fall, although not at the same rate, this should help increase the profit for the company.

The distribution costs appear high, having increased by over 50%, twice the rate of the revenue growth and could be a cause for concern. This could be down to establishing a good reputation for on time delivery or rising fuel costs.

Administrative costs and other overhead heads have also increased although this is more in line with the revenue growth, PAS should be looking for economies of scale in these areas as they continue to grow.

(c)

	Year 1	Year 2
Conversion rate for website visits to number of units sold (%)	5.2	3.0
% sales returned	9.0	21.0
Average price per sale (£ to 2 decimal places)	20.50	23.03

(d)

Report

To: Polina	Subject: Non-financial performance of PAS
From: Accounting Technician	Date: Today

Average selling price

The average selling price per unit has increased in year 2, which answers one of the queries after reviewing the financials, sales revenue has grown through both increased prices and higher volume, while the decline in gross profit is down to escalating cost of sales

Conversion rate

After a fantastic start in year 1 where the conversion rate is well above the industry average, the performance here has dropped well below industry average in year 2. This is a cause for concern for PAS, and could be linked to the increased prices charged discouraging customers from making a purchase.

PAS need to look to understand where the cost increases are coming from and control these so they do not lose more customers in coming years.

It could also be linked to poor internet reviews as returns have increased and there have been fewer deliveries on time.

It could also be due to technical issues with the website, as these have increased this could have put customers off or prevented them from buying the products.

ANSWERS TO PRACTICE QUESTIONS: SECTION 2

Sales returns

The percentage of sales returns has increased dramatically in the 2nd year and is a real cause for concern for PAS, it is now 50% higher than the industry average, for a company looking to get a reputation for quality this is not the way to go.

PAS need to look at the reasons for the returns and look to rectify them.

On time delivery

One of the factors influencing sales returns in year 2 could be the poor performance against on time delivery. Having been well above industry averages in year 1, PAS have again fallen below.

It could be that the accessories were purchased for a special event, but arrived late and so the customer had been out and purchased from an alternative source.

The drop in on time delivery is despite the increasing distribution costs; in fact the returns could well be a factor in the increased distribution costs as a company striving for differentiation would probably pay for the returns costs.

Website performance

One final cause for concern is the number of transactions that were aborted due to website issues. PAS invested heavily in the website in year 1 and for it to be struggling already is not good. Internet security is a key issue for users and they may well be put off buying from the site in the future if a transaction fails.

PAS should go back to the developers to address this issue as there may well be within warranty period.

274 ARCHIMEDES

To:	Finance director	**Subject:**	Various
From:	Accounting technician	**Date:**	Today

(a) Why are the gross profit margins different

Sales Price/Sales Volume

The sales price is higher under Scenario 1 which will result in an increase in the gross profit margin, however the sales volume is half that of Scenario 2, which will reduce the margin because the fixed cost per unit will be higher.

Materials

The materials cost per unit is constant and therefore does not affect the gross profit margin. There is no economy of scale.

Labour

Labour cost per unit is £0.80 for Scenario 1 decreasing to £0.64 for Scenario 2. The more units that are produced the lower the labour cost per unit. This will improve the margin for Scenario 2. It may be because of economies of scale in production or the learning effect.

Fixed costs

Fixed costs are constant in total therefore as the volume of production increases the fixed cost per unit reduces and this will increase the margin.

(b) Why are the operating profit margins different

The operating profit margins are different due in part to the reduction in gross profit for Scenario 2 and in part due to the increased sales and distribution costs in Scenario 2.

(c) Recommendation, with reasons, as to which course of action to take

Based purely on the forecast information Scenario 1 is the best option creating the largest profit. However, the sales volume is lower than Scenario 2 and therefore the market share is lower. It may be worth setting the price lower to gain market share.

275 TEMPEST

To:	Finance director	Subject:	Profitability
From:	Accounting technician	Date:	Today

Why are the gross profit margins not significantly different?

Sales Price

The Sales price in each cinema is the same and therefore the revenue earned per customer does not have any effect on the gross profit margin.

Direct costs

The direct cost per customer is slightly higher at the City centre cinemas (£2.16 versus £2.13 at the out of town sites). This only has a small effect on the gross profit margin.

Fixed costs

The fixed costs per customer are higher per customer at the City Centre cinemas (£3.24 per customer versus £3.00 per customer). This explains the majority of the difference in the gross profit margin.

Why are the operating profit margins different?

Both cinemas have the same administrative costs despite having a different number of customers – this works out at £0.33 per customer at the out of town cinemas and £0.89 at the city centre cinemas. This cost is fixed, and accounts for the difference in operating profit margins.

Which is the most profitable type of cinema and why? (Many different answers could be given.)

The Out of Town sites earn £4.61 per customer and the City Centre sites earn £2.90 per customer. This can mostly be explained by the increased admin costs at the city centre cinemas.

Apart from reducing fixed costs what could Tempest do to improve the profitability of the City Centre Cinemas? (Use numbers to demonstrate your answer if necessary.)

The average spend on food per customer is much lower at the City Centre cinemas – only £0.89. If customers could be persuaded to spend an extra £1.00 when the variable cost of food is only 10% then this would result in an extra £0.90 per customer per visit.

We could try to increase the numbers attending the City Centre cinemas – this would spread the fixed admin cost over more customers increasing profit per customer.

ANSWERS TO PRACTICE QUESTIONS: SECTION 2

Tempest suspect City Centre customers are smuggling in their own sweets and snacks – give ONE way that Tempest could combat it?

Market research – ask the customers – are food prices at the cinema too high?

Look for evidence of food wrappers that aren't sold in cinemas

Tactic to combat smuggling – Offer promotions e.g. 2 for 1.

276 ANIMAL

To:	Finance Director	Subject:	Profit and current assets
From:	Accounting Technician	Date:	XX/XX/20XX

Why are the gross profit margin for the proposed position is higher than the current position:

Sales volume

The sales volume is expected to increase by 100% .i.e. it is forecast to double.

The volume increase will increase the profit margin if the fixed costs remain constant.

In this case the fixed production costs remain unchanged at £60,000 and therefore the increased volume will improve the gross profit margin because the fixed production costs are spread across more units thereby lowering the total unit cost and increasing the profit per unit. This is the principle of 'economies of scale'.

Material cost

The material cost per unit reduces by 20%, from £5.00 to £4.00 per unit, which will also improve the margin for the proposed position. The doubling of the volume is likely to allow the company to purchase in greater quantities and access additional discounts (economies of scale).

Labour cost

The labour cost per unit is unchanged at £6.00 and therefore would have no effect on the margin if the selling price remained constant. However, the selling price has fallen which makes the labour cost proportionately larger in percentage terms, which will reduce the gross profit margin.

There do not appear to have been any economies of scale or any learning effect.

Fixed production costs

The fixed production costs are constant in total at £60,000 but the important point is that they are spread over more units. The proposed position increases the volume by 100% which reduces the fixed production cost per unit. Fixed production costs reduce by 50% from £4.00 to £2.00. This will improve the margin for the proposed position.

What is likely to happen to the current asset position:

Inventory levels

Inventory levels are likely to increase significantly because the volume of demand is expected to be higher and therefore higher inventory levels will be needed to fulfil orders. Based upon the current inventory level in relation to cost of sales the forecast position will be that inventory levels may increase to around £56,000.

(Current inventory days = Inventory/Cost of sales × 365 = 35,000/225,000 × 365 = 56.78 days

Proposed inventory level = £360,000 × 56.78 days/365 days = £56,002)

KAPLAN PUBLISHING

AAT: APPLIED MANAGEMENT ACCOUNTING

> **Trade receivable levels**
>
> Trade receivables' levels are likely to increase because the turnover increases – increased sales will likely lead to increased receivables. The current position is that trade receivable days are 48.67 days (50,000/375,000 × 365).
>
> Therefore, assuming a similar profile, trade receivables will increase to around £88,000. (660,000 × 48.67/365 = £88,006).

277 FRUITY

To:	Manager	Subject:	Profitability
From:	Accounting Technician	Date:	XX/XX/20XX

1 **Why is the gross profit margin of Cranberry less than 50% higher than that of Apple when the gross profit per unit is more than 50% higher?**

The gross profit per unit of Cranberry is 57.5% higher than Apple. While the gross profit margin of Cranberry is only 26% higher than Apple.

The reason for this apparent anomaly is due to the sales price per unit of Cranberry being 25% higher than Apple.

Therefore the calculation of the gross profit margin for Cranberry results in a larger denominator, and therefore 63p per unit as a percentage of £1.25 (50.4%) is not over 50% higher than the calculation of the gross profit margin for Apple (40%).

2 **I was told that the material cost is £0.80 per kilogram for Apple and £0.91 per kilogram for Cranberry. Therefore I do not understand why the material cost per unit for Apple is £0.40 and for Cranberry is £0.50. Is this correct?**

The cost per kilogram is correct at £0.80 for Apple and £0.91 for Cranberry. Apple requires 500 grams (0.5 kilograms) of material per unit, which is why the cost per unit is £0.40 (0.5 × £0.80).

Cranberry requires 550 grams (0.55 kilograms) of material per unit, which is why the cost per unit is £0.50 (0.55 × £0.91).

3 **If the fixed production overheads are constant does that mean they have no effect on the profit margin? And if the fixed production overheads increase will they affect the profit margin?**

If the fixed production overheads were constant in total, because the production volume of Cranberry is 500,000 units greater than Apple this will result in the fixed production overhead per unit being lower. This is because the fixed production overheads are spread over more units, which reduces the cost per unit of Cranberry and therefore the profit margin will be improved.

However, in this scenario, the total costs have increased by 20% (from £100k to £120k), and thus the unit cost is 20% higher than might have been expected (at £0.12/unit and not £0.10/unit).

The impact this has on the gross profit margin depends on sales. If sales reduce, then the cost as a percentage of sales will increase; if sales increase, then the cost as a percentage of sales will reduce, improving the margin.

Comparing Cranberry to Apple, the fixed cost per unit is lower for Cranberry, whilst the sales price is higher, both of which help to reduce cost as a % of sales, and thus improve the margin.

Even if the fixed costs had remained constant, there could still have been an impact on profit margin if the sales had changed.

ANSWERS TO PRACTICE QUESTIONS: SECTION 2

4 Can you explain why Cranberry is more profitable than Apple?

The reasons that Cranberry is more profitable than Apple are as follows:

- Sales price per unit of Cranberry is higher than Apple by 25% which will improve the profit

- The sales volume is much higher for Cranberry which means that fixed costs per unit are lower than Apple again improving the profit

- The variable cost (material) per unit is higher for Cranberry which will have a negative effect and decrease the actual profit for Cranberry

- The fixed production cost per unit is lower for Cranberry due to the volume being greater than Apple which improves the profit for Cranberry

- The marketing costs for Cranberry are 140% (£120,000 – £50,000/£50,000 × 100%) higher than Apple which will result in a higher marketing cost per unit (£0.10 (£50,000/500,000) v £0.12 (£120,000/1,000,000)). This will reduce the net profit for Cranberry. However, since the price of Cranberry is much higher, the marketing costs are only 9.6% of sales (£0.12/£1.25). Apple's marketing costs are 10% of sales (£0.10/£1). This 0.4% difference helps to improve Cranberry's profit margin.

- There are two main reasons that Cranberry is more profitable – the greater sales price and the greater sales volume. These, in combination, outweigh the increased marketing costs and the increased material costs for Cranberry.

278 PI ETHICS

Ethical issues

The manager has clearly received their bonus in qtr 2 having missed out in qtr 1. It appears their objectivity may have been impaired by the bonus and a potential personal need to receive that bonus.

Other financial and non-financial measures have deteriorated, the managers integrity could be called into question about why the selling price has dropped so much in the last quarter. A clear reason could be buying sales through discounts.

To counter this, the manager may well have compromised on quality or service as the number of customers is decreasing, a sign of poor service. This could lead to people questioning the managers professional competence and due care.

Goal congruence issues

In terms of goal congruence, the overall profitability of the company of the company would help here, but the manager looks to have made short term decisions to achieve their bonus which could lead to adverse long term consequences for the company.

Acting in their own self-interest could lead to the company's reputation being damaged and more customers could be lost in future quarters.

AAT: APPLIED MANAGEMENT ACCOUNTING

279 SSS

(a)

	£ per visit
Average price for hair services per female client in 2016	50
Average price for hair services per male client in 2016	25

There were no price changes for female clients between 2015 and 2016, so using the 2015 figures:

Ave price in 2015 = 500,000/10,000 = £50 per visit

If that's the average price for female clients in 2016, then the male price is:

Ave price per visit = (550,600 − (£50 × 8,802))/4,420

= 110,500/4,420

= £25 per visit

(b)

	2015	2016
Gross profit margin (% to 2 DP)	60.50	55.92
Net profit margin (% to 2 DP)	52.50	47.35

To:	Stuart	Subject:	Financial performance of SSS
From:	Accounting Technician	Date:	Today

(a) **Revenue**

Revenue has grown by 10.12% in the last year, which in tough economic conditions and a competitive market place is a good performance.

Of more concern for SSS is that the core customer base (and more lucrative at £50 per visit) customer base is in decline. There has been a 12% fall in visits from female clients. This could be linked to the trainee stylist not performing very well; customers may have chosen to go to one of the competitors leading to a decline in revenue.

The growth is entirely down to the launch of the new male services, with £110,500 revenue being generated from the new services

(b) **Gross profit margin**

Gross profit has grown by just under 2% in 2016, which is disappointing given a revenue growth of over 10%.

The reason for this decline is that Cost of Sales has increased at a higher rate than 10%, this is mainly down to stylist salaries, who all received pay rises and two new stylists were recruited.

The main issue is the additional female trainee stylist, as the arrival increases the cost of sales and coincides with the decline in female clients, making the additional stylist unnecessary.

It would appear that male services command a lower gross profit margin. With further analysis this is not the case. The stylist for male clients is paid £26,000.

This one stylist is generating revenue of £110,500 (4,420 visits × £25 per visit), which is pretty impressive.

ANSWERS TO PRACTICE QUESTIONS: SECTION 2

(c) **Net profit margin**

The net profit for the period has fallen by almost 1%, which is another disappointment for SSS given both the revenue growth and growth in gross profit. This led to a decline on Net profit margin from 52.50% to 47.35%.

Total expenses were up almost 18% in 2016 in comparison to 2015.

The main issue is the increase marketing and advertising spend, which has increased by £6,000 – a 200% rise on 2015. While this is a lot, it is quite normal for businesses launching a new product or service to increase this type of spend and it would be expected to reduce in 2017.

Also, the additional £6,000 may have contributed to the £110,500 revenue generated by the new service, so SSS may consider it to have been worthwhile.

A lot of these expenses are outside of the control of SSS in the short term, for example property rental and rates, combined these have only increased by just over 4%.

The administrative assistant has also had a 1% pay rise in line with the rest of the staff who were present in 2015.

(c)

	2015	2016
Customer		
% of visits that had complaints (2dp)	0.16	1.33
Internal business		
Number of female client visits per stylist	2,000	1,467
Number of male client visits per stylist		4,420
Innovation and growth		
% revenue from new male hairdressing service (to 2 decimal places)		20.07

% revenue from new male hairdressing service = 110,500/550,600 × 100 = 20.07

(d)

Customer

The number of complaints has increased dramatically, a major factor is the new service being offered has upset a lot of the core customer base.

The new trainee stylist may not yet be as good as the experienced stylists leading to further complaints.

Internal business

A business will often look at utilisation of assets, and while Stuart is correct that overall the premises themselves have more client visits, the appointments per female stylist is down over 25%. This will be partly due to the number of female visits being lower but also the increase in number of stylists for female clients.

The male stylist appears to be well utilised although we do not have any comparative numbers here from either prior year or industry averages. It is unfair to compare the number of appointments per male stylist to the number of appointments per female stylist as the service provided to male clients is much quicker.

Innovation and growth

Over 20% of revenue has come from the new service SSS have offered, which suggests the new service has been well received.

The concern is that it has led to a decline in core services of 12%.

SSS need to decide how to continue this new venture; it may be beneficial to set up another salon for male services.

280 COST REDUCTION

Cost reduction is action taken to reduce the cost of goods or services without impairing suitability for the use intended, whereas cost control involves the use of control methods, such as budgetary control and standard costing, to determine whether action is required.

Cost reduction is a technique which has the objective of reducing costs to some predetermined accepted norm or standard, but at the same time maintaining the desired quality of the product or service.

It is a concept which attempts to extract more 'value added' from the resources without loss of effectiveness.

Cost reduction programmes require the support of the senior management team and should embrace the full range of the firm's value adding activities and products.

Focus on a number of issues should be considered.

- Reduction of waste.
- Streamlining activities.
- Product improvement.

Cost reduction compels planning and good practice and benchmarks for achievement may be set.

Some formal management techniques can be used to implement cost reduction programmes, including:

- variety reduction
- value analysis
- work study
- organisation and method study.

All members of the management team should have a clear perception of cost reduction and its benefits in contributing, other things being equal, to improved profitability.

ANSWERS TO PRACTICE QUESTIONS: SECTION 2

281 VALUE ANALYSIS

Value analysis is an assessment process underpinning the cost reduction technique. It is usually undertaken by a quality team during the design stages of the product or delivery of a service. The team would comprise a number of managers including technical and production personnel together with finance staff.

The task the team undertakes is to design the product, or plan the service, at minimum cost, but meeting the quality standard required.

The assessment is a systematic attempt to eliminate unnecessary cost on every aspect of the product's functions, methods of production and components.

The process involves asking a series of questions which may include the following.

- Can the function of the product be achieved in an alternative way?
- Are all the product functions essential?
- Can the product be made more compact and from alternative, cheaper material?
- Can we standardise components, e.g. some components on the Mercedes 'C' class are also on the 'S' class?
- Can the design or process be modified so that the product or service can be supplied more easily and at less cost?

This is an ongoing process where each of the company's products or services should come under regular scrutiny.

ETHICS

282 ETHICS STATEMENTS (I)

A company that takes a strong ethical stance in the way they behave will usually find their relationship with investors **improves**.

A worker in the accounts department who receives a profit based bonus decides to manipulate some of the expenses, artificially increasing the profits and allowing them to get a bonus has not breached the ethical principle of **confidentiality**.

283 ETHICS STATEMENTS (II)

Consumers may be willing to pay a **premium** price for Fairtrade products, knowing that the products are grown in an ethical and sustainable fashion

An advantage of using life cycle costing is it could help an organisation make more **sustainable** decisions as they will consider all costs throughout the projects including any potential closure and clean-up costs.

284 ETHICS STATEMENTS (III)

Products that have **excess** packaging could be considered unethical because they are using more of the world's resources and could potentially cost the company more money.

Ethical actions by a business may help them achieve long term **success**.

CALCULATING FORECASTS

TREND ANALYSIS, INDEXING, LINEAR REGRESSION AND EXPECTED VALUES

285 TREND

	Q1	Q2	Q3	Q4
Average price	£30	£34	£54	£66
Seasonal variation	−£4	−£8	+£4	+£8
Trend	£34	£42	£50	£58

The trend in prices is an increase of **£8** per quarter.

286 RPI

	2008	2009	2010
Cost per kg of materials	£17.00	£18.60	£19.40
RPI	184	192	200
Cost/RPI × 100	£9.23913	£9.6875	£9.70

£9.70 − £9.23913/£9.23913 × 100 = 4.99 %

Correct answer is **C**

287 PRODUCT Z

		Oct	Dec
Cost	£30	£36	£32
Index	100		107

Index = 100/£30 × £32 = 107

Decrease = (£32 − £36)/£36 = 11.1%

Correct answer is **A**

288 TANZANITE

	Jan	Feb	Mar
Actual price	Actual price was £6.90	Actual price was £7.00	Actual price was £7.40
Seasonal variation	Seasonal variation was −10p	Seasonal variation was −15p	Seasonal variation was 10p
Trend	£7.00	£7.15	£7.30

The trend in prices is an increase of **£0.15** per month.

ANSWERS TO PRACTICE QUESTIONS: SECTION 2

289 MARCH

	Jan	Feb	March
Total cost	£450,000	£500,000	£650,000
Total quantity purchased	20,000 m	25,000 m	27,500 m
Cost per m	£22.50	£20.00	£23.64
Index	100		105

£23.64/£22.50 × 100 = 105.067

Correct answer is **A**: 105

290 COST PER UNIT

	Jan	Feb	Apr
Cost	£50	£52	£56
Index	100		112

(£56 – £50)/£50 × 100 = 12% increase, and an index of 112.

Correct answer is **A**

291 PRODUCT Y

Apr	May	Jun
Actual price was £6.56	Actual price was £7.14	Actual price was £7.35
Seasonal variation was (£0.30)	Seasonal variation was £0.14	Seasonal variation was £0.21
6.86	7.00	7.14

The trend in prices is an increase of **£0.14** per month.

292 A COMPANY

	Jan	Feb	March
Total cost	£100,000	£132,000	£127,000
Total quantity purchased	10,000 kgs	12,000 kgs	11,500 kgs
Cost per kg	£10	£11	£11.04
Index	100		110 (W1)

(W1) 11.04/10 × 100 = 110

Correct answer is **B**

AAT: **APPLIED MANAGEMENT ACCOUNTING**

293 PRODUCT X

		Jan	Apr
Cost per unit	£42	£46	£52
Index	100		123.8 (W1)

(W1) £52/£42 × 100 = 123.8

The increase from January to April is: (52 – 46)/46 = 13%

Correct answer is **A**

294 INDEX

	Past	May	July
Cost per unit	70	82	96
Index	100	117 (W2)	137 (W1)

(W1) £96 × 100/70 = 137

(W2) £82 × 100/70 = 117

Increase from May to July: (137 – 117)/117 = 17%

Correct answer is **A**

295 DEXTER

Base	June	September
1,080	1,350	1,710
100		?

Index in September = 1,710/1,080 × 100 = 158

Increase from June to September 1,710 – 1,350/1,350 = 26.67%

The correct answer is **D**

296 WASTE

	Jan	Feb	March
Kgs	1000	1250	1100
Price per kilo	5	6	7
Total cost	£5,000	£7,500	£7,700
Index	100		?

£7/£5 × 100 = 140

The correct answer is **B**

ANSWERS TO PRACTICE QUESTIONS: SECTION 2

297 FIZZ

Jan	Feb	Mar
Actual price was £550	Actual price was £675	Actual price was £650
Seasonal variation was –£50	Seasonal variation was + £50	Seasonal variation was Nil
£600	£625	£650

The trend in prices is an increase of **£25** per month.

298 ACRID

Jan	Feb	Mar
Actual price was £50	Actual price was £50	Actual price was £65
Seasonal variation was £5	Seasonal variation was – £5	Seasonal variation was Nil
£45	£55	£65

The trend in prices is an increase of **£10** per month.

299 PRODUCT J

Apr	May	Jun
Actual price was £7.20	Actual price was £7.50	Actual price was £6.90
Seasonal variation was £0.10	Seasonal variation was £0.20	Seasonal variation was (£0.60)
£7.10	£7.30	£7.50

The trend in prices is an increase of **£0.20** per month.

300 ABCO

	October	November	December
Total cost	£1,250	£1,390	£1,610
Quantity purchased	1,000 kg	1,100 kg	1,200 kg
Cost per kg	£1.25	£1.26	£1.34
Index	100		(W1) 107

The cost index for December based upon October prices is:

(W1) £1.34/£1.25 × 100 = 107

Correct answer is **B**

301 SOAP

September	= £1,200 × 126/105	£1,440
October	= £1,200 × 119/105	£1,360
November	= £1,200 × 133/105	£1,520

302 ASPHALT

June = X = 26, therefore Y = 125 + (2 × 26) = £177 per tonne

July = X = 27, therefore Y = 125 + (2 × 27) = £179 per tonne

June = 177/175 × 100 = 101.14

July = 179/175 × 100 = 102.29

303 BEST FIT

In June X = 26, therefore Y = 25.97 + (3.56 × 26) = £118.53

304 LEAST

In July X = 49, therefore Y = 105.97 + (12.56 × 49) = £721.41

305 MOST

June = X = 21, therefore Y = 15 + (4 × 21) = £99

July = X = 22, therefore Y = 15 + (4 × 22) = £103

May = X = 20, therefore Y = 15 + (4 × 20) = £95

June = 99/95 × 100 = 104.21

July = 103/95 × 100 = 108.42

306 TEA

	June X7 £	Nov X7 £
Cost per Kg of tea	4.95	5.10
Base cost	4.80	4.80
Index	103.125	106.25

£4.80 × 108.25/100 = £5.20 or £4.80 × 108.25/100 = £5.196

£5.20/£4.80 − 1 = 8.33% or £5.196/£4.80 = 8.25%

ANSWERS TO PRACTICE QUESTIONS: SECTION 2

307 FRUIT

	May X6	June X6	July X6	Aug X6
Cost per 1,000 kgs	£1,000	£900	£700	£800
Seasonal variation	£200	£100	−£100	£0
Trend	£800	£800	£800	£800

850/800 − 1 = 6.25% or (850 − 800)/8 = 6.25%

	May X7	June X7	July X7	Aug X7
Trend	£850	£850	£850	£850
Seasonal variation	£200	£100	−£100	£0
Cost per 1,000 kgs	£1,050	£950	£750	£850

308 YANKEE (2)

The seasonally adjusted sales volume for EACH of the FOUR quarters for Yankee Ltd are:

	Q1	Q2	Q3	Q4
Actual sales volumes	224,000	196,000	215,000	265,000
Seasonal variations	14,000	−24,000	−15,000	25,000
Trend	210,000	220,000	230,000	240,000

210,000	220,000	230,000	240,000

The seasonally adjusted growth in sales volume from Quarter 1 to Quarter 4 for Yankee Ltd is:

14%

(£240,000 − £210,000)/£210,000 × 100 = 14.28%

Should the Sales Manager be paid his/her bonus? **NO**

309 SEB

	Apr X3	May X3	Jun X3
Cost per litre of XYZ	£104.55	£107.70	£110.85
Increase per month		£3.15	£3.15

	July X3	September X3
Cost per litre of XYZ	£110.85 + £3.15 = £114.00	£114.00 + £3.15 + £3.15 = £120.30

AAT: APPLIED MANAGEMENT ACCOUNTING

310 TOAST

(a) Trend figures

	20X3 Qtr 1	20X3 Qtr 2	20X3 Qtr 3	20X3 Qtr 4
Actual	£3,200	£3,020	£3,320	£3,060
Seasonal variation	+£200	−£80	+£120	−£240
Trend	**£3,000**	**£3,100**	**£3,200**	**£3,300**

(b) The value of a and b in the equation Y = a + bX

$b = (3300 - 3000)/(27 - 24)$

$a = 3300 - (27 \times 100)$

	£
b	**100**
a	**600**

(c) Trend for 20X7 quarter 1 and 3:

	Workings	Trend (£)
20X7 Qtr 1	X = 40: y = 600 + 100 × 40 =	**4,600**
20X7 Qtr 3	X = 42: y = 600 + 100 × 42 =	**4,800**

(d) Forecast cost for 20X7 quarter 2 and 4.

	Workings	Forecast (£)
20X7 Qtr 2	X= 41: y = 600 + 100 × 41 = 4,700, F = 4,700 − 80 =	**4,620**
20X7 Qtr 4	X= 43: y = 600 + 100 × 43 = 4,900, F = 4,900 − 240 =	**4,660**

(e) Quarter 1 and 2 of 20X8 expressed these as an index number with base Qtr 1 20X3.

	Workings	Index number (2DP)
20X8 Qtr 1	5,200/3,200 × 100 =	**162.50**
20X8 Qtr 2	5,020/3,200 × 100 =	**156.88**

ANSWERS TO PRACTICE QUESTIONS: SECTION 2

311 COAST

(a)

	20X2 Qtr 1	20X2 Qtr 2	20X2 Qtr 3	20X2 Qtr 4
Actual paid	**440,000**	418,500	572,000	791,000
Quantity purchased	10,000	**9,000**	11,000	**14,000**
Cost per kg	44.00	46.50	52.00	56.50
Seasonal variation	−5.00	−3.00	+2.00	+6.00
Trend	**49.00**	**49.50**	**50.00**	**50.50**

(b) Index = 50/44 × 100 =

114

312 DISADVANTAGES

	Disadvantage of EVs?
Expected values only provides the most likely result	
It ignores attitudes to risk	✓
Only two possible outcomes can be considered	
Probabilities are subjective	✓
The answer provided may not exist	✓

313 STATATAC

(a)

20X6 volume of units (000)	July	August	September
Trend	**90**	**95**	100
Seasonal variation	10	5	**−8**
Seasonally adjusted sales	**100**	**100**	92

(b)

20X7 volume of units (000)	October	November	December
Trend	165	170	175
Seasonal variation	−10	−12	−15
Seasonally adjusted sales	**155**	**158**	**160**

(c) £12 × 1.12 = **£13.44**

(d) 14.50/£12 × 100 = 120.8333 ≈ **121**

314 TEX-MEX-INDEX

(a)

Year	Index	Price per kg £
20X2	105	4.73
20X3	**108**	4.87
20X4	110	**4.95**
20X5	**102**	4.61
20X6	**107**	4.82
20X7	115	**5.18**

(b) The percentage increase in price from 20X4 to 20X6 is **21.74** %

(140 – 115)/115 × 100 = 21.74

The price in 20X7 is **£11.97**.per kg

152/127 × £10 = 11.97

(c)

20X7 volume of units (000)	Quarter 1	Quarter 2	Quarter 3	Quarter 4
Trend	100	**110**	**120**	**130**
Seasonal variation	–50	+20	+90	–60
Seasonally adjusted sales	**50**	130	**210**	70

DIVISIONAL PERFORMANCE

ROI, RI AND TRANSFER PRICING

315 DUST CO

Division A: Profit = £14.4 m × 30% = £4.32 m

Imputed interest charge = £32.6 m × 10% = £3.26 m

Residual income = £1.06 m

Division B: Profit = £8.8 m × 24% = £2.112 m

Imputed interest charge = £22.2 m × 10% = £2.22 m

Residual income = £(0.108) m

	Residual Income
Division A	£1.06 m
Division B	£(0.108) m

	Would choose to invest in the project	Would choose not to invest in the project
Division A	✓	
Division B		✓

ANSWERS TO PRACTICE QUESTIONS: SECTION 2

316 PRO MO RI

£830 m

Controllable profit is 1,200 + 90 + 30 + 50 =	£1,370m
Assets at start of year are £4,500m	
Notional interest charges at 12% (4,500 × 0.12)	£540m
Residual Income	£830m

317 PRO MO ROI

30.4%

ROI = 1,370/4,500 = 30.4%

318 DIVISION B

B

Statement (1) is not true: a price above variable costs will generate a positive contribution but will not necessarily cover fixed costs and make a profit, so will not always be accepted.

319 TM PLC

£12.90

We must set a price high enough for TM to cover its costs, but not so high that RM cannot make a profit.

For TM, an item sold externally has VC of 60% × £24.00 = £14.40. Of this, £1.50 will not be incurred on an internal transfer so it is not relevant here, VC on internal transfer = £14.40 – £1.50= £12.90. We do not know RM's cost structure, so we leave the price at £12.90; this will ensure that RM is not discouraged from taking an internal transfer when it is profitable to do so.

320 JB LTD

£10.50

Division A can sell all of its output on the outside market at £12 per unit. Any internal transfer will be at the expense of external sales. However, the external sales also include a packaging cost of £1.50 per unit which is not incurred on an internal transfer and this saving can be passed on to the buying division. Therefore, the correct transfer price from a decision-making point of view is £12 (the market price) – £1.50 (the saving in packaging cost) = £10.50

321 OXCO

B

Increase in variable costs from buying in (2,200 units × £40 (£140 – £100)) = £88,000

Less the specific fixed costs saved if A is shut down = (£10,000)

Decrease in profit = £78,000

322 ZIG

	A	B	C
ROI%	19	21	25

	A	B	C (W)
Revised Capital Employed (£)	325,000	280,000	430,000
Revised Profit (£)	68,500	48,500	106,250
Revised ROI (% to 1 dp	21.1	17.3	24.7

(W)

As C's working capital is reduced by 20,000, so is the capital employed.

£450,000 – £20,000 = £430,000

Discount given = £500,000 × 0.5 × 0.025 = £6,250.

Profit will now be: £112,500 – £6,250 = £106,250

Ethics

Objectivity – As the managers stand to benefit from the decision they make, they may prioritise their personal financial benefit ahead of the companies benefit.

For example the managers of division B and C may be reluctant to proceed with the proposals or even reject them as it reduces the ROI of their divisions.

Decision making implications

In this particular case it would depend on the target set, for example if the target was 20% then the manager of A would be keen to proceed with the proposal to achieve the target and receive their bonus. The manager of division B would reject the proposal to maintain their bonus.

323 CTD

The current transfer price is (£40 + £20)) × 1.1 = £66.

	Workings	FD £000	FD £000	TM £000	TM £000
Internal sales	15,000 × £66		990		
External sales	5,000 × £80		400		
	15,000 × £500				7,500
Total sales			1,390		7,500
Production – variable costs	20,000 × £40	(800)			
	15,000 × £366			(5,490)	
Selling/distribution – variable costs	5,000 × £4	(20)			
	15,000 × £25			(375)	
Total variable cost			(820)		(5,865)
Contribution			570		1,635
Production overheads	20,000 × £20	(400)			
	15,000 × £60			(900)	
Administration overheads	20,000 × £4	(80)			
	15,000 × £25			(375)	
Net profit			90		360
Interest charge	£750,000\£1,500,000 × 12%		(90)		(180)
Residual income (RI)			0		180
Target RI			85		105
Bonus	£180,000 × 5%		0		9

Section 3

MOCK ASSESSMENT QUESTIONS

TASK 1 (12 MARKS)

This task is about budgetary processes, responsibilities and uncertainties.

(a) Match the data in the first column with the appropriate source in the second column.

Data	Source
Consumer price index (CPI) and other inflation data	Production Manager
Country-specific credit rating	Standard and Poor/Fitch/Moody agencies
Components prices for our star product	Operations Manager
Latest company customer service performance indicators	The World Bank
	The Office for National Statistics
	Suppliers and competitors

(b) As budget accountant, match each task with the person or group that you will need to contact:

- You want confirmation that business operations are efficient in terms of using as little resources as needed, and effective in terms of meeting customer requirements.

- You are concerned about the number of complaints received from customers in the West Country.

- The materials usage budget needs a last minute update of wastage information.

Choose from:

- Regional Director
- Supervisor
- Operations Manager
- Management Accountant

(c) Take each item of cost in the list below and place it into its appropriate budget.

Cost
Website development costs
Training to maintain and develop skills and capabilities
Kindergarten expenses for children of employees
Cost of conducting employee surveys
Cost of acquiring a property for investment purposes
Expected number of hours of idle time
Cleaning supplies
Public relations costs before product launch

Personnel

Cost of production

Maintenance

Capital expenditure

Marketing

MOCK ASSESSMENT QUESTIONS: **SECTION 3**

(d) **Select an appropriate accounting treatment for each of the following costs:**

- Cost of hiring an additional supervisor in factory
- Raw material costs
- Cost of the cafeteria
- Admin salaries
- Computing services
- Production equipment maintenance
- Depreciation of machinery
- Redecoration of the top floor exhibition room

Options available are:

- Allocate to marketing overheads
- Allocate to administrative overheads
- Direct costs
- Charge to production in a machine hour overhead rate
- Charge to production in a labour hour overhead rate
- Activity based charge to production cost centres

TASK 2 (24 MARKS)

This task is about budget preparation, evaluation and revision.

(a) **Complete the following production forecast for product P.**

Units of product P

	Week 1	Week 2	Week 3	Week 4	Week 5
Opening stock	1,800				
Production					
Sub-total					
Sales	5,500	5,000	5,100	5,100	7,000
Closing stock					

Closing stock should be 22% of the following week's forecast sales.

(b) The quarterly production requirements for product 'Zigma' are shown below.

7% of production fails the quality checks and must be scrapped.

How many items of product L must be manufactured to allow for waste?

	Month 1	Month 2	Month 3
Required units	99,000	100,000	101,000
Manufactured units			

KAPLAN PUBLISHING

(c) Raw material purchases:

- 1,100 items of product X are to be manufactured in September.
- Each requires 7 metres of leather.
- 5% of raw material is wasted during manufacture.
- The opening inventory will be 10,000 metres of leather.
- The closing inventory will be 9,000 metres of leather.

How much material must be purchased?

Select from:

7,000 m	
7,700 m	
7,106 m	
8,106 m	

(d) Labour hours:

- 42,000 units of Company A's only product are to be manufactured in October
- Each one takes 19 minutes to produce
- 32 staff will each work 160 hours basic time

How many overtime hours must be worked to complete the production?

Select from:

5,120	
8,080	
8,180	
13,300	

(e) Department X manufactures three products, A, B and C.

Calculate the machine hours required to manufacture these in November.

Product	Units	Hours per unit	Hours required
A	120	1.8	
B	190	1.8	
C	190	3.0	
Total hours for Department X			

There are three machines in the department. Each machine can be used for 260 hours in November. Additional machines can be hired if required.

How many additional machines should be hired? [ ]

MOCK ASSESSMENT QUESTIONS: SECTION 3

TASK 3 (18 MARKS)

This task is about flexed budgets or standard costing

(a) Budget revision

You have submitted a draft operating budget to the budget committee. The committee has asked you to budget for an alternative scenario and calculate the increase or decrease in expected profit.

Complete the alternative scenario column in the operating budget table and calculate the increase or decrease in profit.

Assumptions in the first scenario

Material and labour costs are variable.

Depreciation is a stepped cost, increasing at every 12,000 units.

There is an allowance for an energy price rise of 8%.

Alternative scenario

Increase the selling price by 3%

Reduce the sales volume by 8%

Revise the energy price rise to 4%

Apart from the sales price per unit, do not enter decimals. Round to the nearest whole number, if necessary.

Operating budget	First draft	Alternative scenario
Sales price £ per unit	10.20	
Sales volume	60,000	
	£	£
Sales revenue	612,000	
Costs		
Material	135,000	
Labour	270,000	
Energy	108,000	
Depreciation	24,000	
Total	537,000	
Gross profit	75,000	
Increase/(decrease) in gross profit		

(b)   Variance analysis

Prepare the direct material cost statement from the activity data provided.

Enter favourable variances as positive figures, for example 500.

Enter negative variances as negative figures, for example – 500.

Activity data	Items produced	Kgs used	Cost
Budget	3,000	4,500	9,000
Actual results	2,000	4,500	9,210

Raw material cost statement	£
Standard raw material cost of production	
Variance (adverse shown as negative)	
Material price	
Material usage	
Material cost	

TASK 4 (20 MARKS)

This task is about costing systems to aid control

(a) SCL is a furniture manufacturer and has just received the results of a study on the current interest in their new leather sofa range. The study indicates that the maximum price the average customer is prepared to pay for a leather sofa is £1,000.

The company estimates that 1,200 sofas can be sold in a year.

At this level of production, the fixed overheads per sofa would be £240.

The labour requirement per sofa is 8 hours at a cost of £15 per hour.

The wooden frame and the stuffing material cost £90 per sofa.

The required profit margin is 30%.

One sofa uses 10 square metres of leather.

Calculate the target cost per square metre of leather. (8 marks)

	£
Sales price per sofa	
Profit margin	
Total costs	
Fixed cost per sofa	
Labour cost per sofa	
Wooden frame and stuffing material	
Maximum leather cost per sofa	
Target cost per square metre	

(b) SCL's leather supplier quotes a list price of £30 per square metre for the grade of leather SCL needs. However, SCL has managed to negotiate a discount of 15% on this price.

The discount should be ACCEPTED/REJECTED because the £30 reduces to £ ☐

(to the nearest pence) which is ABOVE/BELOW the target cost. *(Delete as appropriate.)*

The minimum percentage discount needed to achieve the target cost is ☐ %
(to 2 decimal places). (3 marks)

(c) Discuss how SCL could use value analysis if they needed to further reduce the cost of the sofa in the future, identify any ethical considerations they may face. (5 marks)

(d) Explain FOUR ways that cloud accounting could benefit SCL. (4 marks)

AAT: APPLIED MANAGEMENT ACCOUNTING

TASK 5 **(20 MARKS)**

This task is about short term decision making

(a) Appler is considering the relevant cash flows involved in a short-term decision. An important client has asked for the minimum price for the processing of a compound. The compound involves the following:

Material A: Appler needs 500 kg of material for the compound but has 200 kg in inventory at present. The inventory items were bought 3 months ago for £5/kg. Material A is not regularly used in the business and would have to be disposed of at a cost to Appler of £400 in total. The current purchase price of material A is £6.25/kg.

Material B: Appler needs 800 kg of material B and has this in stock as it is regularly needed. The stock was bought 2 months ago for £4/kg although it can be bought now at £3.75/kg due to its seasonal nature.

Labour: The contract requires 100 hours of labour. However, the labourers, who are each paid £15 per hour, are working at full capacity.

There is a shortage of labour in the market. The labour required to undertake this special contract would have to be taken from another contract, Z, which currently utilises 500 hours of labour and generates £5,000 worth of contribution.

If the labour was taken from contract Z, then the whole of contract Z would have to be delayed, and such delay would invoke a penalty fee of £1,000.

Other costs: Processing energy costs would be £200 and the supervisor says they would allocate £150 of their weekly salary to the job in the company's job costing system.

Based upon the scenario information, complete the following table showing the relevant cost for each element to be included in the minimum price calculation (to the nearest £)

(9 marks)

Material A	£
Material B	£
Labour	£
Processing energy	£
Supervision	£

(b) Ace Limited is considering whether or not to cease production of leather-bound diaries.

Which TWO of the following items are valid factors to consider in this decision? (2 marks)

The diaries made a loss in the year just passed	
The diaries made a positive contribution in the year just passed	
The market outlook in the long term looks very poor	
The budget for next year shows a loss	
The business also sells pens and many diary buyers will often also buy a pen	
The business was founded to produce and sell diaries	

MOCK ASSESSMENT QUESTIONS: **SECTION 3**

(c) **Which FOUR of the following are to be correctly included in the considerations in a make or buy decision?** (4 marks)

The amount of re-allocated rent costs caused by using the production space differently.	
The variable costs of purchase from the new supplier.	
The level of discount available from the new supplier.	
The redundancy payments to the supervisor of the product in question.	
The saved labour costs of the production staff re-directed to other work.	
The materials no longer bought to manufacture the product.	

(d) A linear programming model has been formulated for two products, A and B, manufactured by J Co.

Which TWO of the following statements about linear programming are true? (2 marks)

J Co can use linear programming if it starts to manufacture another product, C.	
J Co would not need to use linear programming if there was not a demand constraint.	
J Co should ignore fixed costs when making decisions about how to utilise production capacity in the short run, using linear programming.	
Linear programming models can be used when there is an experience curve, once the steady state has been reached.	

(e) A different organisation has the following contribution function:

Contribution = 15X + 6Y, where

X = the number of units of product X produced, and

Y = the number of units of product Y produced.

A graph has identified that the optimal production plan exists at the point where the following two constraints cross:

Material A: $2X + 4Y \leq 16,000$

Material B: $2X + Y \leq 13,000$

There is a maximum demand of 10,000 units of each product

Complete the following table to calculate the optimum production plan and optimum contribution. (3 marks)

Units of X	
Units of Y	
Contribution (£)	

TASK 6 (14 MARKS)

This task is about long term decision making

One of the extrusion machines in the Plastic extrusion department is nearing the end of its useful life and Sarloue Ltd is considering purchasing a replacement machine.

Estimates have been made for the initial capital cost, sales income and operating costs of the replacement machine, which is expected to have a useful life of three years:

	Year 0 £000	Year 1 £000	Year 2 £000	Year 3 £000
Capital expenditure	450			
Other cash flows:				
Sales income		600	650	750
Operating costs		420	480	510

The company appraises capital investment projects using a 15% cost of capital.

(a) Complete the table below and calculate the net present value of the proposed replacement machine (to the nearest £000). Show cash outflows as negative numbers (minus sign or brackets can be used). (6 marks)

	Year 0 £000	Year 1 £000	Year 2 £000	Year 3 £000
Capital expenditure	(450)			
Sales income		600	650	750
Operating costs		(420)	(480)	(510)
Net cash flows	(450)	180	170	240
PV factors	1.0000	0.8696	0.7561	0.6575
Discounted cash flows	(450)	157	129	158
Net present value	(6)			

The net present value is positive/**negative***

*delete as appropriate

(b) The IRR for this project will be greater than/**less than*** 15% (1 marks)

(c) Calculate the payback of the proposed replacement machine to the nearest whole month. (4 marks)

The payback period is ____2____ Year(s) and ____5____ Months

(d) The machine would have a zero scrap value at the end of the three years. The operating costs are cash flows and so do not include depreciation.

Calculate the ARR of proposed replacement machine using the initial investment method.

(3 marks)

Depreciation	£
Average annual profit (to the nearest £)	£
ARR (% to one decimal place)	_____ %

TASK 7 (20 MARKS)

La Mangerie runs a chain of restaurants in the North of England, and opened a new restaurant on 1 January in London – the first to be opened in the South of the country. Market research suggests that in London, the average selling price of a meal is £30 in similar restaurants.

You are aware of the following:

1. The London restaurant currently has 48 seats arranged in the same density as the other restaurants in the chain. In other similar London restaurants, tables tend to be higher density: the London restaurant could have an additional 12 tables if the existing tables were rearranged.

2. It has been observed that a number of the serving staff forget to offer customers the dessert menu, and often neglect customers towards the end of their meal.

3. A mystery diner (a customer who is employed by the company and visits the restaurant as an ordinary customer) has reviewed the restaurant and commented that the customer service was satisfactory, but not up the usual high standard. In particular, the serving staff were not very friendly and rarely smile.

The management accounts for the new London restaurant for the year ended 31 December 20X0, together with the average La Mangerie restaurant's management accounts for the same period, are shown below:

	London	Average
Number of meals served	14,892	19,710
Capacity of restaurant (maximum number of meals)	17,520	32,850
Average sales price per meal served	£22	£22
Number of main courses served	13,400	15,768
Percentage of customers who purchase a main meal	90%	80%
Number of deserts served	11,169	17,739
Percentage of customers who purchase a desert	75%	90%
Direct Labour cost per meal	£4	£2
Net profit margin	16%	31%
Utilisation of the restaurant (*)	85%	60%

(*) The utilisation of the restaurant is calculated as the number of meals served as a percentage of the capacity.

AAT: APPLIED MANAGEMENT ACCOUNTING

Write an email to the Managing Director in three parts:

(a) comparing the London restaurant with the average restaurant and explaining the assumptions upon which your comparison is based. **(10 marks)**

(b) suggesting other appropriate steps to improve the performance of the London restaurant. **(6 marks)**

(c) explaining which of the planning assumptions are not totally within the delivery manager's control. **(4 marks)**

To	Managing Director	**Date**	(Today)
From	Budget Accountant	**Subject**	Review of indicators

(a) Restaurant comparison

(b) London – Performance Improvements

(c) Controllability

MOCK ASSESSMENT QUESTIONS: SECTION 3

TASK 8 (12 MARKS)

This task is about divisional performance and forecasting

A company has used expected values to evaluate a one-off project. The expected value calculation assumed two possible profit outcomes which were assigned probabilities of 0.4 and 0.6.

(a) Which TWO of the following statements about this approach are correct? (2 marks)

The expected value profit is the profit which has the highest probability of being achieved	
The expected value gives no indication of the dispersion of the possible outcomes	
Expected values are relatively insensitive to assumptions about probability	
The expected value may not correspond to any of the actual possible outcomes	

PQ Ltd is a divisionalised organisation comprising a number of divisions, including divisions C and D. Division C makes a single product, which it sells on the external market at a price of £15 per unit. The variable cost of the product is £10 per unit and the fixed cost is £2 per unit. Market demand for the product considerably exceeds Division C's maximum production capacity of 25,000 units per month.

Division D would like to obtain 500 units of the product from Division C. If Division C does transfer some of its production internally rather than sell externally, then the saving in packaging costs would be £2.50 per unit.

(b) What transfer price per unit should Division A quote in order to maximise group profit? (2 marks)

£ [   ]

A business has costs which follow the linear regression equation Y = a + bX, where X is the output volume.

The following data has been gathered about the costs for the last 2 months:

Output (units)	Total costs (£)
500	4,600
900	7,000

(c) calculate the values of a and b. (2 marks)

a = [   ]

b = [   ]

KAPLAN PUBLISHING 355

AAT: APPLIED MANAGEMENT ACCOUNTING

(d) **Insert the three month moving averages into the table below. Round to the nearest unit:**
(5 marks)

Month	Sales (units)	Three month moving average (units)
July	2,320	
August	2,400	2,380
September	2,420	2,447
October	2,520	2,533
November	2,660	2,727
December	3,000	2,733
January	2,540	

(e) **Complete the following sentences** (1 mark)

Prediction of a figure that lies within a range of data that has previously been observed is referred to as [   ]

random variations/trend/interpolation/extrapolation

The observation that sales of a particular item are usually higher during the run up to Christmas is an example of [   ]

underlying trend/residual variation/cyclical variation/seasonal variation

Section 4

MOCK ASSESSMENT ANSWERS

TASK 1

(a) Match the data in the first column with the appropriate source in the second column.

Data	Source
Consumer price index (CPI) and other inflation data	The Office for National Statistics
Country-specific credit rating	Standard and Poor/Fitch/Moody agencies
Components prices for our star product	Suppliers and competitors
Latest company customer service performance indicators	Operations Manager

(b) Who would you contact in each of the following situations?

- You want confirmation that business operations are efficient in terms of using as little resources as needed, and effective in terms of meeting customer requirements: **Operations Manager**.
- You are concerned about the number of complaints received from customers in the West Country: **Regional Director**.
- The materials usage budget needs a last minute update of wastage information: **Management Accountant**.

(c) Take each item of cost in the list below and place it into its appropriate budget.

Personnel
Training to maintain and develop skills and capabilities
Kindergarten expenses for children of employees
Cost of conducting employee surveys

Cost of production
Expected number of hours of idle time

Maintenance
Cleaning supplies

Capital expenditure
Cost of acquiring a property for investment purposes

Marketing
Website development costs
Public relations costs before product launch

(d) Select an appropriate accounting treatment for each of the following costs:

- Cost of hiring an additional supervisor in factory: **Activity based charge to production cost centres**

- Raw material costs: **Direct costs**

- Cost of the cafeteria: **Activity based charge to production cost centres**

- Admin salaries: **Allocate to administrative overheads**

- Computing services: **Allocate to administrative overheads**

- Production equipment maintenance: **Charge to production in a machine hour overhead rate**

- Depreciation of machinery: **Charge to production, in a machine hour overhead rate**

- Redecoration of the top floor exhibition room: **Allocate to marketing overheads**

TASK 2

(a)

	Week 1	Week 2	Week 3	Week 4	Week 5
Opening stock	1,800	1,100	1,122	1,122	1,540
Production	4,800	5,022	5,100	5,518	
Sub-total	6,600	6,122	6,222	6,640	
Sales	5,500	5,000	5,100	5,100	7,000
Closing stock	1,100	1,122	1,122	1,540	

(b)

	Month 1	Month 2	Month 3
Required units	99,000	100,000	101,000
Manufactured units	106,452	107,527	108,603

(c) 1,100 items × 7 metres of leather in total = 7,700 metres are needed for manufacture.

This needs grossing up for total number of metres to 7,700/0.95 = 8,106 metres.

Purchases = production requirements + Closing inventory 9,000 metres − opening inventory 10,000 metres.

Purchases = **7,106 metres**

MOCK ASSESSMENT ANSWERS: SECTION 4

(d) (42,000 units × 19 minutes) ÷ 60 = 13,300 hours needed.

32 staff × 160 hours = 5,120 hours available.

Therefore we need (13,300 – 5,120 hours) = 8,180 hours of overtime.

(e) Department X manufactures three products, A, B and C.

Calculate the machine hours required to manufacture these in November.

Product	Units	Hours per unit	Hours required
A	120	1.8	216
B	190	1.8	342
C	190	3.0	570
Total hours for department X			1,128

There are three machines in the department.

Each machine can be used for 260 hours in November. Additional machines can be hired if required.

How many additional machines should be hired?   2

Working:

1,128 hours required when (260 × 3) = 780 hours are available.

Therefore we need additional machines for 1,128 – 780 hours = 348 hours.

Therefore 2 additional machines are required.

TASK 3

(a)

Operating budget	First draft	Alternative scenario
Sales price £ per unit	10.20	10.506
Sales volume	60,000	55,200
	£	£
Sales revenue	**612,000**	**579,931**
Costs		
Material	135,000	124,200
Labour	270,000	248,400
Energy	108,000	104,000
Depreciation	24,000	24,000
Total	537,000	500,600
Gross profit	75,000	79,331
Increase/(decrease) in gross profit		4,331

(b)

Raw material cost statement	£
Standard raw material cost of production	6,000
Variance (adverse shown as negative)	£ fav/–adv
Material price	–210
Material usage	–3,000
Material cost	–3,210

TASK 4

(a)

	£
Sales price per sofa	1,000
Profit margin (30% × £1,000)	300
Total costs	700
Fixed cost per sofa	240
Labour cost per sofa (8 hours × £15)	120
Wooden frame and stuffing material	90
Maximum leather cost per sofa	250
Target cost per square metre (£250/10 metres)	25

(b) The discount should be **REJECTED** because the £30 reduces to **£25.50** (£30 × 0.85) which is **ABOVE** the target cost.

The minimum percentage discount needed to achieve the target cost is **16.67%** (£5/£30).

(c) **Value analysis**

> Value analysis is about reducing the cost of production while maintaining the value to the customer.
>
> SCL could look at the materials used in the construction of the frame or stuffing the cushion and see if there is a cheaper alternative that is as effective as the current material used.
>
> They could also look at the labour used, some of the work will require skilled workers that are paid at a higher rate, but they may be able to do some of the work with lower skilled/unskilled staff.
>
> **Ethics**
>
> The decision about what labour to use or what material to use would not just be about price/cost. They would also need to consider their customers safety and the impact on the environment. Obviously they would have to comply with legal requirements about safety, but if they chose a cheaper type of material that while still safety compliant was more flammable, they would be increasing the risks to the customer.
>
> Often manufacturing overseas can lead to a reduction in labour costs, but SCL would need to make sure that the labour force was not being exploited or treated unfairly.

MOCK ASSESSMENT ANSWERS: SECTION 4

(d) Technology

> Cloud accounting allows for remote access allowing SCL employees more flexibility as they no longer need to be plugged in to the network to access SCL data.
>
> If the leather sofa is successful and SCL decide to expand their furniture operations, it allows for easier scaling, adding additional users and locations much more easily.
>
> Cloud accounting can incorporate data back-ups removing the need for physical devices to back up the data, this could reduce the significant overhead costs, helping SCL achieve target margins.
>
> In terms of the target costing, if one of the purchasing team identifies a new material or supplier that is cheaper, the cost information could be updated quickly allowing for quicker decisions.

TASK 5

(a)

Material A:

Inventory – saving of disposal costs =	(£400)
Bought 300 kg @ £6.25/kg =	£1,875
Net cost	**£1,475**

Material B

Regularly used so replacement cost needed

800 kg @ £3.75/kg	**£3,000**

Labour

Labour is in short supply so there is an opportunity cost. The contribution of £5,000 from Contract Z will still be earned but will be delayed, so it is not relevant. The relevant cost is therefore the wages earned plus the penalty fee.

(£15 × 100) + (£1,000) =	**£2,500**
Production energy	**£200**
The **supervisor** is a sunk cost	**£0**

(b)

The diaries made a loss in the year just passed	
The diaries made a positive contribution in the year just passed	
The market outlook in the long term looks very poor	✓
The budget for next year shows a loss	
The business also sells pens and many diary buyers will often also buy a pen	✓
The business was founded to produce and sell diaries	

The following were NOT to be included:

The diaries made a loss in the year just passed is a sunk event

The diaries made a positive contribution in the year just passed is a sunk event

The budget for next year shows a loss includes fixed costs and these are not relevant

The business was founded to produce and sell diaries – things change!

(c)

The amount of re-allocated rent costs caused by using the production space differently.	
The variable costs of purchase from the new supplier.	✓
The level of discount available from the new supplier.	✓
The redundancy payments to the supervisor of the product in question.	✓
The saved labour costs of the production staff re-directed to other work.	
The materials no longer bought to manufacture the product.	✓

(d)

J Co can use linear programming if it starts to manufacture another product, C.	
J Co would not need to use linear programming if there was not a demand constraint.	
J Co should ignore fixed costs when making decisions about how to utilise production capacity in the short run, using linear programming.	✓
Linear programming models can be used when there is an experience curve, once the steady state has been reached.	✓

The first statement is not true: linear programming is only suitable when there are two products.

The second statement is not true: there needs to be more than one limiting factor, but it is not essential for one of these two to be the level of demand.

The third statement is correct: fixed costs do not change and do not need to be considered.

The fourth statement is correct: a steady state being reached means that variable costs are constant.

(e)

The optimal production plan will have to be determined by using a simultaneous equations technique.

Material A: $2X + 4Y = 16{,}000$

Material B: $2X + Y = 13{,}000$

Deducting one from the other, leaves:

$3Y = 3{,}000$

Y = 1,000

Substituting this into one of the equations:

$2X + (4 \times 1{,}000) = 16{,}000$

$2X = 12{,}000$

X = 6,000

Contribution = $(15 \times 6000) + (6 \times 1{,}000)$ = **£96,000**

TASK 6

(a)

	Year 0 £000	Year 1 £000	Year 2 £000	Year 3 £000
Capital expenditure	(450)			
Sales income		600	650	750
Operating costs		(420)	(480)	(510)
Net cash flows	(450)	180	170	240
PV factors	1.0000	0.8696	0.7561	0.6575
Discounted cash flows	(450)	157	129	158
Net present value	(6)			

The net present value is **negative**

(b) The IRR for this project will be **less than** 15%

(c)

Year	Cash flow £000	Cumulative cash flow £000
0	(450)	(450)
1	180	(270)
2	170	(100)
3	240	140

The payback period is **2** years and **5** months. Months = 100/240 × 12 = 5 months

(d)

Depreciation	**£450,000**
	Net cash inflows = 180,000 + 170,000 + 240,000 = 590,000
Average annual profit	Total profit = 590,000 – 450,000 = 140,000
	Average annual profit = 140,000/3 = **46,667**
ARR	46,667/450,000 × 100 = **10.4%**

TASK 7

To	Managing Director	Date	(Today)
From	Budget Accountant	Subject	Review of indicators

I attach the comparison between restaurants for your consideration and approval.

(a) Restaurant comparison

The purpose of this report is to compare the London restaurant and the average restaurant, and to suggest improvements in the second part.

The average price per meal served is the same at £22, the same as the average restaurant outside of the capital.

We also find that the London restaurant served a total of 13,400 main courses. This is less than the average restaurant out of London; however, it is a good result because it means that 90% of the London customers order a main course, compared to 80% in the average restaurant.

In London, the number of deserts ordered is also lower, in absolute terms and in percentage: only 75% of customers purchased desert. This could be explained by the staff not offering dessert or not providing customer service towards the end of the meal; it could also be linked to the friendliness (or lack of) of the staff.

The Net profit margin is almost half that of the average restaurant (16%). This could be because of London prices – the cost of rent and the manager's salary are probably higher due to the London location, and direct labour. The direct labour cost per meal is twice as high in London, due to wage costs being higher, as the capital is a costly place to live.

The utilisation of the restaurant is 85%, compared to the average of 60% which is very good and probably representative of the London market.

(b) London – Performance Improvements

The average price per meal is the same in and out of London, but we know that the average selling price of a meal in London is £30; Therefore, the London restaurant could put up its prices, in order to improve profits.

Furthermore, high direct labour rates also add weighting to the option to increase the price of the meal to £30.

The obvious action is, with regards to desert, to make sure that guests are attended to, and offered dessert. Simple customer feedback forms could be handed to customers and basic satisfaction ratings recorded in order to motivate staff and hopefully improve the number of customers ordering desert.

Increasing the number of tables would increase the capacity and probably increase the profit as the only additional costs would be some fixtures and fittings, additional labour costs and additional material costs. Additional contribution would probably be made.

The utilisation rates could be improved further by increasing the table density and thus the number of meals served.

(c) Controllability

Although the London restaurant manager should take ownership of its performance, there are aspects of it which are not wholly within his/her control. For example, the restaurant manager cannot control the economy and eating out is a discretionary expense that will be cut by diners in recessionary times.

MOCK ASSESSMENT ANSWERS: SECTION 4

TASK 8

(a)

The expected value profit is the profit which has the highest probability of being achieved	
The expected value gives no indication of the dispersion of the possible outcomes	✓
Expected values are relatively insensitive to assumptions about probability	
The expected value may not correspond to any of the actual possible outcomes	✓

The expected value does not give an indication of the dispersion of the possible outcomes; a standard deviation would need to be calculated, so option 2 is correct.

The expected value is an amalgamation of several possible outcomes and their associated probabilities so it may not correspond to any of the actual possible outcomes, so option 4 is correct.

(b) **£12.50**

Division C can sell all of its output on the outside market at £15 per unit. Any internal transfer will be at the expense of external sales. However, the external sales also include a packaging cost of £2.50 per unit which is not incurred on an internal transfer and this saving can be passed on to the buying division. Therefore, the correct transfer price from a decision-making point of view is £15 (the market price) – £2.50 (the saving in packaging cost) = £12.50

(c) b = (£7,000 – £4,600)/(900 – 500) = **£6**

a = £4,600 – (£6 × 500) = **1,600**

(d)

Month	Sales (units)	Three month moving average (units)
July	2,320	
August	2,400	2,380 (W1)
September	2,420	2,447
October	2,520	2,533
November	2,660	2,727
December	3,000	2,733
January	2,540	

(W1) = (2320 + 2400 + 2420)/3 = 2380

(e) Prediction of a figure that lies within a range of data that has previously been observed is referred to as **interpolation**.

The observation that sales of a particular item are usually higher during the run up to Christmas is an example of **seasonal variation**.